<u>i.e. Patterns of Thought</u>

compiled + edited by Ellen Rowley with Maxim Laroussi

the arts council
5 chomhairle ealaíon
funding
architecture
artscouncil.ie

Designed by David Duff
www.ninepictures.com

Cover image by John Graham, 2010
'Study for Head Complex'(detail), 2004, Etching, 50 x 40 cm.

Drawings by Fiona Hallinan, 2011
www.notalittlepony.com

Compiled + edited by Ellen Rowley (2007-2012)
Project initiated by Maxim Laroussi (2007)

Copy edited by Neil Ardiff
@nardiff

Printed by Plus Print

Published by Architecture Republic, 2012
www.architecture-republic.com

ISBN - 978-0-9555502-1-8

i.e. Patterns of Thought

Compiled + Edited by Ellen Rowley
with Maxim Laroussi

-

Designed by David Duff
Published by Architecture Republic

Contents

Acknowledgments

Thank you to the Arts Council for funding this publication and the accompanying audio pieces. We are especially grateful for the support, encouragement and hard work of Claire Doyle and Louise Duggan on our behalf.

We are very grateful to all the authors included in this collection of writings. We are grateful to the original publishers of the writings for allowing us to reprint all the writings in this new context: Gill + Macmillan, Gandon Editions, the Royal Institute of Architects of Ireland, the Architectural Association of Ireland, Mermaid Turbulence, Lilliput Press, the Irish Museum of Modern Art, Merrell Holberton, Princeton University Press, *Body City* curators (Dublin Docklands Development Authority), Zero-G design, Sean Rothery (for the Moffett pamphlet), Architecture Ireland and Dennis McNulty (*Afterthoughts*). We are grateful to authors' families in some cases: Phyllis Gibney for Arthur's thesis, Simon Walker for Robin's lecture, Ben Gibney for Frank's plan, Julia O Faolain for Sean's article and to the Craig family for Maurice's presentation.

We acknowledge the beautiful line drawings by Fiona Hallinan; the transcribing and fine book design by David Duff; and the thorough copy-editing by Neil Ardiff. Thanks are due to Sean Collins for transcribing and to Emmet Scanlon, Shane O'Toole, Edward McParland, Hugh Campbell, Grainne Hassett, Tom de Paor, Peter Cody, Dermot Boyd and Sascha Perfect for sound advice. Thank you to those working with Architecture Republic during the project.

About This Book

This book presents a miscellany of writing and musings on the subject of architecture, Irish and otherwise.

The culture of architecture in Ireland is rich but we feel it is somewhat fragmented by virtue of the fact that the many critical voices have spoken, and continue to speak, in isolation. As a result, we have collated some of the words encountered through lectures, catalogue essays, building reviews, architectural polemics, a policy document and critical histories. Mostly, we like the idea of the essays having been already written or 'made' and that we are pulling them back out, dusting them off and gathering them together for consumption by a new generation of readers.

The gathering might seem dubiously random. We raise our hands in admission of guilt. This is certainly not a "reader" companion to twentieth-century Irish architecture – its chronology is unbalanced, its tone is uneven and its selection is biased. Whatever else it is a rich mixture - of reflections and critical commentaries and quirky histories of (Irish) architecture and spatial practices by (Irish) thinkers from different but related backgrounds such as architecture, art, history, urbanism, planning and literature.

Other than chronological categorisation, the essays are bound together without editorial intervention. In this way we are not making points-of-commonality explicit nor are we imposing thematic relations upon the reader; rather we intend for this book to be a string of novellas about architecture/space which is at times specifically Irish in context.

Quite simply, this volume is motivated by our own appetite for a single collection of choice texts; and from our initial kernel of

curiosity came the idea to self-publish an unassuming volume
that considers Irish architecture by its broadest definition.

———

Perhaps the unifying aspect of this miscellany is the relationship
(that unwieldy relationship) between architecture and words.
Indeed all of these essays, loosely-speaking, are a string of
words describing architecture-related phenomena. Surely that's
obvious? But nudge this relationship of words and architecture
in a specifically Irish direction, and we're immediately reminded
of the oral tradition in Ireland. Many of the pieces printed in
this volume were never meant to be written beyond notes – in
starting their lives as spoken words through lectures, conference
papers and presentations, they were to be heard not read. Then
we enter an ephemeral territory: spoken words can float, while
written words are anchored. Speaking about architecture enables
a more public or collective experience, rather than the intimate
act of reading and writing. The oral is a form of discourse, a by-
product of rhetoric which easily grows polemical.

In the translation from oral to written, patterns of thought
become patterns of script and patterns of polemic.

By choosing to publish spoken word (the Grafton Architects'
presentation, Noel Moffett's vision, my lectures or Dermot Boyd's
conversation with Patrick Scott) and also, by giving precedence
to words over pictures in this expression of architecture, the
book is celebrating architecture's relationship with language.
In Seamus Heaney's essay - originally a lecture to the Royal
Institute of Architects of Ireland (RIAI) in 1986 - he discusses
how buildings "may be mute but they are potent". Heaney
proposes that buildings are themselves a form of language,

taking us in as images and then forming our backdrops, our shelters, our dream-scapes. Heaney's insistence that architecture is a language reminds us of Dalibor Vesely's dictum that architecture, like language, is fundamental to culture and enables us to communicate in our world, to orientate ourselves in relation to the world. So, this relationship between language and architecture goes far beyond the stringing together of words.

Our volume hopes to leave traces of the poetic patterns of architecture imprinted on the reader's mind.

In its more everyday, perhaps mundane, relationship to architecture, language acts as a descriptor, as a means of elucidating. Adrian Forty outlines this process when he writes in <u>Words and Building</u> (2000, p.13) that "it is generally supposed that what is spoken or written about works of architecture is merely a tracing of them, an always less than adequate reflection of their `reality'". Certainly our collection of essays contains the more pragmatic employment of language by architects and others. We have the urban policy language of Gerry Cahill's "Back to the Streets" proposal; the medieval history terminology of Roger Stalley's thesis on round towers; Robin Walker's drawings from philosophy and the novel so as to describe architecture's condition; or the capturing of a peripatetic poetry so as to highlight the poet in the city, by Sandra O'Connell. But what all of these variants of language show is how words, language, can be more than an accessory to architectural phenomena.

Throughout the essays, language traces architectural narratives and forms patterns of intention.

———

Nudging the relationship between words and architecture yet further in an Irish direction, it becomes about architecture and writing. Of course, out of the oral tradition grew the literary tradition. Pointedly, while a nod to the eighteenth-century city fabric is made, Dublin's bid (2010-11) to be counted by UNESCO is grounded in the place's literary offspring rather than the place's architectural prowess. From the ground up there seeps compunction to write, and in some of these essays, that compunction is made spatial. With Tim Robinson's chapter, words and sentences, the tools of his trade, are like stones piling up a pictorial structure in the reader's mind. We are transported to the intimate domesticity of his home in the West of Ireland, while gaining knowledge of that home's biography; it's as if we've climbed into the house and yard ourselves, using Robinson's words as footholds for our impatient feet, scrambling up a wall.

Another form of compunction greets the reader of John Tuomey's short piece from 1982. Here, the young architect appears to need to write his way around and over and through the squat prismatic forms of rural Irish buildings on the skyline, so as to situate himself and his praxis. And some years later, the critic/architect Shane O'Toole cites Tuomey's earlier essay – O'Toole recognises the urgency in Tuomey's calling forth of the "power" inherent in the "archaic simplicity" of Irish vernacular architecture. These links could seem clichéd or introverted by now, given the stature of both Tuomey and O'Toole, but it is important to acknowledge them; to reflect and pause through old writings. In this way O'Toole (the emerging critic and writer in 1991) encountered O'Donnell Tuomey's pavilion for paintings by Brian Maguire and as he remembers, it was then that he began a new journey with writing where writing became a type of catharsis. That writing about architecture could enrich the experience of architecture...

Does an argument inadvertently emerge from our volume about the power of writing for Irish architecture?

Leaving the problematical "national" aside, certainly another architect-educator Anna Ryan posits a new relationship for architecture and writing. In her essay we are at school, with an interesting and unorthodox proposition on our desks. Can architecture be taught through writing? Is there a third way? John Olley, also an architectural educator, uses the act of drawing as a means of unpicking the language of architecture. His essay, originally written to accompany an architectural drawing exhibition at the RIAI, is bursting with "writerly" references to the creative process underpinning architecture. Here, understanding architecture through writing makes sense. Olley's study is about both the exercise in its own right (writing for writing) and the new presentation of ideas (greater understanding through writing). Though patchwork in nature and different in aspiration, Hugh Campbell similarly sews references together in his paper on the window in architecture. But here, where Olley is academic, Campbell is essayist. Indeed Hugh Campbell, like Robinson, is a wordsmith – writing is his trade. Observing the Gothic novel, the Romantic canvas and the Modernist pavilion, Campbell's meditation is a painterly exploration on the physical and metaphysical potential of the window.

For Campbell, Ryan and Olley, architecture is understood and made richer through the motifs of window, writing, drawing.

———

Compunction to write, compunction to explain, compunction

to reduce: Pat Scott, in conversation with Dermot Boyd, refuses to analyse his craft and reveal his art through words. At another end, Dominic Stevens seems to situate his architectural activism through his words. And Shelley McNamara and Yvonne Farrell (Grafton Architects) demonstrate just how to raise the wrangle of descriptive language to the level of oratory. Grafton's task was to explain the life of their design, an extension to the Bocconi University in Milan, to the judges of the first World Architecture Festival in 2008. Their tag-team discourse, accompanied by slides which are markedly absent from our volume, is included in this book as an exemplar of how to reduce, through language; of how to (re)present architecture dispassionately yet with integrity through words. And furthermore, to do so using bullet-points!

Like a visionary, Stevens' writing up of his thesis on the prospect and meaning of rural existence in twenty-first century Ireland, is feverish and immediate. We are reminded of Noel Moffett and Frank Gibney, two architects practising in 1940s Ireland who peddled utopian propositions in the face of the slum epidemic. In reaction to the swelling of Dublin through intense rural depopulation and in-migration to the capital, Gibney imagines a realigned Ireland with its civic and commercial centre shifted over to Ireland's real physical centre, somewhere near Athlone, Co. Westmeath. Moffett imagines a more efficient Dublin in 2093, staying where it is, but taking on the form of a Corbusian model. We could argue that Stevens' chapter is less hypothesis than thesis but still, the urgent tone and tendency brings him closer to Moffett and Gibney than to his contemporaries. For all three, writing seems a compulsion. Interestingly, in their built preoccupations, all three concentrate on the family dwelling – in an almost Heideggerian sense – but uncannily, all three envisage the happy future for mass housing to be in the realm of self-building and prefabrication.

Robin Walker's lecture to the RIAI in 1978 posits that there is no such thing as progress, just change. This would ring true for the juxtaposition of Stevens in 2010 with Gibney and Moffett in 1943: the horizon is the same and the crisis is a crisis in another form, only the conditions have shifted. In this sense, can Irish architectural history of the twentieth century (i.e., historicism) continue to trade in the terms of *zeitgeist*, that each episode has a different character? It is a questionable ideology and yet many of our volume's essays and lectures are underpinned by the premise of *zeitgeist*. Arguably we learn about socio-political and economic contexts, or the cultural climate for architecture from a particular essay – take Frank McDonald's chapter from his seminal and contentious <u>Destruction of Dublin</u> (1985) or Gerry Cahill's manifesto from 1978 for examples. Indeed, the book's only organising principle is chronological which in itself infers the pedantry of historical change.

Zeitgeist principles guide us through many of the pieces, including my own which describes regeneration in Dublin at two particular times and the cyclical nature of memory making. But, what is more provocative as we leaf through this volume is the connectivity between the essays. We are grateful to Cahill for citing Aldo Van Eyck's point, made at a Team 10 meeting in 1959: "Man is always and everywhere essentially the same [...] Modern architects have been harping continually on what is different in our time to such an extent that even they have lost touch with what is always essentially the same." In this way then, McDonald's account of the underhand development of the 1960s Irish city is poignant in our post-Celtic Tiger repentance; Maurice Craig's calls for conservation and warnings for the safe keeping of our built heritage ring just as true now as they did in the early 1970s; Ray Ryan's account of an urban design competition in 1991 Dublin, on the eve of Temple Bar's iconic reframing, reminds us of our poor (if anything, decomposing) architectural competition culture still in the early twenty-first century... and so on.

———————

Fintan O'Toole is definitely a writer who grapples with the conditions of *zeitgeist*, *volksgeist* and all the rest. His essay "Ireland" (1999) - written to accompany an exhibition of recent Irish art on a jaunt around America – is useful in its abstraction of Irish tendencies (so-called *volksgeist*, spirit of the people). He refers to the map of Ireland and we think of the diagrammatic approach of Frank Gibney's nationalist polemics. But more so, in O'Toole's magisterial account of Kate Murphy in the Irish Fair in New York (1897) and his description of the soil, nature, repackaged as culture, we think of Tom de Paor's N3 pavilion from 2000, Venice Biennale. This tiny yet complexly construed structure of peat briquettes, consumed and considered through a series of cards placed in one of its chambers, is precisely about packaging Ireland's natural resource as an aestheticised experience of Irish architecture.

N3 is a conceit. Not really written, it is presented in our book through the architect's drawings and a sound bite of information around its conception(s)... patterns of concepts, i.e., patterns of thought. The iconology of the poetic briquette house is evoked by art historian and curator, Catherine Marshall in her story of dislocation – an artist pingponged from urban to rural. In this Marshall is rather like the rest of us: not quite knowing what to do with N3, but being very aware of it all the same. Marshall does however write about Dominic Stevens and places her artist, Juliana Walters, alongside Stevens' experience in <u>Rural</u>.
Place, places, to displace.

In a volume which is about "writing architecture", we could not forget that detective branch of the business - architectural history. Edward McParland's essay on the Christ Church Deanery presents us with a tidy, almost perfectly formed study of architectural history: how to retrieve a building from complete obscurity? With only a photograph from 1912 as evidence, the historian sets off. The subsequent writing must be layered. McParland writes the processes of the archive into his account, all the while we are learning about the disappeared building's physiognomy and the conditions of its commissioning. The building has been investigated and its exterior and plan retrieved for the moment.

Roger Stalley's exploration is colourful and full of fruity hypotheses around the meaning (origin and primary function) of the round tower, reputedly Ireland's only true indigenous building typology. The writing is akin to a release; in this instance a release of scholarly findings and questions. For both historians, writing architecture is the only option. It is not cathartic or an accessory to the craft: it is the craft. It is the means of exposing the archival enquiry and the site excavation. With Stalley's unafraid approach, the round tower is at last stripped back and hopefully, laid bare. By asking the most basic questions, our architectural culture is enriched.

———

The aspiration for this book is that it might be a small but full volume which would accompany architects through their lives: a *livre-de-poche*. If that is to work it should be full of little surprises. The reader should find for instance a short review of C.I.A.M. from 1953 by the young Dorothy Cole (later Walker); or a rant about the poverty of Irish architecture compared to its American counterpart in the early 1960s by Sean Ó Faoláin. That a literary giant like O Faolain commented so directly on architecture, or that the architectural community in Ireland was in tune with the post-war rhetoric of C.I.A.M. (International Congress of Modern Architecture) in Aix-en-Provence are two surprises, contributing to the spicy flavour of this collection of writing. Presenting younger generations with the student writing and sketches of Arthur Gibney from 1957 - with his calls for a situated modernism for Ireland, pre-empting the churches of Liam McCormick and the rooted practice of Andy Devane – will surprise. None of these examples constitute a wholesale revision of twentieth-century Irish architectural history but they do suggest an architectural culture lurking in 1950s Ireland.

Editorial intervention throughout the book has been minimal. Sometimes, in the translation from spoken words to writing, there has been a need to shift punctuation. But the editors have maintained a light hand, thus contributing (we hope) to a textured collection. Idiosyncrasies have been maintained. For instance, authors' systems of footnoting have been left alone, unless incomprehensible!

The line drawings in this book are by artist Fiona Hallinan. They have been specially commissioned in reaction to particular writings and the process of the commission was motivated by our aesthetic/ethic vision for the project; that it would be a monochrome, non-glossy and tactile book; again, something of a *livre-de-poche* that could become a companion read for students and architects alike; to be picked up and put down over a lifetime. i.e. patterns of words, patterns of space, patterns of thought...

- Ellen Rowley, April 2012

One.

Frank Gibney

Framework for a National Plan, 1943

Published Pamphlet 1943

Designed by Raymond Unwin with his partner Barry Parker, both Letchworth Garden City and Hampstead Garden Suburb were proposed as planned alternatives to the byelaw street environment that had appeared across vast swathes of the British landscape in the latter stages of the 19th century. With Unwin's writings arguing that the act of making establishes a rich relationship between a man and his surroundings, and the garden suburbs providing space for such making, the partnership's work can be read in particular as a reaction to the byelaw street's deficiencies in providing for man's mental faculties. Such deficiencies had long been established as a political issue by commentators such as Dickens. Addressing members of parliament in a short anonymous tract as early as 1836 he reminded the ruling classes of their duties to the working man:

> *You offer no relief from listlessness, you provide nothing to amuse his mind ... he saunters moodily about, weary and dejected. In lieu of the wholesome stimulus he might derive from nature, you drive him to the pernicious excitement to be gained from art. He flies to the gin shop as his only resource.*

The garden suburb movement was one of many middle-class responses to such calls. It might be useful therefore to offer a definition of the state of mind that Dickens describes – that of monotony or boredom. In 1934 the psychologist, Otto Fenichel defined the affliction as 'an unpleasurable experience of a lack of impulse' related to man's need for 'intense mental activity'. He was of the opinion that boredom resulted from an inadequate environment, and claimed that '*we have the right to expect some 'aid to discharge' from the external world. If this is not forthcoming, we are, so to speak, justifiably bored.*'

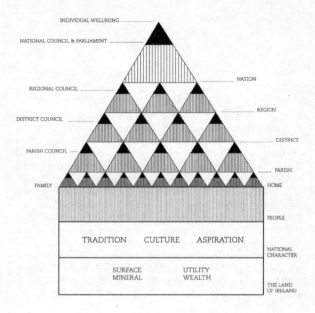

INDIVIDUAL WELLBEING

NATIONAL COUNCIL & PARLIAMENT

NATION

REGIONAL COUNCIL

REGION

DISTRICT COUNCIL

DISTRICT

PARISH COUNCIL

PARISH

FAMILY

HOME

PEOPLE

TRADITION   CULTURE   ASPIRATION

NATIONAL CHARACTER

SURFACE
MINERAL

UTILITY
WEALTH

THE LAND
OF IRELAND

Constitution of Ireland.

Article 6.

'All powers of government, legislative, executive and judicial, derive under God from the people, whose right it is to designate the rulers of the State and, in final appeal, to decide all questions of national policy, according to the requirements of the common good.'

Article 41.

'The State recognises the Family as the natural primary and fundamental unit group of Society, and as a moral institution possessing inalienable and imprescriptable rights, antecedent and superior to all positive law.'

Article 45 (2).

The State shall, in particular, direct its policy towards securing
1 / That the citizens (all of whom, men and women equally, have the right to an adequate means of livelihood) may through their occupations find the means of making reasonable provision for their domestic needs.
2 / That the ownership and control of the material resources of the community may be so distributed amongst private individuals and the various classes as best to subserve the common good.

Stress diagrams of Ireland.

Today.

Political democracy.
Vested interests.
Individual outlook.
Inequality.
Poverty & plenty.

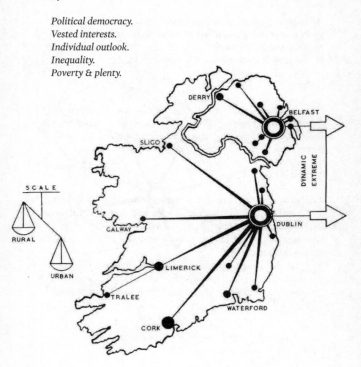

Amputated body.
Heart-each part.
Anaemic & high pressure extremes.

Stress diagrams of Ireland.

Tomorrow.

Politico-economic democracy.
National production, distribution & consumption.
Community outlook.
Equality of opportunity.
National wellbeing.

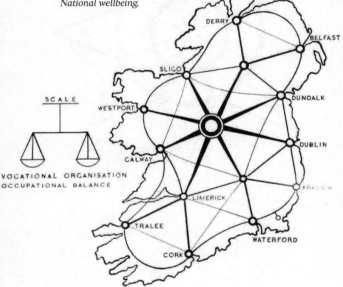

Whole body.
Healthy circulation.
One heart.

lat. 53° 35' 25' N.
long. 7° 56' 30' W.

'Dark was my dream, though many a gleam of hope
through that black night broke.
Like a Star's brightest form through a whistling storm,
or the moon through a midnight oak!

My dream grew height as the sunbeams light,
as I watched that Isle's career.
Through the varied scene and the joys serene
of many a future year'

- Denis Florence McCarthy, A Dream of the Future

The above diagram illustrates the first basic approach to the Plan which is assessment and recognition of Ireland's proportionate and relative place in the World Scene, geographically, economically and socially.

'Though patriots flatter, still shall wisdom find
An equal portion dealt to all mankind ;
As different good, by art or nature given,
To different nations makes their blessings even'

-Goldsmith

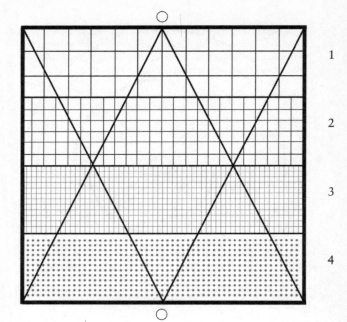

34

1

2

3

4

This diagram illustrates the second basic approach of
the plan which is the engendering of a community sense in the
individual (local, regional, national and global), by the graduated
upward and downward interdependent filtrations of: -

1 / World concerns affecting the nation.
2 / National concerns affecting the region.
3 / Regional concerns affecting the locality.
4 / Local concerns affecting the individual.

'The good things which God has created for the
benefit of all men should find their way to all alike
in a just proportion.'

-*H.H. Pope Pius XIIth*

Eighth Reading
(government, administration & planning)

Planning

3
2
1

Government & administration

Genesis & evolution.	**Territoral.**	**Administrative**
The People.	Locus.	centre.
	The Land of Ireland.	

Representative voice.

The Family.	The Home.	Parish centre.
Parish council.	Parish.	District town.
District manager.	District.	Regional capital.
Regional council	Region.	National capital.
National council &	National territory.	
parliament		

'When we see a lot of framed timbers, different portions of which we know have been gotten out at different times and places and by different workmen, and when we see these timbers joined together and see they exactly make the frame of a house or a mill, we find it impossible to not believe that all understood one another from the beginning and all worked upon a common Plan.'

-Lincoln

'All our activities should be co-ordinated in a way to produce a coherent pattern and a single machine of national endeavour, wherein all parts work in unison without friction and waste and geared to the power of the State. The Plan visualises the States as a pyramid, the base being our National Resources, the body the Population, and the point, or summit of the whole design, the well-being of the individual.'

- extract from the Author's plea for an Irish National Plan published in *Irish Times* of February 17th, 1940, and *Irish Independent* of March 1st, 1940.

Sixth Reading (culture)

Education

Parish & district schools	5
Regional vocational colleges	2
National university	3
National art galleries & Scientific institutes	3
Archaelogical studies (whole country)	-
Local art galleries, civic museums, folklore institutes & libraries	1,2,3
National archives	3
Naval academies	2
Physical cultute & institutes of hygiene	1,2,3

Religion

Parish churches	-
Diocesan cathedrals	-
Pilgrimage centres & wayside shrines	-
National shrine & cathedral of Christ the King	3
Missionary college	3

Seventh Reading (recreation)

Regional & national

Landscape, scenic coastal and nature preserves; national parks: developed holiday resorts; bathing: boating: parkway drives: camping and caravan locations: canoeing and walking: sea & inland fisheries: game preserves & bird sanctuaries: mountain climbling: hunting: planetarium: aquarium: botanical and zoological gardens: youth hostels: open air theatres: motion picture locations. *(whole country as determined)*

Local recreational centres

Parks, playing fields, swimming pools, village & community halls, drama, dancing singing, golf & race courses	1,2,3
National theatre	3
State opera house & concert hall	3
National stadium	3

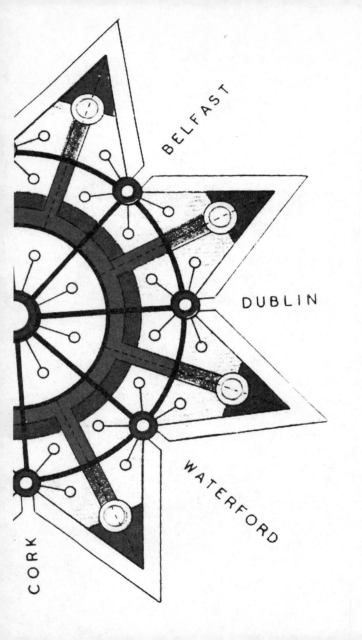

BELFAST

DUBLIN

WATERFORD

CORK

Two.
Noel Moffett
Dublin 2093 AD, 1943

From two previously unpublished lectures to
Dublin and Cork Literary Society, 1943

'Planning' is a terrible word – to some people. The word symbolises for them rigid control, the freedom of the individual gone for ever, totalitarianism. They see themselves as automatons, thinking, moving and speaking as human cogs in a vast inhuman machine, their thoughts and actions predetermined for them by some inspired dictator or group of dictators with supreme power.

I am making an attempt here to show that planning does not mean that. It means the converse of that. It can provide mankind - every man, woman and child - for the first time, with a human environment. It can do more than that. It can make man conquer the machine and abolish war and its horrors.

FACTS

I am not going to appeal for planning. I am merely going to state briefly a few facts about our world as it is today, or rather as it was in 1938, which may, I think, be taken as a normal year. These facts tell their own tale of a world unplanned.

- 1% of Irish farms are supplied with electricity. In Norway the figure is 90%. Just now, owing to lack of paraffin and candles, how many thousands of Irish families are sitting every evening in the dark with their fire the only source of light?

- If you walk down Gardiner Street at 11 o'clock any night you will see small groups of children aged 1 year to 10 years huddled together shivering, sitting on the edge of the pavement. Why? Because their parents don't go to bed till 12. And they all sleep in the same bed.

- Flats built by the Dublin Corporation cost £900 to £1000 per flat on the average. Similar flats, giving better accommodation cost £500 to £600 in Sweden, Finland and Denmark. Why?

Because the design is simpler and modern synthetic materials and methods of construction are used. And the rates in Dublin are 20/6d in the £, almost the highest in the world.

PLANNING IS LONG OVERDUE

Perhaps I have cited enough facts about the world we live in. Perhaps you will agree with me that planning is long overdue. And my submission is that planning and planning alone, can cure these evils and make that world a better place for all who live in it. Some wise men among us go further than that, and state that man has now reached the stage when, unless he plans – and plans mighty fast, he will be exterminated as a species, exterminated by machines and objects of his own invention. Be that as it may, one thing is obvious: up till now society has not changed fast enough to make use of the tremendous technological advances made by science in recent years. And the result is war – two world wars in one generation.

I am assuming, here, that we in Ireland will change with changing conditions and that we will use, when we build, the thousand and one new materials which science has given us (continuing to use many of the old ones, but in a new way).

I am assuming too, that after the present war an international order will gradually come into being and that Ireland will take her place as a unit member of that order, and will develop simultaneously along national, regional and international lines.

It is Ireland's physical development which concerns me here and I shall try to describe, in brief outline, what I think this country will look like in the year 2093, that is after another 150 years development. And I say straight away that it will bear no resemblance to the Ireland of 1943. 'Why?' you exclaim with horror, but, I hope, some curiosity. The chief reason is the recent tremendous development of these thousand and one new materials which I mentioned. And now I want to tell you a little about 1 or 2 of the more important of these.

NEW BUILDING MATERIALS

All over the world at the moment factories and laboratories are converting these materials into armaments. As soon as peace is declared, many of these same factories and laboratories will make them into building materials with which to build a better world. Ireland cannot afford to ignore that international reconstruction; she must use these new materials; and therefore I say that the Ireland of tomorrow will look very different from the Ireland of today.

PLASTICS is the great building material of the future. Already today it answers almost every building problem. And there are hundreds of plastics. The raw materials for most plastics are timber and coal (or turf) – Irish native materials. As long ago as 1937, at the Paris Exhibition, I saw a house built entirely from by-products of turf, from walls and windows to cushions and curtains. The best-known plastic at the moment is Bakelite – our light switches, brightly coloured Woolworth tumblers and salt-cellars, buttons and buckles are made from Bakelite. If you want one material which is transparent, translucent, sound-proof, weather-proof, heat and cold insulating, you have it – a plastic material which even bends rays of light.

PLYWOOD is today a structural material as well as a decorative one. We can span 300 feet with plywood arches. It can be bent to any shape, is weather-proof and sound proof, and can be faced with any metal, glass, veneer etc.

Our fathers boasted of spanning 50 feet. Today we span one thousand feet, nearly 1/4 mile with a reinforced concrete flat arch 8′ thick in the centre. The house we were born in took 2 years to build. The house our sons will be born in can be built in less than 2 days, and speed is no longer synonymous with poor construction.

There are hundreds of synthetic metals designed in the laboratory to withstand any stress or strain and to take any load.

The chemist today is the builder's best friend. He can solve all his problems. The materials are there to be used, if only he will use them.

PREFABRICATION and MASS-PRODUCTION are the key-stones of tomorrow's buildings. The parts of every building (including the structure or framework) will be made beforehand in the factory or laboratory and put together on the site. The production of these parts in large quantities, for world distribution, will reduce the cost of every building to a fraction of what it is today.

NOT FANTASY BUT FACT

I ask you now to project your minds 150 years into the future, and to imagine that you have just flown over from America. Your aeroplane, with 500 passengers, is flying slowly over the Irish countryside so that, with me as your guide, you may observe what that countryside looks like. Presently we will approach Dublin and I shall briefly describe the layout of the city. We shall land at Collinstown airport, and fly again, in a number of small *autogyre* ('plane-cum-car-cum-boat') air-taxis, right to the centre of the city, and shall examine some of the buildings at close quarters.

Let me say immediately that the buildings I will describe are not architectural fantasies, but all of them either exist already in other countries, or can be built today. The rural and urban environment which I shall describe is a logical and practical outcome of the application of modern thought and building technique to the solution of national, regional and local problems.

THE COUNTRYSIDE

Well then, here we are, looking down on the Irish countryside from the air. We notice three things immediately –

1 - The farms are no longer scattered over the country. They are grouped together.

2 - The roads are either straight or gently curved. The old turns and twists are gone.

3 - Large sections of the country have no buildings at all. These are national parks – Connemara, parts of Mayo, Clare and Kerry, Wicklow, part of Waterford, the Glens of Antrim, the Donegal Highlands.

Gradually Irish farmers have realised that the old 20- to 100-acre farm was uneconomical and the fact that the small farmer had to rely on the kindness of his wealthier neighbour for the loan of reaper, binder, thresher. Now the farms are larger, and are clustered together in small groups on the periphery of the village or parish community enabling every farm to have abundant electricity and piped water-supply. Every Parish Council owns all the larger farm implements and machines necessary for modern farming on scientific lines, and loans them every year to the local farmers, at a nominal charge.

THE VILLAGE

The village is the centre of parish activity, and is a properly-planned self-contained unit, designed to satisfy the needs – physical, social, spiritual and cultural – of the farming community. It contains schools (for children and adults), churches, cinema, theatre, dance-hall, library, museum, agricultural college, shops, public houses, cafes, market hall, everything planned to make the village as attractive to the rural dweller as the city is to the urban dweller.

The modernising of farming meant that one machine now does the work of 20 farm-hands, and the output is a hundred times greater. Unemployment is a thing of the past as every village has a compact industrial centre situated on its outskirts, where industry – mostly of a kind connected with agriculture - absorbs the young men not needed for farming. Rural production and consequent wealth, is thus greater at a minimum of effort; leisure is increased and happiness is abundant. Now, once again, we have time to 'stand and stare'.

THE TOWN

The villages are, in their turn, rural satellites attendant, as it were, on the urban star – the country town - and looking to it for the more concentrated brightness of community life on a larger scale.

The centre of each town is a large park with municipal and public buildings, larger shops and stores, cafes, restaurants, etc., grouped about it. Beside the park, too, is the central bus station, and everywhere, alongside the main roads, are situated small landing-grounds where Dr. O'Toole and Mr. Murphy go up or come down in their own *autogyre* ('plane-cum-car-cum-boat'). The railway is a thing of the past. All internal transport of people and things is now done much more conveniently, efficiently and economically by air or by road. Residential areas surround the 'town centre'. These are of 3 kinds:

1 - Detached houses, each in its own garden.
2 - Terrace houses, with a common garden or with individual gardens.
3 - (In larger towns) 5-to-20 storey residential blocks designed on the cellular principle, the blocks spaced wide apart and set in parkland. Each dwelling unit has its own garden beside it, on every floor level.

The roofs of all buildings are flat and are used as gardens, sun-loggias, etc.

All towns are surrounded by a green belt, where building is forbidden other than that connected with recreation. In this green belt too is situated the town's principal passenger aerodrome, and beyond the green belt to the east of the town, is a compact industrial centre with its own road, rail, canal and air communications.

Where old villages of special historic or aesthetic interest have remained, they have been preserved as such, and have not been spoiled by modern development. Where old towns have developed to most modern needs, ancient buildings of importance have been moved to new sites, if their original sites did not fit in with later planned development.

ROADS

All main roads pass through open countryside for their entire length. They link together villages and towns, but do not pass through them. A single wide road takes the traveller from these main roads to each village and town. Two roads crossing at right angles pass over or under one another. Contact between the roads is indirect, and is affected by means of a clover-leaf crossing. High speeds are thus maintained on all roads, without fear of accident.

Generally speaking, the countryside presents an ordered appearance to the traveller by air and by road. Monotony is non-existent, as the scene is ever-changing. The whole country is at last developed, along sane, human lines, for the benefit of ALL its inhabitants, rural and urban.

THE CITY

Our plane is now approaching Dublin. We circle over the city once or twice, and examine its layout. We land at Collinstown airport where our own small *autogyres* await us. We jump in and alight anywhere we please in the middle of city or on its residential outskirts, for we find small landing-places everywhere, alongside roads and streets. Private aeroplane becomes private motor-car, as the wings telescope against the side of the chassis, and wheels are lowered from the undercarriage. The same machine is transformed into a boat by another simple adjustment. For almost every citizen now possesses his own amphibian 'plane-cum-car-cum-boat'.

Well, then, let us see what Dublin looks like from the air. At first glance we cannot believe that we are approaching a city at all for we can see no buildings. Everything is green – trees and grass everywhere. For the whole of Dublin is a park. Then we see more than green. We see the colour, bright colour, which, on closer inspection we discover comes from flowers, planted everywhere, and from the buildings themselves.

IN THE CENTRE OF THE CITY

In the centre of the city are 6 tall pencils of buildings pointing to the sky, grouped on the north side of a winding blue ribbon which is the river Liffey. Each office building is 100 storeys high, and is situated in the centre of a square formed by a grid of wide streets at ¼ mile intervals. The shadow cast by each pencil, even when the sun is low, never reaches a neighbouring pencil, ¼ mile away. Each office building accommodates 9,000 people, so that

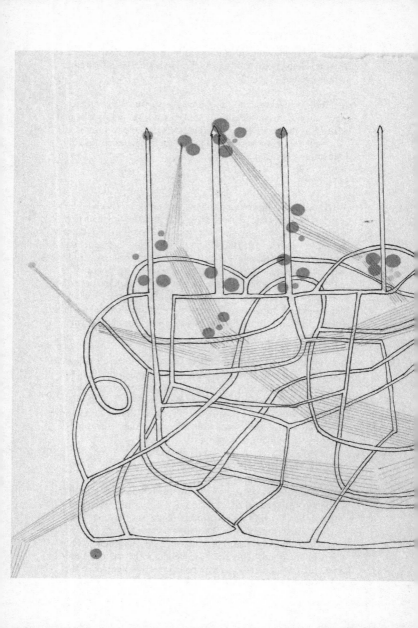

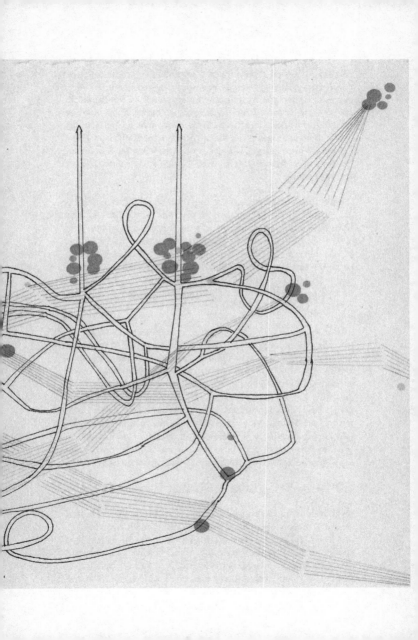

the density in the centre of the city is higher than it was in the bad old congested slum days of 1943, and at the same time the centre has gradually been thinned out - now it is a huge park, gay with colour and brightness, for the walls of the buildings are of plastics, transparent or brightly coloured. Each building offers ideal working conditions for its occupants, and at 2 o'clock in the afternoon, when the day's work is done, the lifts take the workers to ground level, where electric buses or their own plane-car-boat take them swiftly to their home or their club or their sports pavilion.

Situated among the trees at the foot of these tall office buildings are parking places, shopping centres, cafes, restaurants, clinics, libraries, churches, cinemas, theatres, and ancient buildings of special interest. The old Renaissance Four Courts and Customs House have been preserved as museums. The metropolitan cathedral forms the nucleus of an ecclesiastical centre. All these buildings are set right back from the main traffic arteries, and are approached, through the park, by smaller informal roads and paths.

To the south of the river we find a central electric-bus station, government administrative buildings, municipal offices, and buildings connected with national, regional and international affairs. Dublin's old cathedrals and churches have been preserved in settings worthy of them. Here, too, near the river, we find a hotel centre, with its gardens, swimming pools, tennis courts and summer-houses, every bedroom and living-room with a magnificent view and sunshine all the time. And here two large educational centres have developed around Dublin's old universities, where adolescents and adults study together an ever-increasing number of subjects. This is the centre of the city.

HOUSING AND A GREEN BELT

Surrounding the centre, in a wide circle, are long residential blocks, 5 to 20 storeys high, designed on the cellular principle, and described in greater detail in a moment. Surrounding these residential quarters is a 3-mile wide green belt, a protected zone of woods and fields and market gardens. Here all building is forbidden except that directly connected with agriculture and horticulture, recreation and sport. Thus the city is assured of a fresh supply of meat, fruit, vegetables and dairy produce every morning. And here, right beside his home, every citizen spends a very great part of his time – his leisure hours - playing games, swimming, boating, fishing, making love, or just strolling about in a rural environment. In this green belt are situated all the hospitals and also Dublin's two great aerodromes – Collinstown on the north side and Baldonnel on the south side – both of them 4 times as large as they were in the 20th century.

All buildings have long since been removed from Howth Head and Killiney Bay. Both are permanently reserved as seaside open space, to be enjoyed by everyone.

Beyond the green belt, at intervals along the circumference of the city, are the garden cities or residential satellites – two-storey houses, detached or in the form of terraces, each in its own garden, and all properly orientated to make the most of sunshine and good light. The main roads from the city serve these satellites but do not run through them. Schools, playgrounds and parks are provided so that no child or adult has to walk more than ¼ mile to school or play. Small neighbourhood centres are dotted among the housing development and each contains churches, more schools and training centres, library, dispensary, cinema, health centre, cafes and restaurant, local shops and public houses. Dun Laoghaire is no longer a packet station as most of the cross-channel transport of passengers and goods is now done by air. The town has become a residential satellite of Dublin and separated from it by the green belt.

Thus the citizen of Dublin has the choice of living in two kinds of environment. If he insists on a house in its own garden at ground level, then he must travel in to the city in the morning to his office or his factory, and back again in the afternoon. If he wishes to live nearer his work then he has a flat in one of the residential blocks surrounding the centre of the city.

The long residential blocks vary in height from 5 to 20 storeys, and in size from the minimum 'bachelor' flat to the very large 7 bedroom 'family' type. All the blocks run east and west so that the living-rooms, most of the bedrooms and the gardens face south and every room has a wonderful view. Each flat has its own garden beside it, and all the rooms overlook the garden, so that the housewife can see her baby in the pram in this enclosed garden from every room in the flat. And she hasn't to go to the window to look out – the whole wall is transparent.

Editors' note: This is not the full lecture but only an excerpt. Clearly Moffett was writing in reaction to the contemporary development of Dublin following the publication in 1941 of Sir Patrick Abercrombie's (with Sydney Kelly and Manning Robertson) latest Sketch Plan for Dublin.

Three.
Dorothy Cole

Review of CIAM, Aix-en-Provence, 1953

From *Irish Architect & Contractor*, 1953

- Note to reader: C.I.A.M. is the commonly used French abbreviation for International Congress of Modern Architecture.

The 9th International Congress of Modern Architecture took place at Aix-en-Provence from 19th to 26th July [1953]. The setting was ideal. Aix is the capital of Provence and has quite an air of grandeur. The heat and sunshine of Provence in summertime is tempered by the shade of great plane trees and the splashing of many fountains, and the mingled feeling of untidy humanity and 18th-century elegance in this southern city provided just the right atmosphere for some of the too-theoretical CIAM city planners.

Whether it was the southern ambiance which influenced the Congress or not, I don't know, but although among some of the younger architects there was a tendency towards a cold theoreticism, in general the feeling of the projects presented was a very human one.

The theme of the Congress was 'The Dwelling' (mainly the city dwelling), and it was interesting to see the extremely comprehensive study which had been made by various CIAM groups from every continent (except, strangely enough, North America) of the way people in countries all over the world like to live. Although, inevitably, an attempt at organisation in providing ideal dwellings for large numbers of people in large cities is likely to involve a certain amount of repetition in dwellings at the expense of individual taste, the schemes submitted at CIAM 9 retained a live consideration for the individual while incorporating him into large units of dwellings such as the *Unité d'Habitation* at Marseilles, which I shall be describing in more detail later.[1]

From a study of the schemes presented, two points are evident:

1 - That large buildings are more in keeping with the scale of population in large cities than a number of small ones. It is

more suitable, in a large city, to have thousands of people living separately in one large, fine building of combined dwellings, than to have thousands of people living separately in thousands of tiny identical dwellings spread for miles over a large area of land. Furthermore, apart from the purely intellectual satisfaction of the ideal relationship of scale, it is becoming increasingly urgent, on the strictly practical side, to stop the devouring of land by cities, as populations increase and new networks of small dwellings spread over the countryside in a most uneconomical manner.

2 - The importance of the architectural treatment of buildings. It was very obvious that mere good town-planning is not a sufficient solution to the dwelling problem. The benefit of CIAM in this respect is enormous. Although composed of the most eminent city-planners, such as Le Corbusier, it is primarily a group of architects to whom the design of a building is all-important. In this, CIAM 9 differed greatly from meetings of town-planning organisations where the town-planners are content to consider general amenities for town-dwellers but attach very little importance to the architectural quality of the buildings. A scheme for housing 2,362 people at Paddington in the heart of London, now almost completed, illustrated the CIAM point perfectly. The architects, Drake and Lasdun, have provided every possible amenity within the unit which is comprised of blocks of varying heights on a slightly sunken site which gives traffic peace and a feeling of seclusion in the centre of London's ten million people, but together with that, the design of their elevations is excellent, so that the man who gets up in the morning and looks out of his window, instead of seeing some grim creation of his local municipal authority, receives a pleasant impact of well-designed lines, forms, planes, a harmony which cannot but soothe him every time he sees it.

It must be admitted that CIAM 9 was dominated by the spirit of Le Corbusier. All the projects have been influenced by the Marseilles building. He is still so far ahead of everyone else that even the young architects and students of whom there were a great number at the Congress and who fought with all the other elderly architects, had nothing but admiration for him. An interesting side-shoot of the Congress was the list of suggestions from architectural students. There was a report from the Dutch group of students on their university course and the method of teaching, which would seem to resemble quite closely the course at the National University [NUI, University College Dublin]. Their suggestions for improvements might also be applicable.

Footnotes

1 - Cole is referring here to her review of Le Corbusier's Unité d'Habitation for *Irish Architect and Contractor*, published in August 1953. In this CIAM 9 review, she concludes 'The highlight of CIAM 9 was the visit to Le Corbusier's Unité d'Habitation. This building will be described in the next issue of the *Irish Architect and Contractor*.'

Four.

Arthur Gibney

Towards a National Architecture, 1956

A thesis submitted by Mr. J Arthur Gibney, Student.
(from *Royal Institute of Architects of Ireland Yearbook*
1956 – 57)

- The drawings reprinted here are by Arthur Gibney and they accompanied the original publication of his thesis. Gibney went on to become one of the most distinguished architectural draftsman, specialising in watercolours, in the history of twentieth-century Irish architecture.

One of the basic characteristics of the modern movement in Europe is its cosmopolitan and international character. Yet an investigation of any of the great styles of the past would prove that all good architecture, including good classicist architecture, must always be subject to a national and even regional influence. And even in the short time elapsed since the modern movement came of age, it is possible to detect the effects of such influence. It is not difficult for instance to distinguish an Italian office block from a German or Brazilian one, and in those places where traditions are strong, a new richness and maturity have arisen to grace the stark and pristine forms of the modern ethic. In some parts of Europe there is visible a considerable opposition to such growth and a tendency to consider it a violation of the modern ideology. Yet any attempt to carry the already overloaded abstract principles of modern architecture further, without an awareness of environment or without recourse to traditional or organic limitations, will end in a facile and over-mannered expressionism. The introduction of such a national awareness in Ireland is essential. It is particularly necessary at the moment when the initial fervour of our introduction to the modern idiom has nearly died and when our shops and cafes have succumbed to a rash of black glass, chromium plating and all the glittering necessities of the pseudo-contemporary face.

Poland is a country which has much in common with Ireland. It is small, it is on the outskirts of Europe's cultural zone, it has had a very troubled history and it has preserved its Catholic religion from its conversion. In an examination of Polish post-war architecture, the rebuilding of her blitzed cities or the published work of her architectural students, we find a unique national character. Polish architects are not inhibited by the doctrinaire prescription of mechanical functionalism. Their sense of what is appropriate goes beyond the satisfaction of elemental necessities. Fundamentally the spirit that permeates the work is Baroque - the spirit that has permeated the arts and peasant crafts of Poland for centuries. It is because that spirit persists that Polish architects are still able to do what their contemporaries in many countries find very difficult - to design easily and unselfconsciously in monumental terms and to make effective use of the resources of painting and sculpture. Another source of strength is the consciousness of the continuity of their traditions and their strong decorative sense which they are able to gratify by drawing on the rich store of motifs afforded by the Polish peasant crafts. The forms they use have all the familiar structural and material qualities of the modern movement but they are given an unmistakable Polish inflexion.

In the short history of European Modernism there have arisen many attempts at national expression, though few could be compared with the condition of Ireland as well as can that of Poland. Sweden and Denmark have characteristic styles, and Aalto in Finland and Moser in Switzerland have provided brilliant and modern national architecture. Logically enough, one of the greatest lessons in hereditary expression comes from France. The work of Auguste Perret is distinguished by his lucid and rational expression in ferroconcrete. This expression was not merely personal, it is essentially French and was the outcome of such French pioneers as Toni Garnier and [Henri] Labrouste and the writings of Viollet Le Duc. His own style was the fulfilment of a great national tendency. His awareness that reinforced concrete had a dignity of its own, and that architectural forms are essentially structural forms, though capable of infinite and subtle modifications in the interest of proportion, was part of a national outlook deflected from its course by the Renaissance. For Perret is the continuation of the great Gothic builders of the *Ile de France* and he is essentially of the structural North. His rational outlook and his sensitivity to profiling are completely French, as is his precise and logical use of texture and decoration. The lesson he teaches is now nearly lost behind the eager and poetic fallibility of Corbusier's internationalism.

What have we in Ireland to offer the demands of a national style? From the Georgian tradition (the nearest thing to hand) we inherit a love of proportion, a refinement of detail and a magnificent precision of craftsmanship. But these are the inherent qualities of all Palladian architecture and indeed are some of the basic requirements necessary for the success of any modern school of thought. Beyond the eighteenth century we have little architectural tradition to inspire us. We have no early classical period, no era of great Church building, no medieval grandeur to rival the Gothic of England or France.

For a complete appreciation of our native sensibilities it is necessary to go back to our ancient Celtic tradition and the works of the early Christian era. From a purely architectural viewpoint, these eras are completely undistinguished. Churches, the only important architecture to be attempted, were of a very simple character, small in size and usually just a background for the other arts. However, it is not the style of architecture we want to perpetuate by our study. (This has already been attempted by that gullible movement known as 'The Hiberno Romanesque' and was brought over from Germany by Cormac McCarthy.) Irish art is the most advanced and magnificent development of Celtic Europe and shows us the human mind in one of its most fanciful and daring aspects. It is conceivable that from the investigation of such a natural and indigenous development, we might arrive at a more precise evaluation of our inherent tendencies and contribute to the enrichment of our architecture. By this I do not mean to encourage the meaningless application of trumpet spirals, zoomorphs, and other antiquarian and unsuitable motifs to modern carpets, tapestries, Christmas cards, etc., or the preposterous idea (which is known to have been tried) of re-using the Celtic vocabulary as decoration for our modern buildings. But from the study of such a lengthy and brilliant tradition it must be possible to keynote the schematic qualities inherent in our cultural fibre and so to determine the direction of our modern ideas.

It is quite obvious from the briefest studies of our ancient glories that we have at one time been possessed of a magnificent decorative instinct, a love of colour and texture and a mastery of surface and of natural material. Nor is this of the type of tranquil decorative detailing we find in Georgian buildings which in its objective calm and essentially symmetrical nature shows its Hellenic parentage and the essential simplicity of the Mediterranean mind. Irish art in its tenseness of pattern and

Doorway Clonfert

Capitol
Clonfert.

compare with the carved
Swans on Smiths Head of
the Lagan.

animal
Book of Durrow.

62

Newgrange

Cross at
Bedun

The Mask of the River Lagan by Edward Smith (Custom House Keystone). Compare the tense intertwining swans with some of the early Christian spiral carvings.

Newcomen's Bank: Ivory's preoccupation
with duality for its quality of tension.

Project for East Punjab Parliament, from
sketch by Polish-born Matthew Nowicki.

Project for Chapel of Three Faiths
at Brandeis University, from sketch
by Nowicki.

1/50

asymmetrical development belongs to the subjective north and shows much of its early Eastern influence in its sinuous and dynamic rhythm. Nevertheless, these tendencies did break through our Georgian reticence and are responsible for much of its unique charm. An example is the typical Georgian terrace. Upon examination it will be found that every house is of different design, although they are all bound together in the further unity of the terrace block - this would be a very unusual sight in England. Our sculptures too are of a different character to the essentially imitative and humanist tradition of the Greeks. Carvings had an extraordinarily sensitive feeling for flattened but modulated relief and an almost fierce elegance of design. In their curious intaglio-like decoration one is constantly reminded of the fantastic and shallow carving on Oriental Temples.

It is significant that our arts are not only Celtic but Christian also. Considered from this aspect their study might be of benefit to the insipid fusion of our present Liturgical arts with our modern churches. The two periods of greatest achievement were the eighth century which saw the creation of the Ahenny Crosses, the Ardagh Chalice and the Book of Kells - and the tenth century, the era of the figured high crosses. Yet this art embodied a persistent pre-historic tradition. It is a Christian art with a strong pre-Christian background and an early medieval art to which the points of view of the Iron Age are still familiar. In its early phase it lived on false pretences. It was a pagan decoration masquerading as an ecclesiastical art. The ornaments which were used for croziers, shrines, church lamps, or which were entwined around the initials of Gospel Books, were none other than the old *La Tène* spiral, Germanic animals and half-disguised figurations of Celtic Gods. It was only in the ninth and tenth centuries that art became conspicuously directed to its Christian ends and there emerged from the endless draperies of Celtic ornament the purposeful images of the 'Cross of the Scriptures'.

The strange and subtle beauty of the Celtic tradition is now no more, and all the elaborate iconography has disappeared forever. They did not develop into a splendidly decorative Romanesque Church Art, a carved and jewel-encrusted Gothic beauty, or a purposeful and original native culture to precede the classicism of the eighteenth century. The sudden withering of so powerful and so ancient a tradition is strange enough in itself but it can doubtlessly be readily explained by the vicissitudes of history. But it is more than strange that our native genius for Pattern and Decoration, that coherent spirit that so powerfully persisted in all our works for many centuries should also die and leave us with a barren future. It is inconceivable that something of this spirit did not survive in our later works and lies still dormant in our race, awaiting the opportunity (which our troubled history could seldom have allowed) of sympathetic expression. From this viewpoint it would be worthwhile to make some brief investigation of that later history.

In our long and painful association with the *Sassenach*, we find the cause of much of our cultural poverty and of the moribund condition of our arts. Yet they can hardly be blamed for the complete disappearance of the authentic *La Tène* tradition and the withering of our early Christian art which gave so much to promise to our early medieval years. For in truth the great traditions of our Golden Age were already lost before the English gained a foothold and there remained only a pale shadow of that irreducible individuality which characterised our monastic civilisation. Francoise Henry writes:

> Irish Art, for all its wild background, was in execution a fragile, delicate thing, a fairy construction erected in a calm atmosphere, too frail to stand the violence of the Viking Cyclone. Its incredible balance was incompatible with terror and flight. It was a work of patience, the product of subtle minds working in peace and leisure. With the insecurity of the Viking wars, the very possibility of making works like the Ardagh chalice and the XP page of the Book of Kells was destroyed forever.

And not only was it destroyed in spirit, but the material conditions on which it was based also disappeared. The workshops were wiped out and with them the marvelous technical knowledge, the product of centuries of experiment. Never again will Ireland see the artistic brilliance of the eighth century. Secrets were lost, enameling died as an art, and *millefiori* work and the exquisite combinations of filigree of the Ardagh Chalice disappeared, never to be attempted again.

Such was the country the English started to colonise in the twelfth century. With the decline of the originality and independence of the native style, foreign influence came to be felt. Romanesque columns and capitals replaced the low even chiseling of our portals, and, in Dublin, we see the commencement of a watered-down Gothic style brought by the colonists, and having neither the structural ingenuity of its birthplace nor the decorative enrichments of the 'Old Irish style'. The early Normans did bring the art of woodcarving with them, though their successors destroyed any hope of it blossoming into a native tradition, by cutting down all our forests a few hundred years later. In the intervening centuries there was little creative activity in any style, with the exception of the unexpected carvings of the fifteenth- and sixteenth-century altar tombs which show something of our ancient instincts. This lethargy at such a time is very strange. Warfare was still a cursory affair of skirmishes between Irish and Irish, Irish and Anglo-Irish or Irish against English. It was not until the seventeenth century that we saw any signs of real war and the English use of scorched earth policy which prevented creative artistry in any form. This inactivity of three centuries is a reflection on the visual sensibilities of both sides and we find its effects continuous up to the Georgian Period.

The Renaissance came to us mainly through England, a new England, awakened to the Italian past and it was undoubtedly the Anglo-Irish ascendancy who, through their patronage of foreign and native genius, gave us the delightful purity of our Georgian capital. Nevertheless, the difference in the style here and in England is worth noting and is frequently a source of amazement to English architects. The Irish style is distinguished by its purity, simplicity and complete continuity of the Palladian tradition which gave way in England to Baroque vagaries and the frilly elegance of the Adams' period. These differences are partly due to this tradition, and partly to our own native tendencies which, though curbed as they were by centuries of frustration and by the disciplined limitations of the Palladian style, nevertheless insisted on expression. Such expression as they were afforded, however, was confined architecturally to our more modest buildings and when present in more important projects was confined to detail.

Symmetry and monumentality are foreign to the Irish spirit. All our ancient works show a horror of such obvious and static qualities. The internal logic of all our art was governed by infinitely more subtle laws. The use of deceptively similar curves disposed inside identical frames avoided this regularity without recourse to the equally obvious unsubtlety of complete asymmetry. Symmetry and monumentality were essential ingredients in the Palladian formula, which depended for its effect on a mathematical perfection of geometric ratios which was just as strange to the subjective Celt as the Platonic ideal it embodied. Most of our Georgian monuments are of this ideology. It is significant, however, that most of them were actually designed by Englishmen. In the case of the Irish Georgian terrace we often find a departure from such rules. The door and windows are rarely symmetrical in arrangement.

Neither are they obviously asymmetrical but come between the two in a subtle and unmistakable harmony. In spite of the cellular character of the terrace and the classical rules, no two houses are exactly alike. Neither are they completely unlike one another for they vary in minor and devious ways. Such developments are traditionally Irish in character and are unknown in English architecture. It is significant that such terraces were not built by English architects but by local builders and craftsmen. (It may be worthwhile mentioning here the work of two Celts in America, that of [Louis] Sullivan and [Frank Lloyd] Wright. Sullivan in his glyptic and plastic ornament showed his Irish inheritance. Wright's own ornament showed harsher and cruder influence but his obvious fear of symmetry and monumentality in his architecture are symptomatic of his race.)

The case of [Thomas] Ivory and [Francis] Johnson [sic], two Irishmen who did get a chance of designing civic buildings, is also worth investigation. Newcomen's Bank, by Thomas Ivory, is unique in its deviation from classical ideals in a period when such were sacred. In its façade he exploited a strange and sensitive duality, whose tension-giving qualities are reminiscent of the linear drawings of Celtic work. The detailing and decoration on this building are highly original, having little connection with classical motifs at all, but typical of the low delicate chiseling of our early Romanesque period. With the exception of a certain preference for Grecian ornament, Johnson's classical work was anything but eccentric in character and successfully rounded off a period of brilliant achievement. Yet for a Georgian Classicist and an outstanding practitioner in what must have been a very academic circle, he exhibits a strange side to his character. His decision to build the Chapel Royal in the 'Romantic Gothic' style is very strange. It is even stranger to find him placing it in the middle of a completely Georgian quadrangle and within full view of [John/Jan] Van Nost's *Justice* over the castle gates.

The appearance of this 'Romantic Gothic' style coincided somewhat with the decline of the Georgian era. It was almost completely confined to the architecture of small Protestant churches. It was also completely confined to Ireland and represented something of an original and national development. It was characterised by a severe and disciplined unity, a forced structural emphasis, and a delicate and imaginative fantasy of detail. The extensive use of rhythms of pointed pinnacles (usually atop the buttresses) and simple unadorned spires gave it a curious appearance of sharpness and solidity. I do not intend to find a direct connection between this unusual outbreak and our native genius. Although it would be extremely difficult to do so, it does seem that the fantasy and the very incongruity of the style can be related in a perfectly definable way with our national temperament if not with the exact spirit of our archaic work. It is sufficient to call attention to it, creating as it does a unique and original vernacular many years before the insincerity of the Gothic Revival appeared in England.

Another unusual phenomenon was the amazing standard and variety of craftsmanship to be found in Ireland during the Georgian era. In its formation it showed certain foreign influences and particularly the influence of travelling Italian artists. In the development of our Georgian plasterwork many Italian names (the Francinis, Bossi, etc.) are eminent but in its ultimate brilliance it became a great Irish tradition and the names of Michael Stapleton and Robert West are synonymous with this splendour. Stone carving, too, flourished at this time, though, unlike the plasterwork, it nearly always remained subdued by architecture and never attained that disciplined effervescence or lyrical imagery inherent in Celtic carving. Yet it exhibits some lively flourishes and in the work of Edward Smyth (the greatest sculptor we have produced) we find an animation and feeling unequalled in the 'Three Kingdoms'.

We have nearly arrived at our own era and there remains only one development of our popular arts to which I would like to draw attention. This is the unusual and highly evolved tradition of decoration on our public houses, in imitation of coloured marbles and with geometrical patterns deriving from that type of rustication in which the face of each stone is given the shape of a flattened pyramid. These patterns have given the style the name of 'Irish Pub Wall'. Mr. Osbert Lancaster, writing on the subject, suggests that it may have arrived in the country with the certain Italian plasterers in the earlier part of the eighteenth century. He continues,

> But whatever its history the Irish art of pub-painting is marked by characteristics which relate its products in a definable way to the Book of Kells and other Irish work of the early Christian Period, while today it has a twofold significance - for Ireland, as a genuine and surviving folk-art; for the world at large, as an example of what external colour can achieve when uninhibited by consideration of 'taste' and yet controlled by a sense of structural logic.

There is nothing else that I can add to this history. In conclusion I must admit that a national style based on the modern movement and the ingredients of Celtic culture is a difficult synthesis to visualise. All big commercial undertakings must remain international in the expression of their structure and development of their functions. Yet it must be remembered from our recent investigation of the past styles that the dominant Irish trend is a decorative one, a tendency to decorate in a lively but subtle manner, based on organic and animated abstraction.

Our national style would have a highly developed sense of abstraction, a passion for colour and richness, and sculpture (there should be a vital sculptural style) would be architectural in inclination, in the form of decorative screens and panels. These carvings would not be in the round, or applied to the buildings but would be organically part of it, a low and even chiseling of the architectural planes. It would not be difficult to make use of such qualities, even in the case of commercial architecture, no matter how international in outlook, or determined in structure.

But it is not in commercial architecture Ireland would look for the purest and most complete expression of Nationality.

Modern churches are not international in character, no matter how universal they are in liturgical concept. Nor can it be said that the modern movement has as yet developed a mature and satisfactory style of church architecture. The development of such requires the forming power of a great religious tradition and sufficient vitality to ensure the adaption of that tradition to current interests. Without such adaption, the tradition grows obsolete and archaic. These factors were predominant in Gothic France and are responsible for what good churches can be found in modern Italy. Ireland more than any other place in the world today has that responsibility and sincerity of religious tradition necessary for such development. We are notably lacking in the other factor, the vitality to ensure the adaption of this tradition to our contemporary culture. Yet this is a logical outcome of our troubled history and its relief is only a matter of time and education. Ireland seems admirably fitted for the development of a moving and significant church architecture. It should be remembered too, that what claims we have to artistic greatness in the past came through our early Christian art and it was the fervour of our belief which produced such brilliance as the Book of Kells, the Ardagh Chalice and the great crosses. In the development of a new church form, we would also have a great opportunity for our national genius of decoration, and in the unity of fusion of all our talents we would have the promise of a significant and valuable contribution to the culture of our time.

Five.
Sean Ó Faoláin

Is Architecture a Was? 1962

Forgnán (vol.1 no.5, May1962)

To return to Dublin from a period of residence in the United States and to as much as hear the word 'Architecture' (with the big A) is to be held up for an instant as by a foreign word. One says 'Architecture?', looks expectantly around, and there it is. 'That stuff!' The word has taken on, at once, another and conglomerate meaning, blended of such various senses as quaint, elegant, rather silly, uncomfortable, expendable, costly, nice-to-look-at, historically interesting, affected, photographable, anachronistic. Then one looks around for the sort of thing one had got used to, which is a construction, and it is just not there. Then one begins to think. And one gets back, very quickly, to the primary postulates on which American architecture, like everything else in America, is based, and all becomes more or less intelligible and, if not wholly acceptable, falls into place. The American way of life is, as I see it, based on, chiefly, two ethical propositions: that every man is equal to every other man, and that work is the cardinal virtue. From these elements one could trace outward a wide ramification of effects.

The frozen limit

For example, on the egalitarian principle, mass-production is not only necessary but admirable - to each man his bit of bread, clothes, radio, automobiles, education, pink telephones, housing, and so on and on. From this there follows some odd effects. One is that quality and equality do not go together. For example, the mass-produced bread of America seems to be made from coast to coast of farinaceous chewing-gum, preserved (I have been told) by the same chemical as is used by embalmers to preserve corpses. Preservation is a by-product of mass-production - the goods have to travel far and wide.

Hat trick

Neither have our American friends solved the problem of how to give every man, and woman, a bit of real variety inside the normal conformity of mass-production, e.g., in dress. They have created, as Simone de Beauvoir was the first to point out, an extraordinary illusion of variety in women's clothes. The villain is again mass-production plus egalitarianism. An English woman-friend has told me an interesting experience which illustrates how it works. She saw a charming green velvet hat in a shop window on Fifth Avenue. Accompanied by a New York buyer for a big store, she went in to price it. 'Ridiculous!' said the New Yorker. 'Come with me! I'll get it for you much cheaper elsewhere.' They went from store to store. The hat reappeared in each store, ever so slightly changed - a feather, a button, a tuck - and it also became cheaper and cheaper as they went from the most classy stores to the least classy. The hat also lost some of its quality as they went from store to store, until at the end of the journey, now a fifth cheaper, it just was not worth having, though still (quote-unquote) 'the same hat'. Within a couple of weeks the original and charming hat would have been unavailable - priced out of the market by mass-production - priced, indeed, out of existence. Everybody had it, and nobody had it.

The jerry-hat trick

One need not elaborate about the effects on architecture. We have only to look around Dublin to see jerry-built Georgian doing the hat-trick on the real stuff. (Now we are the geriatrists of the jerry-hatrists). If it comes to that, there was once a type of home called a villa. To Cato, Cicero or Horace it meant a country-seat, or a mansion at the seashore, or near the city. Now everybody in these islands may have a villa, meaning a detached, or semi-detached suburban dwelling of no pretensions at all, more-or-less mass-produced. It is about as significant socially or intellectually as the mass-produced title of B.A. In the same way, skyscrapers can now be produced out of any architect's bottom drawer, at the turn of a wrist.

The great American highways

But this is where the work-equals-virtue comes in, to infuse a tremendous energy, ambition and inventiveness into the formulas of mass-production. The drive of America is - even when misguided - undeniable. One of the most exciting forms of deconstruction, for example, is the American highway. These three-lane or four-lane, double highways sweep through the country from coast to coast, from north to south, bounding over great rivers, shamrocking out, to, and in from lesser roads, tunnelling under or winding over high hills. (The paintings of de Kooning, slashing and criss-crossing great canvases, reflect this inspiration.)

Energy and its exciting progeny

From this energy comes the habit of tearing down and building up again, in higher and more compacted forms, buildings that are still perfectly sound and have for years returned a decent income. From this at first glance seemingly reckless energy, comes the New York skyline as seen from the New Jersey turnpike or the Triboro Bridge route out of Manhattan. It is, as an American friend - architect - once said to me in disgust, an architectural mess. From any angle, level road or soaring helicopter, it is also excitingly beautiful.

One force behind this energy is, no doubt, wealth, or the possibility of more wealth, or the spur of success measured in terms of wealth. Witness the new skyscraper going up on top of the Grand Central Terminal in New York City, on 42nd Street and Park Avenue. This is right in the heart of the city, which is always at present crowded and traffic-jammed! What the streets around will be like when this mammoth is completed everybody hates to think.

American inventiveness

But wealth is not the only spur. Inventiveness, once born, operates out of its own energy. An instance to illustrate: north of Chicago at Evanston, on Lake Michigan, North Western University, finding itself hemmed between roadway and lakeshore, on very expensive land, has now discovered - that is, its architects have discovered - a solution to its problem. It is about to build out over the vast lake between a series of man-made lagoons. I have forgotten where a building is at present being constructed above ground into which it is planned to sink foot by foot as its weight increases. Maybe it is beside the Liffey?

When [Eero] Saarinen was invited to design a triumphal arch for the city of St Louis to commemorate its historical role as the Gateway to the West across the Mississippi he took a small piece of aluminium strip, bent it into an elliptical arch, laid it on his desk and said (in effect), 'Enlarge that by a thousand'. I have only seen the architect's drawing. To a layman it looks magnificent, and impressive. We may be very tired of Mr. Stone's grilles, and everybody is copying them now, but what a saving in warm climates this simple idea effects on air-conditioning bills, and they do look striking.

Large-A Architecture

There is a lot of large-A Architectural stuff in the United States, and very odd it looks nowadays. The oddest examples of it I saw were Frank Lloyd-Wright's quaint Byzantine-Moorish buildings in Rice University at Houston, Texas. Equally strange are the various McKim, Mead and White Renaissance palace jobs one comes across, though they are now taking on an unexpected quality of old-time appeal where the great glass-boxes climb on each side to the clouds - literally to the clouds, for on foggy days sky scrapers do scrape the sky. The Racquet Club on Park Avenue has begun to look more and more appealing since the Seagram Building and the Lever Building appeared close at hand. These probably owe something, too, to the contrast. I notice, by the way, with interest, a tendency among architectural critics to suggest that F.L. Wright went a bit batty towards the end. (Do they like his earlier work at Rice?) Witness, they say, the Guggenheim Museum. Yet, compare its simplicity with the messy maze of the Museum of Modern Art on Fifty-Third Street, which is always uncomfortably crowded because the rooms and the stairs are so small. Here is space, light and air. Visitors circulate freely. The spiral idea is quite sound. It works beautifully in his fine-arts store in San Francisco and nobody every complained there that they had to stand with one foot higher than the other. If, as is suggested, Wright hated modern art and this is his revenge, his revenge backfired. Large-A architecture (v. H. H. Richardson and Stanford White) never had a future in America, where requirements are indigenous. The work of [Louis] Sullivan lasts because he recognised this fact.

With the work-energy naturally goes the competitive spirit and endless change, which is not always a matter of *plus ça change*, though it also often is. (The Seagram Building is a real innovation; the later bank-building north of it is the same old thing all over again. The new, unfinished, apartment building rising around a central round-elevator-tower hard by the Wrigley Building in Chicago looks like an innovation.) The point is they welcome change, always, no doubt, within the limits of their social and economic needs and the profit-principle. What these last seven or eight words mean I would not know, but we may safely presume that certain 'laws' do operate.

Hotels, motels and architecture

Some such law, for instance, must lie behind the odd fact that New York has only recently opened its first-built hotel in many years. Obviously there must be some sickness in the hotel business in New York. Elsewhere - New Orleans, Chicago, San Francisco, Dallas, Las Vegas, Memphis, Philadelphia, Washington - you can find first-class hotels that really are first-class. I have never stayed in a New York hotel - and I have sampled a dozen of them from the Plaza down - which is not either a factory or a dump once you get beyond the first floor. It is all due to labour costs, I suspect. The great modern American invention in hotels is the motel, where there is no labour cost, i.e., no service and no food. I am all for them. So are most Americans, a thrifty people who do not like paying high for poor service. In this regard it is, I think, a significant detail that many residents in big hotels do not eat in the hotel, not even breakfast: they walk across the street to a cafeteria. Architecturally these motels are often amusingly inventive, but, basically, they are not what we call Architecture. They are simple constructions.

An active and work-absorbed people - the two most often used words in America are go and problem ('Let's go!...There's no problem...You gotta problem?') - they are, to an astonishing degree, anti-aesthetic, or a-aesthetic. Which, depending on whether you utter the word with a beam or a sneer, might not be altogether a bad thing. Not that they are not 'interested' in Art - they have some of the finest galleries in the world which, unlike ours, are always full of people - but 'interest in' is a very different matter from being 'absorbed by'. By and large, interest in Art in America is an interest in a was. And Architecture is a was.

A featherbed of wasness

To come back from all that to Dublin is to come back to a delightful featherbed of wasness, until one shuffles over the edge of its beautiful centre and falls plonk on one's behind on the cold, cold linoleum of our 'modern' age. Then to preserve Georgian Architecture at the price of preferring Crumlin Constructionism seems a high price to pay for wasness.

What, by the way, is our way-of-life's basic postulate, proposition or priority? Look at the name of the journal and you will see. Can you buy it? Can you eat it? Can you smell it? Can you sell it? Can you do anything with it except wonder at its non-materialist approach to the business of building for the here and now? Can you translate it? I can. It means Twelve Inches off the Ground. Well, why not? That too, could be an interesting form of construction, like lake-dwellings.

<u>Six.</u>

Maurice Craig

Attitudes in Context, 1974

From *Architectural Conservation: an Irish viewpoint* (a series of papers read to the Architectural Association of Ireland (AAI) by Irish authorities, between October and December 1974)

In a sense I have the easiest task of this series, that of introducing the subject of architectural conservation, on which my colleagues will later elaborate in the light of their particular specializations.

Nobody can escape having an opinion of some sort on this subject. Dublin, in particular, has been brought up against this problem during the past ten or twelve years in a way unprecedented in her history. I shall speak mainly of Dublin; but I want to say also a certain amount about buildings in the country at large and to begin with some reflections on the social and historical background of the whole subject.

There is nothing new about a desire for preservation. The Emperor Hadrian is one of the earliest in European history of whom it is recorded that he took positive steps to conserve and restore notable buildings of the past. He is also - and I emphasize that this is not, very definitely not, the same thing - one of the earliest figures who actively promoted building new buildings in the revived styles of the past. A great deal of damage has been done and is still being done by this confusion between the desire to conserve the masterpieces of the past and the desire to produce counterfeit copies. To me, at least, it seems that the latter of these motives is, at least nowadays, more frequently the enemy of the former than its ally.

The motives for preserving old buildings are very frequently mixed. Many of us have a sentimental attachment to what is already there simply because we have known it all our lives. This, I submit, is nothing to be ashamed of. But we shall obviously have to do better than that if our desire to preserve is to survive the first critical scrutiny, whether by ourselves or by our opponents. There is a considerably smaller, but usually more articulate group of people whose critical sense, and experience of enjoyment, tells them that a particular building is a work of considerable art, and who resent being robbed of a work of art just because it belongs to someone else, when the art of the past in other forms, such as poetry, easel-pictures, music, plays, silver and glass, not to mention motor-cars, clothes and films remains accessible for our enjoyment.

I shall return to this aspect - perhaps the most important of all, later on.

There is another group, a group to which I often find myself tempted to belong: those who are mistrustful of redevelopment because they fear that, even though the buildings threatened with demolition may not have any very high value, their successors are likely to be positively offensive. This school of thought reminds me of the child in one of Belloc's cautionary tales which left its nanny and got eaten by a lion. Belloc, you will remember, ends his poem with the couplet;

Always keep a hold of Nurse
For fear of finding something worse.

Though I am prepared to admit that such fears are, all too often, justified nevertheless in the event, this attitude seems to me to be an ignoble one, and I do not think we should ever let it, by itself, rule our notions. In other words, I do not believe in playing for safety, except on very rare occasions when I admit it does seem to me to be sensible. There is, on the other hand, a more refined version of this doctrine which has, I think, great value and importance. I quote from an American political speech: 'The US is the most powerful nation the world has ever seen. But we are not omnipotent. While there are no limits to what we can destroy, there are limits to what we can build.' This applies with equal force to the business of architecture in our own small country, and not just for economic reasons.

I need not tell an audience of architects how many things there are which an architect can admire if they were done a hundred or two hundred years ago, but which it would be psychologically quite impossible for him to do today, even if his client had all the money in the world. Like every generation in human history, we are imprisoned in a strait-jacket of limited options. We should trust our architects, and the more we trust them the better they will be; but they will still be able, at best, to produce only mid-20th-century architecture. But we cannot live only in our own narrow time-band. We are not animals, we are men; and we look before and after. Sir John Summerson, who, like the rest of us, is not always wise, was nevertheless wise when he wrote that 'Man can form no picture of the future except by reference to the past'. Remember that the present is an infinitely thin slice of time, and that, even as we experience it, it becomes the past. No matter whether it is five minutes ago or five hundred years ago, it is still the past and we owe it certain duties because we are its children.

I am well aware that there is a school of thought which holds that henceforth all artifacts including buildings should be designed to be expendable, like so many bottles of stout. (I mean the stout rather than the bottles, though increasingly we have the expendable bottle as well.) I do not propose to join issue with that one frontally. Most of you, I am sure, feel that this metaphysical digression has gone on long enough. I will content myself with saying that I respect this attitude because it is an absolute attitude and I have a weakness for absolute attitudes. But I reject it. I do not see why I should be expected to do without the works of Sir Edward Lovett Pearce, any more than I should be expected to do without those of Jonathan Swift. Nor do I see why my descendants should be expected to, nor, for that matter, to do without the works of whatever future Swifts or Pearces may be living among us at this moment.

To return to the more specific problem of the replacement of old buildings by new, in, for example, Stephen's Green: this may be seen - in much more acute form than we have yet had the misfortune of seeing it in Dublin - in most parts of London, for example Berkeley Square, or in the high street of practically every town in England. Looking at these examples, I am convinced that it would have been better to leave moderately well alone.

But of course it could not have been left alone. If for no other reason, the fact that very few people now live or desire to live in the centre of any English town, and that the central sites are more profitable when used for all sorts of purposes which had never been heard of a century ago - chain-stores, supermarkets, cinemas, banks, post-offices, office-blocks, car-parks, cafés - or if they did exist a century ago, then they have now entirely changed their scope and scale - these facts would in any circumstances have exercised their pressure on the visible scene, first, by utilitarian adaptation of basically unsuitable buildings, later by their demolition and replacement.

If we want to freeze the appearance of any street or any precinct in or near the centre of any of our towns, it is essential that we should know exactly what we are doing. We are asking a certain number of people or institutions - the owners of the buildings in question - to forgo a certain amount of the profit or convenience which they might otherwise expect to have, so that we may continue to enjoy something which is in fact someone else's property. We cannot stop them getting out and going somewhere else, where there is more room in which to provide themselves with a tailor-made environment for whatever it is that they do. And when they do get out, we may well find that the empty buildings are of no particular use to anybody, or that the only takers will be concerns which are short of money, unconcerned about status, and anxious only to get low-cost accommodation on which they will spend as little as possible in the way of maintenance. If, for example, there are zoning regulations which are enforced to prevent light industry moving into such buildings as it is very prone to do, the resulting stagnation does nothing to help the building: quite otherwise. It is common in English towns, and increasingly common in Irish country towns, to see nice old three-storey buildings with a shop on the ground floor and the floors above quite empty: usually because there is no adequate independent access to the upper floors. When there is any room in the back, it is usually covered with a squalid jumble of sheds and lean-tos, half-heartedly used for storage or simply falling down more or less slowly.

I have deliberately painted the picture in its gloomiest colours. In practice it is not always as bad as this. But supposing we had the power, would we knowingly bring about such a state of affairs as I have described, in which we hog other people's property for our own enjoyment, to its ultimate detriment? I have used three words or phrases which ought to be looked at a little more closely.

One is the phrase 'other people's property'. Leaving aside those buildings which belong to the government or the corporation or to other public bodies - who presumably owe us some sort of duty - does anybody nowadays really believe that other people can fully 'own' buildings in the sense that you and I can own a car or a television set? Even the ultimate legal owner, the ground-landlord, cannot insist on the buildings remaining in being, as the Fitzwilliam Street affair demonstrated. Even those of us who have no money in the Bank of Ireland feel that it belongs to us, and not only for historical reasons but for architectural reasons as well.

But we are still stuck on another of the words that I used - the word 'enjoyment'. Suppose, for example, that I enjoy whiskey, as I do. The community says to me: 'All right, you enjoy it, you pay for it, and every time you buy a bottle the Government will see to it that you pay a good deal of money towards social services, education, housing and the roads'. So far, so good. But now suppose that the scotch whisky industry, with its greater financial and promotional strength, manages to undermine the taste for Irish whiskey in Ireland, to the point at which the Irish whiskey distillers either go out of business or concentrate their resources on making imitation scotch? Would the community consider itself under any obligation to keep Irish whiskey artificially alive just to please me and a handful of other people who shared my taste? Not very probable, I think.

I should make it quite clear that this argument is not based on nationalistic feeling, though, by the way, I would not give much for a nationalistic attitude which was not fed by a large number of similar attachments to things and institutions which are in fact Irish. The point is that Irish whiskey already exists, and we have a taste for it. It came into existence quite naturally and it is very different from anybody else's whiskey. But it will not last for ever unless we continue to think it is worthwhile. In other words, unless we can fight back and persuade enough people to share our taste, it will die a natural death.

This brings me to the third of the words I want to examine: the shortest, and, as so often happens with short words, the most important. I mean the word 'we'. Who are 'we' who are asking our fellow citizens to help us to carry the burden of conservation of what belongs to us all? The number of people who notice or care about architecture in any country is always very small. It sometimes seems, in these islands at least, that they are outnumbered by those who positively dislike it. But, however that may be, it is certain that both sides are always vastly outnumbered by those to whom it has no meaning at all: those who do not even see it. At least, that is how it looks.

For myself, I am not so sure. I think that a great many people have a strong feeling for the difference between the atmosphere of one town and another. Most of what is acting on them is in fact architecture: the trouble is that nobody has so far taught them to recognize it when they see it. Mr. Ruairi Quinn is beginning to do so, in his excellent feature 'The Living Street'. They would notice quickly enough if it were all taken away overnight: the trouble is that it is, in fact, filched from them year by year and bit by bit so that by the time the process is complete they have not noticed that they have been robbed. In so far as such people resemble ourselves and differ only in the lack of visual training, it seems to me that we have a duty to act on their behalf, and should not be ashamed to do so.

This is not an easy thing to say in a country which has a deeply-rooted democratic tradition. Most of us are very reluctant to come out into the open and say to our fellow-citizens: I know better than you do.

But one of the features of a mature democracy is that the knowledge of experts under suitable political control is continually being turned into political action and applied for the common good. We spend our lives giving in to experts, from our dentist who tells us we must have that tooth out, up to the Government which says we must pay three pounds odd for our bottle of whiskey and buy it before eleven o'clock at night, or do without. Architects are, or should be, experts in environment, and environment is a commodity which, like the air we breathe, surrounds us whether we notice it or not, and will surround our children and their children.

I am not ashamed to say that we - and this time by 'we' I mean not only the architects and professional advisers but the lay members of preservation societies and pressure groups - have the right and the duty to ensure that the environment is not needlessly impoverished.

Here, I'm afraid, we must look rather closely at a word, or rather an idea: that of poverty. A country may be poor in respect of its standard of living and the spread of personal wealth, yet rich in the accumulated deposits of past civilization. Civilization, in turn, means not only good drains, good administration, efficient trains and telephones, but also (and this, by the way, is its primary meaning) the art of living becomingly and enjoyably in cities, with good libraries, concert-halls and so forth, not to mention the art of co-existing with your political opponents without finding it necessary to shoot them. In some of these respects we have obviously done quite well: but in the middle one, the art of living in cities, we are now facing the crisis which has already hit most of the rest of Western Europe. This is the impact of prosperity on poverty, and the threat which prosperity paradoxically directs against our inherited architectural wealth. For technological reasons, this threat is much more radical than it has ever been before.

The survival, almost intact, of Dublin down to, say, 1950 was a very freakish circumstance. It was directly due to our relative poverty in the twentieth century, coupled with the great wealth of the city, if not of the country, in the eighteenth. I remember thinking, at the time, what a freak it was, and reflecting that when prosperity, in its twentieth-century sense, hit this country, there would be a landslide of formidable proportions. I remember hoping against hope that by the time it began we should have evolved some machinery, of a practical rather than a visionary kind, to deal with it. After all, there had been Town Plans at intervals of about twenty years since the pioneer Abercrombie effort of 1913; we had been, before the First World War, very early in the field, under the old Georgian Society, in the business of published survey and description; after the Troubles the young Government had tackled, in the right spirit if not always with precisely the right results, the formidable problem of the reconstruction of the Four Courts, the Custom House and the GPO. There was a Civics Institute in being, which in 1925 had published an impressive large book on the future of Dublin. There was a Planning Act on the statute book. The Corporation, in the late forties, was carrying out, in Gardiner Street, Summerhill, Sean MacDermott Street and elsewhere, a scheme of urban renewal which, whatever may be with justice urged against it, had at least the merit of some sort of coherence.

Well, now we know. The avalanche is upon us with a vengeance, and it seems that after all our machinery is very feeble, and we have learned very little from the experience of other countries, and from our own have perhaps drawn the wrong conclusions. All hell, and here and there a little bit of heaven, seems to have been let loose upon our unfortunate city, which is beginning to look as though blind impersonal forces had laid hold upon it and were tearing it apart. Let me break off for a minute to put the case for the opposition. I shall do it as fairly as possible. If I fail to put it as forcibly as it should be put, I hope that someone else will get up after I have finished and put it as it should be put. It runs something like this: here is a city built by a rich landowning aristocracy, supported by a largish army of craftsmen and tradesmen, to be the political, administrative, commercial and educational capital of an oligarchy. If it was suitable for their purposes, it cannot possibly be suitable for ours. We are an increasingly middle class social-democracy: increasingly we work in offices during the day, and want those offices to be habitable workplaces, not a converted reach-me-down made out of someone else's house. After work we want to go home to somewhere where we have a bit of garden and somewhere to put the pram and hang the washing, where we are more likely than not to stay all evening watching the telly and drinking beer out of tins. Furthermore more and more of us have motor-cars and want to use them, and the local suburban supermarket looks after most of our shopping needs. In any case, the buildings you are making such a fuss about have reached the end of their useful life and are uneconomic to repair.

Let me take the last of these points first. It is in fact extremely rare for a building to reach a point at which it cannot be repaired. Almost any building, with money and suitable skill, can be brought back to life and made to last indefinitely. Serious structural decay is much rarer than most people, including many architects, think it is. I know this because for sixteen years I worked for a government body in England whose job is to help owners to repair and rehabilitate old buildings, many of which are much older than our Dublin buildings. Quite often it is actually cheaper to rehabilitate such buildings for present-day use than to build a new one. The English Historic Buildings Council, for which I used to work, had five years ago a budget of only about £800,000 per annum to cover the whole of Great Britain. This is not big money by today's standards, and with one-twelfth of that sum we could do a very great deal in Dublin and the provinces.

If you consider the City of London, and that of Amsterdam, you have two cities which, during the past three hundred years, have been very similar in their functions. Both are great trading and mercantile cities, both, in the seventeenth century were run by mercantile oligarchies, both are financial centres full of specialized businesses and trades closely packed together. Yet, on the average, nearly all the City of London has been rebuilt about three times since 1680, while Amsterdam during the same period has hardly been rebuilt at all. There is no doubt in my mind which is the pleasanter place to visit. Yet Amsterdam is not a dead museum: it lives and works at least as hard as London. It may, for all I know, work in a good deal less comfort: I dare say it does. After all, as we know very well, if a large eighteenth-century house in Dublin becomes an office, the senior partner has nothing to complain of, sitting there in the front drawing-room with a nice view over the square and a handsome chimney-piece and perhaps a few rococo birds and twiddly-bits overhead: and the clients envy him, as well they may. But the drawing-office staff and the typing girls may well be not so happy. In the end they may well move out in order to get and keep suitable staff.

I remember, many years ago, being very amused at a Spanish friend who told me that when he first came to Dublin he had digs somewhere out on Merrion Road. During his first fortnight he came two or three times as far as the Dodder at Ballsbridge under the impression that he had reached O'Connell Bridge and the Liffey. How absurd this seemed, as indeed it was. Similarly, many of you have no doubt played, as I have, the game of Monopoly, in which you buy and sell places like Ailesbury Road, Shrewsbury Road, Kimmage and Crumlin, and if you have enough money you build hotels there. I can well remember thinking how absurd it was to build hotels in such outlandish places. But it doesn't look so absurd now.

It is nearly fifty years since the RDS which used to live in Leinster House moved to Ballsbridge. Now, a number of other large and very central concerns have appeared to keep it company - an embassy, not far away the Telefís Eireann studios, and University College, Dublin, not to mention various large and very grand hotels, and probably quite soon the headquarters of Allied Irish Banks. There is nothing in all this which should surprise any student of Dublin's past history. In the seventeenth century, all the major concerns of Dublin were in Christchurch Place and Cork Hill: in the eighteenth they tended to be in Dame Street or College Green: in the nineteenth they started creeping along Nassau Street and to Dawson and Kildare Streets - remember that the National Museum, the National Gallery and Library and College of Art, as well as the Kildare Street Club, are all nineteenth-century creations. Within my lifetime Hodges Figgis, which started in Dame Street, has moved eastwards and southwards at least twice, and all the central-city restaurants which existed twenty-five years ago have disappeared. There seems to be some kind of irresistible long-term natural force at work here, like the precession of the equinoxes. In fact it is nothing so mysterious. It is the natural tendency for pressure to transfer itself to areas of lower density. And once such a movement has started to go in a certain direction, it tends to continue in the same direction until something stops it. Or, of course, till somebody stops it, supposing, that is, that it is desirable to stop it. I offer no opinion on this last question, except to suggest that it is difficult to imagine Ballsbridge, however remarkably transformed, looking like the centre of a city. To that extent my Spanish friend's naive mistake still seems ridiculous. But no doubt Dublin is at last in process of acquiring a secondary centre. This is a very common happening in English cities: Bristol, for example, which is roughly comparable in size to Dublin, and has spread in all directions, is completely shapeless and incomprehensible in the middle. In a desperate attempt to make sense of it they carved out a very grim 'Civic Centre' in the thirties. Much the same thing was done in Birmingham and in Nottingham, with equally horrible results. All round the edges of inner Bristol there are tracts of semi-derelict Georgian property which look at least as lugubrious as anything Dublin has to show, or to hide. The outlook in Bristol is in fact worse than in Dublin, because the scale in Bristol is so small. Two of Bristol's eighteenth-century squares have had screeching motor-roads driven diagonally across them. If ever a city needed the application of [Sir Colin] Buchanan's principles, it is Bristol.

Dublin, also, badly needs the application of Buchanan. But it does start with an enormous advantage over most English cities, that most of its centre is already on a generously large scale. Indeed this is an advantage which many quite small Irish towns enjoy: we have only to think of Birr, Mitchelstown, Armagh, Gorey, Roscommon and Blessington. Very often they seem to be all centre and no periphery. There are good historical reasons for this striking difference between Irish and English towns. It seems to me that we ought to foster the characteristic aspect of Irish towns, which is the provision of leisurely and enjoyable space surrounded with unpretentious but agreeable buildings, and resist very strongly the temptation to turn them into imitations of English towns. especially as very few people in England yet seem to have a coherent idea of what an English town should look like. We should, I think, beware of the up-to-date solution, because we know from experience that it may not remain up-to-date for very long, especially if it is based on current ideas and estimates about motor-traffic. I can well remember, about fifteen years ago, when everybody used to shake their heads wisely and say that before long it would certainly be necessary to cut a link-street through from South Great George's Street to cross the river and join up with Liffey Street. This would have meant the destruction of the Metal Bridge and the Merchants' Hall, and probably also of the Commercial Buildings. I don't suppose anybody now thinks this would have done any good at all, but it is a sobering thought that it might well have happened.

Let me tell you a cautionary tale from London which illustrates the danger. In about 1770 the architect George Dance laid out, south of the Thames, a very sensible piece of town-planning in which six streets, three of which lead to bridges over the Thames, a fourth to a ferry (where there is now a bridge) and two others to the south and east, are united in a single circus like many of those in Paris, and called it St George's Circus. In the middle of this was erected an elegant obelisk carrying inscriptions on its faces telling the traveller how far he is from various important places such as Charing Cross and St Paul's Cathedral. Thirty or forty years ago it was thought that this obelisk got in the way of the traffic, so it was moved and re-erected about a quarter of a mile away where it is quite meaningless and none of the inscriptions tell the truth any more. But before many years had passed, somebody invented the roundabout; so the middle of the circus was filled up with a large mound of earth with a rustic retaining-wall round it. So the obelisk might as well have been left where it was, and a lot of money would have been saved. Needless to say it has not been put back. Before we feel superior about this we should remember that for nearly two hundred years the elegant Phoenix Column put up by Lord Chesterfield used to stand proudly in the middle of the Castleknock Road in the Phoenix Park, facing towards Parkgate, until, in about 1930, it was thought to be an obstruction to the Grand Prix Races which were held there for a few years. So it was moved to a rather pointless situation to one side of the great avenue. But the races were only held for a few years. In the meantime, the Rush Hour Grand Prix continues with unabated fury in south London, with this difference; that instead of the roundabout there is now one of those very large invisible roundabouts consisting of a lot of one-way streets, which seem to be the only sort of rough-and-ready half-way-house towards the full Buchanan solution which we are likely to get until someone starts spending some real money.

Of course the mere moving of an obelisk or a column is a much less serious matter than the destruction for similar short-term reasons, of a building of real architectural quality. I hope that we have now reached the stage where no building of obviously outstanding architectural merit will be destroyed without a determined - and I should expect usually a successful - fight being put up to save it and give it good prospects for continued use. Of course there will be borderline cases, and among them there will be some losses. I know in advance that among the losses there will be some - I hope a very few - which could have been avoided. No system can be expected to work perfectly. But the point is that so far we do not even have a system. Until we have we shall continue to be at the mercy of blind chance and economic pressures and of whatever protection the County Development Plans may succeed in providing.

I dare say that, even with the law in its present unsatisfactory state, there will be some successes in the saving of individual buildings of high quality; but if that is all we can do it will be a pretty poor result. There are many parts of Dublin where the buildings, though not individually of remarkable merit, create a splendid effect because of the scale, the harmony of the materials, and the general overall observance of certain elevational standards. I think that at least two, and probably three, sides of Stephen's Green are of this quality. In Merrion Square and Fitzwilliam Street the fact that the houses are not quite uniform is an important ingredient in the effect: in Dublin at that period those who took the building-leases built two or three houses at a time, and there is endless enjoyment to be got from the subtle variations in the detailing of houses which are to a standard general specification. But once you allow nibbling away and partial rebuilding, a large part of the quality of the environment evaporates. Mr. McParland's recent article has shown this very clearly.

Consider, for example, such a street as Pembroke Road. Could anything be more splendid or civilized than this? The superb scale, the part played by greenery, the contrast between the unbroken run, with its rank upon rank of external steps, on the north side, and the detached articulated blocks on the south side, the intersections with Wellington Road and Raglan Road, the light and airy harmony of the whole: if we allow that to be cut about and mutilated we will not lightly be forgiven. Already two houses on the Lansdowne Road corner have been demolished and replaced by a modern building. I am quite sure that no more of this should be permitted. I gather that the building at present levelled is to be replaced by a facsimile. It may not be so very difficult to safeguard such areas as this. It is going to be more difficult, or at least proportionately more expensive, to rehabilitate such an area as Henrietta Street. Yet here, too, I am quite certain that it must be done. The Henrietta Street houses are among the earliest and finest houses in Dublin, and are equal to the finest that any city has to show. Besides, the relationship of the street to the King's Inns makes it an essential part of the setting of that lovely building. If you think that rebuilding on the old building-lines would meet the case, just take a look at Hardwicke Street and Hardwicke Place, the rebuilt setting of St George's Church. Better than nothing, I suppose, but not good enough for a city of Dublin's pride and quality.

The Quays present a problem of an altogether special kind: a unique challenge and a unique opportunity. I love the Quays, even in that state of tottering and gap-toothed decrepitude, which has been their condition ever since I have known them and for long before that. But even I can see that they are not long for this world. It may be - I hope it will be - possible to save some little patches of their old higgledy-piggledy charm, perhaps at the west end of Batchelors' Walk and possibly on Ushers Island. Every city needs some areas of unimproved property in which small useful trades can be carried on: trades which could not pay the increased rents which could follow from rebuilding. The gaps in such patches could be fitly filled in with modern buildings, small in scale but totally modern in style. As for the rest of the Quays, it seems to me that some bold imaginative strokes are needed: something as bold and imaginative as Gandon did when he built the Four Courts. Perhaps we are going to get such a stroke in the new Civic Offices? I am going to offer an opinion on the subject of point-blocks in general. In any case, the time has gone by when it would have been possible to insist that central Dublin should keep a horizontal classical skyline as has been kept in Leningrad. In the old days, when you stood on Grattan Bridge and looked eastwards down the Quays, you saw the Metal Bridge, beyond it O'Connell Bridge, and at that distance the Loop Line Bridge was all but invisible. Over O'Connell Bridge you saw the dome of the Custom House, marking the gateway to the world. It was only a faint and distant accent, because it is quite a long way off, and after all, the Custom House Dome is not quite the dome of St Paul's. Nowadays, when you look in the same direction, O'Connell Bridge appears to be framed between the two verticals of Liberty Hall and O'Connell Bridge House. Now I know perfectly well that these two buildings are not in the same plane and that only one of them is strictly a point-block. Nevertheless, from up river they do suggest the gateway to the Port of Dublin, and this symbolic suggestion seems to me not without value.

Of all the point-blocks which have sprung up in London in recent years I find the Vickers Tower by far the most attractive. I suspect this is not entirely because of its architectural qualities, but is at least partly owing to its relationship with the river. It suggests to me that Dublin might well be able to take a few more point-blocks in such situations as Upper Abbey Street and the Cattle Markets. In short, I don't see why quite large areas, even of Central Dublin, should not be totally transformed, in a mid-twentieth-century sense without robbing us of anything that we ought to value: and indeed there is a good chance that we will end up very much richer. After all, it has already been pointed out by people better qualified than I that all the historic buildings of value in Dublin put together take up only 2½ percent of the area of the city. (This, of course, depends on how you define them: I should think 5 to 7 percent more like it, and, I would add in the spaces between the buildings, which are as important as the buildings themselves.) Their value is out of all proportion to the small space they occupy. But again, and as a last word on this subject, I repeat that we must not think only in terms of architects' masterpieces: there will be many situations in which buildings of no very extraordinary value in themselves will demand to be treated with the same sort of reverence which we readily enough accord to the grandest works of a Gandon, a Cassels, a Johnston or a Pearce.

I think that in this country we are still some way from understanding the importance of ordinary buildings and especially of their insides in certain circumstances, and more especially of their plan-forms. It is not enough simply to keep the facade of a building as a kind of back-drop, though I think this is sometimes a reasonable compromise. But the Brazen Head, for example, turns out on close examination to be a purpose-built hotel of the first quarter of the eighteenth century, with a plan-form of exceptional interest, far more interesting than its elevation or even than its undoubted atmosphere. There is often, also, much to be learned from the constructional techniques used in old buildings, and this will not be learned by taking snapshots of their fronts. The backs are often more interesting and more informative. Naturally, of course, I have a vested interest in the saving of this kind of material because it is the subject-matter of an architectural historian's activity, and helps to keep us in business.

As a general rule, most eighteenth and early nineteenth-century buildings are more adaptable to new purposes than are their successors, because they were built to serve a more generalized set of requirements. There is very little difference in this period between a hospital, a college, an almshouse and a barracks, and even a lunatic-asylum or a school. They are often very nearly, and sometimes completely, interchangeable. A neat illustration of this principle is the fact that in the proposed reorganization of the central Dublin hospitals, the only one at present destined to survive is Dr. Steevens', because apparently its plan still works perfectly well for hospital purposes. Late-Victorian hospitals, and late-Victorian schools, like late-Victorian houses, are proving less adaptable, principally because they were more closely tailored to a more closely studied set of requirements which have since changed.

Florence Nightingale, you may remember, was the effective designer of St Thomas's Hospital which used to face across the Thames to the Parliament House in London. There used to be a guide who used to point across the river to those six red-brick blocks and inform credulous visitors that they were built by Henry VIII for his six wives. Now, alas, they have been replaced by a new purpose-built hospital which will in due course go out of date.

In the not very distant past some of our architects left a lot to be desired in the way they restored old buildings. The Board of Works architects who had to deal with the Custom House and the Four Courts did their best, more or less, with the outsides of these buildings which were, we must remember, almost completely gutted. But they could not resist the temptation to replan the insides, and, perhaps worse than that, they ignored whatever evidence remained of the internal detailing, and substituted their own brand of twenties detail for that of Mr. Gandon. There was even less excuse for the Corporation's architects in their treatment of Charlemont House, for, without the excuse of previous destruction, they swept away more than half of the building and even presumed to monkey about with Chambers' exterior apparently in the confidence that they were improving it.

We must remember that the twenties and thirties were a more permissive age than ours: in those days you could get away with murder. Nowadays, not only are there more vigilant spies among the laity, but there are certainly some architects who have more humility in these matters. The other side of the coin is that they have more pride also; pride in the achievements of their predecessors and in their own ability to rise to the challenge of respecting them, not by lip-service but by a practical response to the challenge they present.

<u>Seven.</u>
Robin Walker
Man & Matrix 2,
Reason, Intuition & Change, 1978

A paper read at the RIAI Conference, 1978

This paper is an enquiry into the basic philosophy which underlies the 'conservator - preservator' and 'developer' attitudes towards our environment. I must state at the outset that I am not a member of An Taisce, not because I do not consider that much of the work, and successful work, which your body has undertaken is of no significance, but because I cannot subscribe fully to your attitudes, particularly those which have to do with change -inevitable change. I do not really believe in progress (except perhaps material progress) but I do believe in change. I do not believe that the Greeks and Romans and by inference the artists of the Renaissance were so much superior as different from us; and, particularly in the area of abstract thought and art, I believe that they were simply different. In materialistic terms, quite clearly inferior, but in spiritual terms I believe not superior, simply different.

In that distinction, I have touched directly on the theme of this paper. I am concerned with change; with change and not with progress. I believe that change is meritable and something with which, in our attitudes towards our environment and in particular our built environment, we have to cope with and accept, indeed enthusiastically accept. Change no more means regress than it means progress. This demands from us a degree of tolerance which is foreign to Western culture; foreign because we subscribe to the existence of a dualism, we accept quite naturally an exclusive dualism of material and spiritual things, a philosophy of mutually exclusive objective and subjective substances and thought, reality and surreality.

The antagonisms that frequently flare between architects and preservationists could perhaps be more easily reconciled if a better understanding of the motivations of both parties prevailed. I can speak, I think, for architects but whilst sympathetic I do not understand fully and therefore cannot speak for the preservationists' motives.

It is hard for a sincere architect to be untrue to the materials he works with. Brick, stone and glass; steel, reinforced concrete and glass are the materials, the stuff of architecture. Brick and stone in the past, steel and reinforced concrete now. If Francis Johnson [sic] were alive today, he would unquestionably build like Mies van der Rohe, with steel or reinforced concrete and glass. I like to call him Ireland's 18th-century Mies. Similarly if Mies had lived in Johnson's time, he would have built in brick and stone and glass. In both cases, however, it is the basic order underlying the use of materials that constitutes the substance of architecture. I do not accept the late-19th-century view as propounded by the Arts and Crafts Movement that form is determined by material. I do not accept, in fact find laughable, Michelangelo's statement that in his sculpture he was 'releasing' from the stone its hidden form. Henry Moore, in his semi-abstract forms could claim more assuredly such a pretension but, in fact, both Michelangelo and Moore, like any mere architect, do not just work with (that is express) their material but inevitably impose on their chosen material their own preconceived designs. This shows itself very evidently when one tries to analyse the content and form of their work, the substance of the work. In our 18th-century buildings it is not the decorative doorways, porticos, cupolas, domes, etc., but the disposition of the brick joints, the patent reveals, the glazing bars; the spacing of windows in the wall, the surface and mass of the body of the building - as in Townley Hall or the Old Library in Trinity, which are the substance. In our age, it is the disposition of the steel frame, the detail of the corner and the jointing of steel to glass, or other infill materials and again the body of the building that constitutes the substance.

Superficially, of course, Johnson's [sic] 18th-century (and 19th-century) buildings are different from those 20th-century buildings of his alter ego. But intrinsically they are the same because of the basic concept of order. That is why, if looked at understandingly, they can be seen to harmonize the one with the other.

To me, as an architect, it is less important to try (and inevitably fail) to create a superficial harmony with the traditional externals of our cities (and here I am not speaking of those areas of the city which because of their unquestionable beauty must be treated with great care) than to surround oneself with beautiful things. Because to do so, to deliberately distort the nature of a building for that reason, for which one may be esteemed by the laity, is to put oneself in a contemptible position: as Françoise Sagan writes, *'I don't think it's all that important to preserve one's self-esteem or to think of oneself as an entity with precise distinguishing marks. I merely think that one shouldn't put oneself in a contemptible position (by contemptible I mean very precisely a position in which one despises oneself).'* [1] This would be the view of a conscientious architect and should be the view of his patrons and of the public. There is a compulsion to do right. Do right? In what context? Rousseau? Nature as the source of Truth? (An idea which became and largely remains one of the great revolutionary concepts of present society.) Again one comes face to face with the problem of change, of birth and death, no birth identical to the previous birth, no death identical to the previous death and not even the rising and setting of the sun, so rhythmical and certain, escapes difference and change.

Each dawn and each sunset is different, just as the sun itself is in a state of change. Is the source of all evil - as Rousseau postulated, in *Society* - the individual (as opposed to man)? Surely, however, the Truth, as exemplified in Nature, can be construed to include the natural individual as well as, with what we now know from the researches of anthropologists and sociologists, natural society.

To believe as Rousseau did, as John Weightman writes, that *'if only we could change the 'system' and eliminate the wicked 'they' who have plotted to make things go wrong, we would reconstitute the Garden of Eden and reinstate Paradise Now,'* is patently false. [2] The 'system' as with all man's processes and procedures is certainly a part of nature. There is no more a 'Noble savage' than a 'nobleman', and the same holds true for architecture, there is no 'right way' outside of and independent of the introvert nature of the material; there is only man's way which is the way. And how does one discover that? How then does one reconcile the work of Frank Lloyd Wright, Le Corbusier and Mies van der Rohe? Which of these men understood man's way? They all theorized with authoritarian zeal almost identical philosophies in their writings but produced contrastingly different architecture, great architecture.

Perhaps one has then to fall back on Rousseau's contemporary Voltaire and profess his philosophy of tolerance. If one puts these two philosophies together - Rousseau's cult of the individual and Voltaire's insistence on tolerance, one might expect chaos as the result. But one might equally anticipate a perfect seed bed for the expression of Truth.

Lack of tolerance expresses itself in the arrogance of the proponents of the modern movement in architecture and equally in the negative attitudes of the conservationist/preservationist. If tolerance were to be cultivated and an awareness of the inevitability of change accepted and understood then we might all subscribe to this dictum: *TOLERANCE IS THE WOMB OF CHANGE.*

If this tolerance were achieved we might with temperance be able to capitalise on the triumphs of the 19th century when PROGRESS was thought to be a realisable goal, and accept and promote enthusiastically change, for the sake of change whilst understanding the futility and absurdity of such an attitude if unaccompanied by some idealistic aim.

What idealistic aim?
Ideals are inevitably the expression of some kind of philosophical cultural attitude. I should stress a cultural attitude, for in fact I believe that ideals are as much subjective phenomena or substances and just as insubstantial as the conventions of any particular civilization or culture (cultures, in the sociological sense, can be uncivilized).

Here I return to the subject of dualism which I have previously mentioned. Our whole tradition, the roots of our tradition, are based on, I suppose you can agree, the philosophies of various periods which developed after the Greeks had had their say and those philosophies are totally circumscribed, limited, trapped, snared and distorted by the underlying assumption that there is such a quality as REASON by contradistinction with another quality called INTUITION.

Reason and intuition: mutually exclusive attitudes to thought and ethics. These two aspects of our culture have been so far distinguished and polarised that it has become almost impossible for us to analyse our motives without a preconditioned acceptance of the validity of these apparently mutually exclusive attitudes. Validity? I accidentally used this term and suddenly find myself in the sphere of value, value judgments, a supposedly inexcusable admission of irrationality into any philosophical discussion. Perhaps metaphysically acceptable but certainly not something of which one can speak, let alone consider seriously in any philosophical, in Western terms, argument.

Since the time of the Greeks, since Aristotle and Plato, the philosophies of the Western world have accepted without question the two aspects of thought termed rational and intuitive (theoretic/empirical, etc., are qualifications of this duality) and have proferred, in the area of aesthetics, a way of harmonization of these two antithetical qualities, the quality of reasonableness or at its best the Golden Mean. From period to period since then we have tended to describe each age as leaning more towards one pole than the other and have tended to admire any period which has seemed to us to synthesise the two extremes. But I do not accept that reasonableness (or the so-called Golden Mean) are what we are searching for. I believe that we are, or should be, searching for some quality which surpasses this average. We should search, I believe, for something which not only encompasses but, as I said, surpasses (rather than transcends), these two apparently exclusive poles, the rational and the intuitive.

As an architect, and in practice, I find this a perfectly natural goal and I think that most architects (all artists) in fact pursue this approach, but when called to account for, or professing the aims of their work, tend to try to justify their struggles in terms of the purely rational or (shamefacedly in our particular period) the intuitional.

Any design problem can generally be solved in many ways and the architect or designer in proposing a particular solution in favour of the other alternatives does so on the basis of intuition. This is not to say that his choice is wilful; his 'correct choice' is intuitional but in so far as all the alternative solutions are to varying extents rational, wilfulness cannot be ascribed to his choice. His choice, therefore, is neither entirely rational nor entirely intuitive but may more properly be described as aesthetic. This almost sounds like tautology since I have used the term 'correct choice' to describe what amounts to 'aesthetic choice'.

But let us see if we cannot be more precise, particularly in searching for a satisfactory solution of what surpasses rather than transcends Reason and Intuition. First, I think it is necessary to establish that there is a viewpoint that enables one to deal with the subjective and objective, reason and intuition, without contending that one is more valid than the other. In his book *Religion and the Modern Mind*, which I have used as material for a previous paper delivered to the RIAI Conference in 1976, the author W. T. Stace - arguing that subjectivism, naturalism or the scientific method is not in conflict with the mystical view - suggests that there are two standpoints from which one can confront the truth: the one, the temporal or space-time order; the other, the eternal order, and that both are equally true as frames of reference. This would, of course, by-pass, so to speak, the problem of the irreconcilability of reason and intuition, but leaves us still in a situation where we are caught in a dualism.

Stace's thesis however has the benefit of suggesting to us that there may not be an essential conflict between reason and intuition. And if one could find somehow a philosophy which could cope with Reason and Intuition in a confluence of Change, one might be able to put those apparent antagonisms of which I spoke earlier - between the conscientious innovative architect and the conservative preservationist layman - into a harmonious forward-looking perspective, or better still, perhaps into a Byzantine plane.

Two books which I have read recently can help towards this search; one by Robert M. Pirsig called *Zen and the Art of Motorcycle Maintenance* and the other (on which the former, I suspect, draws largely for its philosophy) by F.S.C. Northrop called *The Meeting of East and West*. Both works try to escape the dualism: the former by transcending to instate what he calls Quality (capital Q); the latter by side-stepping and surpassing by a form of immersion, by submerging the dualism in what Northrop, rather scholastically, calls the 'indeterminate aesthetic continuum'. Although a clumsy terminology, it has inherent in it the elements which I take to be important if we are to find a philosophy which is adequate to cope with our present and, indeed, historical dilemma. It can cope with change in its indeterminacy and also with reason and intuition by their comprehension in aesthetics.

I will consider Pirsig's *Zen and the Art of Motorcycle Maintenance* first because I want to dispose of, if I can, the notion of a hierarchical structure which strikes against, to put it politically, our idea of democracy; and which despite the apparent humility of his thesis leads inescapably to an elitism which derives not from nature (where elitism is an obvious occurrence) but from a superimposition of the *'homo sapiens'* syndrome on Rousseau's 'noble savage' description of reality. Having described Pirsig's thesis I will, I hope, be able to expand Northrop's thesis to comprehend what I have concluded are the essential ingredients of a valid, functional philosophy comprehending Reason, Intuition and Change.

Pirsig's story is set in a framework of Technology, in the modern romantic fear of technology on the one hand and the equally romantic reverence for technology on the other. The former is the preservationists' attitude, the latter the progressivists' attitude. Neither is a balanced view such as the view which Pirsig's hero takes about technology - simply that it is a useful tool which society has developed.

The fear and the reverence for technology derive from the part that the scientific viewpoint has played in our traditions; indeed they spring from the fact that Science is at the root of our tradition. The fear and the reverence are both expressions of an intuitive feeling that the scientific viewpoint is not the only viewpoint from which one can perceive reality. But,

> it's completely natural to think of Europeans who believed in ghosts or Indians who believed in spirits as ignorant. The scientific point of view has wiped out every other view to a point where they all seem primitive, so that if a person today talks about ghosts or spirits

he is considered ignorant or maybe nutty...my own opinion is that the intellect of modern man isn't that superior...Those Indians and mediaeval men were just as intelligent as we are, but the context in which they thought was completely different. Within that context of thought, ghosts and spirits are quite as real as atoms, particles, photons and quants are to modern man...Modern man has his ghosts and spirits too...the laws of physics and of logic...the number system...the principle of algebraic substitution. These are ghosts. We just believe in them so thoroughly they seem real.[3]

Pirsig is here stating what I have previously stated: that progress is a myth and that change is the reality. Intuitively, I think we know this and again on the intuitive and change I will paraphrase Pirsig talking of a motorcycle.

Each (machine) house has its own, unique personality which probably could be defined as the intuitive sum total of everything you know and feel about it. This personality constantly changes, usually for the worse, but sometimes surprisingly for the better, and it is this personality that is (properly) the real object of city renewal.[4]

An aside: the purely visual personality of the city consists, in the layman's eyes, of the brick of the houses, the fancy doorway and fanlight, the up-and-down sash windows and, if he is perspicacious, the patent plaster reveals. But I do not think that the layman understands how, or indeed the fact that, all these elements belong to a technological system. An 18th-century system which, perhaps unfortunately, is no longer useful today.

The condemnation of modern technology is quite simply ingratitude; just as in the 18th century, completely improbable though it would have been (pace Jean Jacques Rousseau), it would equally well have been ingratitude. Perhaps improbably because 18th-century western man understood his technology whereas today most people simply do not want to know. Voltaire would have said 'intolerant'.

But unfortunately to know this does not change it. It is unfortunate that most laymen and many architects are unable to distinguish the immediate appearance of a form from the underlying meaning of that form. Mies's R.S.J. mullions on the 860 flats; who likes to think of a block of luxury flats faced with rolled steel joists? But how many like to think of an upper class town house faced with lumps of baked mud? There are two realities:

> ...one of immediate artistic experience and one of underlying scientific explanation and they don't match and they don't fit and they don't really have much of anything to do with one another.[5]

Pirsig pursues this theme of the two realities, he says:

> ...the world of underlying form is an unusual object of discussion because it is actually a mode of discussion itself. You discuss things in terms of their immediate appearance or you discuss them in terms of their underlying form, and when you try to discuss these modes of discussion you get involved in what could be called a platform problem. You have no platform from which to discuss them other than the modes themselves.[6]

That platform is what finally emerges in Pirsig's philosophy as Quality which stands above the immediate appearance and the underlying form, above this dichotomy which is more properly the dichotomy of the classic and romantic.

> A classical understanding sees the world primarily as underlying form itself. A romantic understanding sees it primarily in terms of immediate appearance.[7]

When the layman and the commonly untutored architect look at, for example, the Bank of Ireland in Baggot Street in its 18th-century setting they are, I think, seeing the setting from a Romantic standpoint (the immediate appearance) and are seeing the 20th-century building as an unharmonious intrusion of a modern classical (that is, scientific) order. But the 18th-century setting was 18th-century classical order; the underlying form is the same and that is why there is in fact a harmony. And the order is rational not, essentially, intuitive. This kind of rationality [as Northrop puts it],

> ...has been used since antiquity to remove oneself from the tedium

*and depression of one's immediate surroundings. What makes it
hard to see is that where once it was used to get away from it all,
'.... (the Casino at Marino) .... the escape has been so successful that
now it is the 'it all' that the romantics are trying to escape.*[8]

I do not have the time to develop fully Pirsig's philosophy to
the point where he superimposes what he calls Quality on the
dichotomy of Classical and Romantic, or reason and intuition,
subjective and objective. It is sufficient to say that he arrives at
a kind of trinity consisting of Quality (that is reality) from which
depend subjective reality and objective reality. Actually it is more
complex: there is Quality (Reality) from which depend Romantic
Quality (pre-intellectual reality) on the one hand and Classic
Quality (intellectual reality) on the other, and from the latter
depend Subjective Reality (mind) and Objective Reality (matter).
What I find inadequate in this is that it is a hierarchical trinity,
not really three in one so much as two depending on or from
one. I do not like this kind of order, I do not think that it is a true
picture of reality which I find to be, certainly in architecture, of
a much more complex kind, and closer to the Christian idea of
the Trinity, one in three and three in one. For this reason I am
more convinced by F.S.C. Northrop's 'indeterminate aesthetic
continuum'. Pirsig refers to Northrop noting that he sees the
division between East and West as principally a division between
what Northrop calls the theoretic component of man's existence
- which is primarily Western - and the aesthetic component -
which is primarily eastern - and which correspond to what Pirsig
calls the classic and romantic modes of reality. According to
Northrop,

> *...science designates a factor in knowledge and in things at the
> opposite pole from their intuitive aesthetic component ... science,
> and Western common sense and religious belief following science,
> direct knowledge to the inferred factor devoid of its aesthetic
> immediacy.*[9]

In other words Pirsig's underlying reality.

Northrop terms this the theoretic component. The aesthetic
component is the immediately apprehensible and the theoretic
component is scientifically verifiable. We still however have a

dualism, a dichotomy between the theoretic and the aesthetic whereas I am searching for, in Northrop's words, *'the true relation between intuitive, aesthetic, and religious feeling and scientific doctrine'* which is one of mutual supplementation.[10] But I do not like the suggestion implicit in his analysis that the theoretic component is somehow unaesthetic and that only the intuitive is aesthetic. But, momentarily accepting this division, he is right in suggesting that *'a philosophy grounded in both the aesthetic component and the theoretic component of things as equally primary, defines the idea of the good.'*[11] By postulating an indeterminate aesthetic continuum, an intervening medium, within which the person and the object rotate and outside of which the theoretic and aesthetic components reciprocate, it becomes possible to see how there is in fact, as all architects in their practice know, no conflict between reason and intuition.

> *Within the aesthetic continuum there is no distinction between subjective and objective.*[12]

> *All determinate natural objects, whether they be persons or flowers, or mountains or streams, are made up of two aesthetic factors ... (one) is the undifferentiated aesthetic continuum which is in all objects in their purely empirically given, immediately apprehended component as well as in all persons; (the second) is the limiting principle, or the sensed differentiations distinguishing one object in the complex aesthetic continuum from another, and the determinate self from its determinate object. It follows from this that it may be possible, by some experimental technique to eliminate (the sensed) differentiations from the complex aesthetic continuum, so that only the emotionally moving, aesthetically ineffable, indeterminate field factor in it remains, then all distinction between the knowing subject and the known object, and between the personal self and the non-personal natural object, would be escaped. The knower would be identical with its object, and the object would be identical with knower. It is precisely this which the Oriental method known as the Yoga attempts to achieve.*[13]

In this situation of course the dualism inherent in our preoccupation with Reason and Intuition, the subjective and objective, Classic and Romantic, and also the problems associated with change, of mortality, immortality and infinity, cease to exist.

This very sketchy description of Northrop's thesis points to the fact that there is a viewpoint from which in particular terms it would be possible to understand the 18th-century component of 20th-century architecture, and to realise that the views of the romantically moved conservationist and the classically moved developer concerning the relationship between our modern glass-and-steel boxes and the glass and stone boxes of the 18th century, are reconcilable harmoniously. It entails however adopting a different context of thought from the traditional context, a context in which Reason and Intuition are seen to be reciprocal and mutually tolerant in a continuum of change. Since change is inevitable one should be open to it, not just for the sake of change but for the sake of discovery. In that sense, one might perhaps accept the notion of progress, one comes near to it.

But in the sense in which progress suggests improvement, betterment, superiority I reject it and revert to my belief in change as simply difference. However, the difference to be of value to us must be Revelationary. And to achieve this within the indeterminate aesthetic continuum - which is in itself neither static nor dynamic so much as fluid - one must seek the most up-to-date revolutionary rationalism and the most ecstatic transcendental intuitiveness, so that change becomes charged with an excitement and potential achievement which can grab the enthusiasm of an epoch: an epoch-making endeavour ceaselessly fluid; in motion in an inevitable state of change; in the continuum of change, a continuum which is tolerance, which is the Womb of Change.

Footnotes

1 - Sagan, Françoise. *Scars on the Soul*, trans. Joanna Kilmartin,
Penguin Books Ltd 1977, p. 88 (Des Bleus à l'Ame, Flammarion 1972)
Weightman, John. *The Observer*, 6th August 1978
2 - Pirsig, Robert M. *Zen and the Art of Motorcycle Maintenance*,
The Bodley Head, London, 1974, p. 39
3 - ibid. p. 50
4 - ibid. p. 61
5 - ibid. p. 73
6 - ibid. p. 73
7 - ibid. p. 76
8 - Northrop, F.S.C. *The Meeting of East and West*, The MacMillan Company,
New York, 1947, p. 163
9 - ibid. p. 64
10 - ibid. p. 434
11 - ibid. p. 333
12 - ibid. p. 368

Eight.
Gerry Cahill
Back to the Street, 1979

From *Back to the Street* (Dublin : Housing Research Unit, School of Architecture, University College Dublin/Cement Roadstone Ltd., 1980)

APOLOGIA

People always like to be near to the action. Traditionally this action has existed where culture, society and commerce have merged – namely, the centre of any large city. This centre has been attractive because it has been both fixed – those who live there – and transient – those who come to it to work or relax. The life of the city is at the interface of the two; without one there is no dynamic, only decay. Without an inner city population, the urban life blood is drained, resulting in a place without identity or meaning except when the office workers or theatre and cinemas goers are present. Such is the state that Dublin's inner city is rapidly approaching, the city communities are disappearing, and the dereliction grown more noticeable every day.

So much of Dublin, apart from the very few privileged streets and squares, looks like the bombs have just stopped falling. Redevelopment, where it does occur, merely appears to follow the pattern of other western cities, and produces an ever-growing office and commercial district, structures that the micro chip will one day make redundant. These developments rarely follow the ethic of quality, bowing instead to the new dictate of quantity, so producing a soulless environment as well as soulless facades. But this need not be so. Inner city communities wish to stay where they are and to help their areas improve, grow and develop – not be forced to abandon them. But they must be aided by Government policies to remain. Urban communities are the soul of a city. Without them the city is dead.

This truth has been documented by researchers throughout Europe and the United States. Too often, however, the wider understanding of the problems the city faces gets lost in academic publications. In order to avoid this, I chose to use the Fellowship not only for book research but also to examine the issue at community level. The problem of the decay of city neighbourhoods is of such importance that it needs to be communicated to the public at large. By going back to the street, this problem can be understood, assessed, and recommendations made that are pertinent to specific and familiar locations. Undertaking research through involvement with a community work team in a city locality helped me to understand how much communities identify with their area and how important are the familiar street patterns. In revitalising any urban district, these patterns must be respected. Architects and planners must also get 'back to the street' as their main vehicle for imaginative urban renewal. Such an approach, allied with creative management, administration, funding and public participation programmes will return to the city the quality of environment so sadly lacking in recent times.

THE VALUE OF THE CITY STREET
Reactions to urban living

The city is sometimes loved, sometimes hated by its inhabitants. To ask the members of a city community about their area they will tell you where it's nice to have a drink in the evening, remark that it's great to have good neighbours to rely on, the shops, schools, and churches so 'handy' and point out pleasant walks and items of interest on streets they know well. All of this, of course, is termed by planners as good 'infrastructure' but that does nothing to capture the variety of sights, sounds and smells that the city contains on busy days.

To the opposing viewpoint this is seen as confusion and chaos. The streets are too narrow to handle the volume of traffic, the pavements are too narrow to handle the volume of people, shops cannot be properly serviced and industry proximate to housing is merely a pollutant and health hazard.

Following this thinking, the view arrived at is that *'the older city appears to be dying – functionally, structurally, politically, and eventually, ideologically'*.[1] Many city planning policies have compounded this opinion through massive urban clearance projects and a decanting of the population to the surburbs where the shops, pubs, schools and churches (where they exist) are miles away via ill-made roads over terrain which the bulldozers have recently de-landscaped.

THE ROLE OF THE STREET –
STRUCTURE & DIVERSITY IN THE CITY

We must be sensitive to the role of streets as the prime location for the human interaction which is the soul of the city. The street is integral to the life of the city itself. It could be held that in the attempt to find a new expression, the street was largely ignored by Architects and Planners. However, a fresh attitude which recognised the need for a philosophy sympathetic to the urban past, was expressed by Aldo Van Eyck when he wrote

> *Man is always and everywhere essentially the same. He has the same mental equipment though he uses it differently according to his culture or social background, according to the particular life pattern of which he happens to be a part. Modern architects have been harping continually on what is different in our time to such an extent that even they have lost touch with what is always essentially the same.*[2]

Recently, analysts have attempted to define what were the ingredients that gave the city its liveliness, safety, convenience and interest. This analysis often involved the examination of each element (housing, industry, etc) totally removed from the others that contribute to its existence. Jane Jacobs remarked on the folly of this in saying

> *No single element in a city is, in truth, the kingpin or the key. The mixture itself is kingpin and its mutual support is the other... A city's very structure consists to its structural secrets when we deal with the conditions that generate diversity.*[3]

The city street is the generator of diversity. Its value is the city's value. *'If a city's streets look interesting, the city looks interesting, if they look dull, the city looks dull.'*[4]

TOWARDS A BETTER CITY - THE WAY FORWARD

If the city is to have industry and commerce, those employed must have a place to live. At present, the only agency providing housing on an appreciable scale is Dublin Corporation. Housing produced by private agencies is mainly limited to the residential element in new office developments. Hence we have a situation where there is an increasing quantity of public housing for generally low income groups together with a minuscule amount of luxury rented apartments. If we are to retain the present population and yet avoid social homogeneity in new city housing, we must provide dwellings for the middle income owner-occupier and tenant bracket. If we can make the inner city desirable as a place in which to live we may go some way to stemming the growth of our 'commuter society' through providing homes for, among others, the ever-growing worker population employed in city centre locations.

The local authorities may consider it is not their responsibility to provide housing of this nature. Private speculators do not consider it profitable to provide medium-priced housing in the inner city. But there is the real possibility for local and central government to help people to help themselves. The following proposals taken singly or collectively allow for a diverse response to a diverse economy. If acted upon, they could support and improve the operation of existing organisations and harness the drive and initiative of the entrepreneurial investment community. To quote Wallace F. Smith: *'Public agencies should learn to appreciate the value of accomplishing their housing sector aims by indirect means.'*[5] One of these indirect means would be increased encouragement for the Co-operative Housing Movement. This movement has been growing in popularity on a worldwide basis over recent years; its purpose being to encourage people in need of housing to provide homes for themselves and others through co-operative methods.[6]

In Ireland, the National Association of Building Co-Operatives (NABCo) is the representative and promotional body for co-operative housing, and receives grants aid for its administrative expenses from the Department of the Environment. The aim of NABCo is to provide *'a means for people to obtain access to financial assistance (loans and grants), building sites, professional legal and architectural advice'* and to enable them *'to participate in the design and costing of the housing they intend to purchase.'*[7]

The community can be very greatly aided from the energy generated through Co-op housing activity. Smaller co-operatives are self sustaining, and, once started, concern themselves with constructing a limited number of houses for their own members at particular locations. That these would significantly contribute to the physical character of an area is without doubt, but an ongoing Co-operative Housing Society could contribute to the solution of housing needs in general. It could have a community development role working in partnership with the statutory authorities towards improving the range and sources of housing. To assist the development of the co-operative housing movement Dublin Corporation could:

1 - Integrate co-operative housing into the forward planning for an inner city area. Co-op housing efficiently supplements a public sponsored programme through providing a feasible alternative for those on the waiting list so alleviating the burden on public expenditure.

2 - Designate sites for Co-operative housing. If well chosen their development would provide a much-needed injection of enthusiasm into a decaying neighbourhood. Such a step could help halt the decline in Inner City population through rekindling a belief in the value of an old area.

3 - Encourage house improvement. A Co-op need not confine itself to new housing. It can be made up of existing house owners combining to renovate their properties. This they can part finance through a savings scheme from monies held in common in the Co-operative Housing Savings and Credit Union Ltd. But the Corporation should provide an incentive for this through the reintroduction of an improvement grant for first time house improvers. This could match the grant for first time house-purchase and would help house owners renovate rapidly since the abolition of the Department of the Environment's house improvement grants.[8]

Co-operatives are flexible; their ability to adapt to changing social and economic forces qualifies them as suitable agencies for undertaking any one of the infill developments proposed. No

major legislative change is needed for their increased operation; they would assist in activating improvement neighbourhoods as proposed in the Inter-Departmental Committee Report on the Inner City. Through these, action on housing would not be taken *in vacuo* but would be considered in conjunction with industrial and commercial development and the provision of educational and recreational facilities.

An Inner City Renewal Agency (consisting of local and central government representatives and professional consultants) would identify designated neighbourhoods. These would be divided between Priority Action Areas - where there is increasing decay and little investment activity - and Overall Improvement Areas - where there are fewer physical problems and development interest but there exists a need for a co-ordinated approach.

The agency could undertake a full land use and building condition survey (similar to that carried out in the Liberties) with the added information of a full profile on land ownership.

Through the knowledge gained on the location of vacant land and vacant buildings a 'land and building bank' could be established so identifying properties in need of renovation or renewal. Multi-disciplinary area teams appointed by the Agency consisting of a Community worker, Social worker, Lawyer, Economist and Architect could liaise with community groups and representatives to determine the optimum use for derelict or decaying sites and buildings.

This team would be responsible for determining housing need and demand and identifying existing and projected job requirements. Through co-operation with the IDA and AnCo, small-scale industry for establishment in the Inner City could be helped to find premises.

In order to encourage private developers into an area that they have heretofore viewed as unattractive, it has to be made attractive through some Inner City Renewal Agency sponsored action. Ideally this action has to cost nothing, or next to nothing in real terms. Such action could be in the form of setting up a revolving fund programme.[9] A programme of this nature simply means investment in enterprises that are expected to pay their way. These enterprises could entail the purchase of a derelict building or site, its rehabilitation or redevelopment and the sale of the completed building. Loans that were advanced for the project are repaid after the sale and the balance is re-invested to repeat the procedure. So the money 'revolves'. Similarly, such a fund could purchase a number of properties, convert them to living accommodation and rent the finished units at a variety of rates. Thus people who cannot afford market value payments could be subsidised to remain in the area.

The fund must be administered by a non-profit organisation. Such an organisation could be established by one of the area teams with the Directors being from the neighbourhood. The funding should come from the locality – two or three major sources plus a broad community campaign to raise money. It is important that local donors see the immediate tangible evidence of what their contributions helped support. As a gesture of positive goodwill, the Agency should commence the fund through injection of 'seed money' so that the community has something from which to work. The ball will roll from there.

Often the major discouragement to private developers is in the high cost of Inner City Land. Incentives in the form of Site Subsidies which cover the difference in purchase cost between city centre and green-field sites could be introduced from the central exchequer.[10] This again would give impetus to commercial activity, which after, say, five years would maintain its own momentum. This is less contentious than encouraging Dublin Corporation to sell their land for cost to a private agent and then being forced to replace it at a much higher figure. Such subsidies could initially come from the Inner City Fund to which £1 million was allocated through the Inter Departmental Committee in May 1979. Similarly, higher central city development costs could be taken into account through the introduction of tax concessions for those operating in this area. These could be in the form of lower tax being paid on income and profit earned from providing housing and industrial development in a deprived urban location.

The section of the Dublin Draft Development Plan [1976] which indicates that the local authority may assist a private developer states,

> Where the established pattern of ownership and tenure does not permit comprehensive private development the Planning Authority may take the initiative to secure such development by the use of its powers of compulsory acquisition.[11]

The Local Authority should make use of this power and aggregate parcels of land suitable for use as community housing and industry rather than speculative office development.

Returning to the income tax theme, there could also be a scheme for private individuals who are on a high income tax band to take out investment bonds in a government sponsored community renewal programme. This is an idea which has been tried out in the United States and for every £1 invested (which would be on a minimum term, fixed interest rate basis) there would be £1 worth of tax relief.[12] Such an inflow of funds would aid the liquidity of urban projects and enable action to be taken sooner. And, action is, after all, what is immediately needed to arrest the further decay of our inner city.

This study has attempted to illustrate methods of tackling the problem of urban blight. Whether the problem will be solved depends on the positive will of our legislators. Perhaps this would be forthcoming if they went back to the streets and observed at first hand the need for renewal in our city neighbourhoods.

Footnotes

1 - Scott Greet, 'The Changing Image of the City' from A. Blowers, C. Hamnett, and P. Sarre (eds.), *The Future of Cities* (London: Open University Press/Hutchinson Educational, 1974)

2 - Aldo van Eyck, 'Otterlo Meeting of Team 10, 1959', in Alison Smithson (ed.), *Team Ten Primer* (Cambridge Mass: M.I.T Press, 1968)

3 - Jane Jacobs, *The Death and Life of Great American Cities* (New York: Random House, 1962)

4 - Ibid.

5 - Wallace F. Smith, *Housing: The Social and Economic Elements* (California: University of California Press, 1971)

6 - John Hands, *Housing Co-Operatives* (The Society for Co-Operative Dwellings Ltd, 1975)

7 - Information Documents from the Educational and Advisory Service, National Association of Building Co-Operatives Society Ltd.

8 - Department of the Environment, Grant Information, *A Home of your Own* (Dublin: Stationery Office, 1979)

9 - Arthur P. Ziegler Jr., Leopold Adler II and Walter C Kidney, *Revolving Funds for Historical Preservation, A Manual of Practice* (Pittsburgh: Ober Park Associates Inc., 1975)

10 - Site subsidies were initially proposed by the Inter Departmental Committee on Dublin's Inner City in order to encourage the establishment of job creating projects for inner city residents

11 - *Dublin City Development Plan: Draft Review* 1976, Section 2.8.17

12 - John Sharratt described the concept when delivering his paper on 'Redevelopment – Community Based Action' to the National Housing Conference, Dublin, April 1979

Nine.

John Tuomey

Images of the Past, 1982

From John O'Regan, *Annexe 4 (1982)*

- George Steiner

I intend in this short essay to raise an issue which is, in my opinion, of great importance to architecture. It is not yet a developed argument, capable of withstanding detached intellectual scrutiny, but it is, I believe, fertile ground for future, more detailed work. It is also an attempt to describe the background and sources of inspiration for my own recent work and that of some colleagues. I will refer mainly to rural examples, but the argument is equally applicable to towns and villages.

There is a tradition of vernacular architecture to be found in Irish towns and settlements which has been largely ignored by architects in recent years. If we study this indigenous tradition, disregarding the conventional art-historical and archaeological categories and terminologies, and apply only architectural criteria, we begin to see that there was a consistent attitude applied to building form by past generations which has been lost or abandoned by our own. An innate classicism is common to so many Irish buildings that it allows us to generalise about the formal qualities shared by religious buildings, farm buildings, industrial buildings, etc.

For example: at Kilmacduagh, Co. Galway, there is a round tower in a graveyard surrounded by seven ruined churches. Across the road are two barns side by side, identical in plan form; one with a vaulted metal roof, the other a pitched slate roof. On the horizon, seen across a lake and a landscape criss-crossed by innumerable stone walls, is a tower house.

These disparate buildings are from different periods, built for different purposes, yet they have an architectural presence which transcends their time or function. All share the same elemental character given by prismatic and cubic forms, and they have a power which is to do with the archaic simplicity of these forms seen in relation to the landscape. These obviously man-made objects influence the landscape which is also in some way man-made. The apparently contrasting buildings and land enhance each other and merge to form a desolate and poetic image that seems specifically Irish, a proto-architectural image containing a message which could help us to discover an architecture appropriate to this island. This does not inhibit creativity in any way but gives a basic context linking the vagaries of time and taste.

The circular hedge garden in Kilruddery is obviously a reference to French Baroque gardens, but it also suggests the memory of ancient ring forts and stone circles which locates it in a specific way in an Irish tradition.

The house and farm buildings at Kilcarty are the work of an extremely sophisticated architect who employed Palladian methods of formal composition while using traditional forms in a most restrained and urbane way. The architect has isolated and perfected certain aspects of the indigenous rural type while at the same time addressing himself to contemporary architectural ideas.

The urbanity of the Irish rural building tradition is being denied by modern architects. When asked to build in the natural landscape they seek to camouflage their buildings or else they produce superficial parodies of the imperfections and irregularities of the vernacular. The resulting chaos is blamed on the difficulty of working in the absence of a common language. This problem arises out of a misunderstanding of the architect's role and the value of architecture to society. People are under the impression that the architect, by definition, should produce an extraordinary invention as a particular response to the special demands of the site, climate, client, etc. Happily, this arrogant and anti-historical view seems to be losing sway following its disastrous effects on towns and countryside.

To advocate research and examination of existing vernacular architecture is not to suggest the simple reproduction of these buildings. Nor is it to say that we must try to reattain a now ravaged 'garden of civility' as if such a thing had once existed. It is to assert that the continuous tradition of building with typical forms according to tectonic principles is a *sine qua non* of meaningful architecture, and also to propose that there is that innate classical tradition existing in Ireland before our eyes which is in danger of being totally lost.

If we could develop a way of seeing that indigenous architecture as an inspiration to work, then we could build with certainty and imagination in a spirit of contribution to the continuum of architectural culture.

Ten.

Frank McDonald

A Handyman, his Son & a Ladder.
excerpt, 1985

From *Destruction of Dublin*, 1985

You must remember that Ireland is a very backward county and most buildings that are required here can be built by a handyman, his son and a ladder.

Nothing has so changed the face of cities in the modern age as high-rise buildings. Until well into the 20th century, London was still recognisable as the city rebuilt by Christopher Wren after the Great Fire of 1666, with the dome of St. Paul's as the dominant feature of the landscape. Viewed from Waterloo Bridge today, the city now looks much the same as Pittsburgh or some equally forgettable Middle American town, with a host of tower blocks vying with each other for supremacy of the skyline.

As far back as 1962, Lewis Mumford roundly condemned the mass of undistinguished buildings, which had, even then, so disfigured the face of London. 'The present investment in high buildings is primarily a financial phenomenon; architecture is secondary and civic design noticeably absent', he wrote. Mumford might just as easily have been referring to Dublin. For just as London was repeating the worst mistakes of American cities, so we were preparing - as usual - to ape the dismal example set for us by our old masters across the Irish Sea. It fitted the mood of the time, however. There was a feeling that Dublin was somehow emasculated as a city because it didn't have its share of 'skyscrapers.' There was something macho about these architectural phallic symbols and we had to have them, if only to show that our capital had grown up at last.

Contemplating the prospect of Liberty Hall and the other tall blocks then under construction, the *Irish Builder* wrote glowingly about 'progress' and 'the advance of architecture' in Ireland:

The wind of architectural change has at last reached our shores, and the fight to establish the modern movement has been won.

Architects were now posed to improve the standards of the background against which we live, to provide the cheerful and even exciting structures that elevate the spirit and turn the mind towards higher ideals. Another commentator talked of the erection of 'these clean-lined modern structures' as marking 'the first stage in the transformation of Dublin from a rather shabby town dominated by crumbling slum areas into a 20th-century city'. Only 'outmoded ideas' were standing in the way of Irish architects doing 'equally well, if not better, than has been done in Caracas, Birmingham or Sydney', he declared. Dublin Corporation could have stopped this movement dead in its tracks, but it lost its nerve when confronted by the clamour for change. Musty Victorian by-laws carefully restricting the height of buildings in the city were cast aside and architects were given free rein to 'express themselves.'

Liberty Hall was the first big breakthrough. A seventeen-storey tower, rising to the height of 197 feet, it was planned to replace the old headquarters of the Irish Transport and General Workers' Union at the corner of Eden Quay and Beresford Place. This historic two-storey building, dating from the 1820s, had served the union well since the heady days of Jim Larkin and the 1913 lockout. It had been faithfully restored after suffering massive blast damage during the 1916 rebellion. In 1958, however, it was found to be 'unsafe' and was demolished without any hint of nostalgia. The union then engaged Desmond Rea O'Kelly, a structural engineer, to design a new headquarters incorporating a large conference hall, shops at street level and 35,000 square feet of office space - much of it intended for letting to civil servants or private firms. Given that the amount of office space in the building is relatively small and that the union didn't need all of this space for its own use, there was no practical reason why Liberty Hall had to be so tall. Indeed, the ITGWU's requirements could easily have been accommodated in a five-storey building on the same site. But the union wanted to cut a dash, and the foundation stone for the new building was laid on 12 May 1961 - the 45th anniversary of James Connolly's execution - with the expression of hope that it would prove 'worthy of past sacrifices'.

Dubliners watched with a mixture of awe and excitement as the reinforced concrete structure rose higher and higher from Eden Quay. When it was finally completed in 1965, commentators fell over each other in their rush for pithy phrased to sum up its virtues. It was described as 'an inspiring monument', 'a crystal tower' and 'a truly contemporary architectural composition'. The *Irish Builder* was swept off its feet. '*Under the changing skies of our climate - at night lighted up, or in the daytime - it always looks handsome; when seen against a blue sky with white clouds sailing over, it has a gossamer quality as charming as a Japanese print scene.*' As usual it took a foreign visitor to bring us back to earth. Writing in the *Architectural Review* in 1966, Ian Nairn described the building as an outrage and said the 'silly flippancy' of the roof was 'a particularly harsh slap in the face for the dome of the Custom House.' But then, we had allowed Gandon's masterpiece to be defaced by the construction, in the 1890s, of the Loop Line railway bridge and then compounded this terrible mistake by permitting the steel lattice-work to be covered with crude advertising hoardings.

Much of the initial infatuation Dubliners had for Liberty Hall can be explained by the fact that, uniquely, it afforded them an unparalleled opportunity to view their city from a great height. High-speed lifts took visitors to an observation terrace on the top floor and this quickly became one of the city's main attractions. But with the outbreak of the Troubles in Northern Ireland, the terrace was closed to the public for security reasons. Then, in December 1972, a bomb went off just outside the building, shattering most of the windows. In the subsequent repair work, the original clear glass gave way to dull reflective glass, and whatever airy, transparent quality Liberty Hall once had now disappeared. And with the mosaic cladding on the edge beams of each floor visibly peeling off, it has become a decidedly shabby memorial to the tower block mania of the early 1960s. In its current state of near-dilapidation, Liberty Hall would provide an even more appropriate setting for Oisin Kelly's bronze men gazing skywards in awe and perplexity. This amusing sculpture was originally commissioned by the ITGWU for the pavement outside their headquarters, but an unamused Dublin Corporation refused planning permission on the grounds that it would be 'an obstruction'. And that's why the two larger-than-life figures ended up outside Cork's County Hall, which had been deliberately designed to beat Liberty Hall in the height stakes - by a matter of inches.

The second of Dublin's motley collection of high-rise office blocks was O'Connell Bridge House. Twelve storeys high and bestriding the bridge like a colossus, this utterly prosaic building (Ian Nairn called it 'weary new City of London') is the principal legacy to the city of John Byrne, the Kerry-born property developer who became one of the richest men in Ireland. Byrne, the eldest of a family of twelve, was born on a small farm near Lixnaw and he first showed his entrepreneurial flair by cutting turf during the Emergency and selling it house-to-house from a donkey cart. Like so many others who would find their way into the property world, he went to London after the war and made his first fortune in the ballroom business. On returning to Ireland, he built up a string of dancehalls, but he was always on the lookout for new opportunities. As a result, he was among the first to appreciate the significance of the 1958 Office Premises Act. It would, as he correctly foresaw, produce a demand in the marketplace for functional, modern office space. Just two months after the new Act came into force in April 1959, Byrne had plans drawn up for a large office block on the site of the Carlisle Building, at the corner of D'Olier Street and Burgh Quay. This building was even grander than the Ballast Office, on the corner of Aston Quay, though both had been designed for the Wide Streets Commissioners in 1800 as part of a unified composition centred on Carlisle (now O'Connell) Bridge. Having served for many years as the offices of Independent Newspapers, the Carlisle Building was put up for auction in August 1957, but withdrawn after bidding stopped at only £26,000. John Byrne bought the property shortly afterwards - purely for its site value - and probably didn't pay much more for it. Indeed, records show that his site acquisition costs - including the purchase of McDaid's pub next door in 1961 - came to a grand total of just £53,000.

For this astoundingly small sum, Byrne had bought himself one of the most prominent sites in Dublin and he immediately set about maximising its value. That is the main goal of all property developers, but Byrne was the first in Dublin to try, and he was breaking new ground. Obviously, he would need the services of an architect to design the new office building and get it through the planning process. He already had a solicitor in Christopher Gore-Grimes, who had helped to set up his property company,

Carlisle Trust Ltd, and Gore-Grimes recommended Desmond Fitzgerald, the professor of architecture at UCD. Fitzgerald also happened to be Gore-Grimes' brother-in-law.

Fitzgerald was impeccably well connected. His father had been Minister for External Affairs in the Cumann na nGaedheal government during the 1920s and his younger brother Garret was making a name for himself as a leading economic commentator through his weekly columns in the *Irish Times*. Desmond, known more commonly as 'Dem' or 'The Prof', had received the RIAI gold medal for the original terminal building at Dublin Airport, a very fine example of early modern architecture, designed in the late 1930s and completed shortly after the end of World War II. Though he was a brilliant mathematician and could be very persuasive on planning minutiae, he affected an image of vagueness as if his head was in the clouds all the time. At UCD, where he had been Professor of Architecture since 1951, his students found him remote, even disdainful. When the architectural society at the college invited an expert from London to give a lecture on technology, then very much a new-fangled subject, the Professor pronounced that technology had little relevance here:

> You must remember that Ireland is a very backward country and
> most buildings that are required here can be built by a handyman,
> his son, and a ladder.

Throughout the 1960s and 1970s, however, Fitzgerald would busy himself designing large, complex structures, mostly for his friends and mentor John Byrne. O'Connell Bridge House, the first venture of this unlikely pair, consumed 500 tons of structural steel, 90 tons of steel-reinforcing bars and no less than 7,500 tons of concrete - not to mention the Portland stone cladding. It cost £1 million, kept more than fifty men at work for two whole years and, in the end, stood 145 feet tall - eleven feet higher than Nelson Pillar. So much for that handyman, his son and a ladder.

But the most incredible fact about O'Connell Bridge House is that it was built at all. Although the building contains a total of 45,000 square feet of office space, there is not a single place to park a car. Yet at the time, the Corporation was insisting on the provision of one car parking place for every 500 square feet of office space. On that basis, O'Connell Bridge House should have had ninety car places. Instead, it had none. Fitzgerald told the planners, who bitterly opposed the scheme, that it would be 'quite impractical' to provide any car parking accommodation on the site. Despite this, the Corporation waived its sacrosanct car parking standards as well as the more fluid height restriction bye-laws and granted permission for the scheme. It is difficult to explain this strange turn of events other than that it came about by political influence.

John Byrne's close relationship with Fianna Fáil politicians was well known. Notable among these was Charles J. Haughey, who gained his first cabinet post as Minister for Justice in 1961. Haughey had married the daughter of Seán Lemass; he was a chartered accountant by profession, in which career he had been immensely successful prior to his entry to the political field. Along with Harry Boland, who would later become secretary of Taca, the notorious Fianna Fáil fundraising group, he established the firm of Haughey Boland and Company, with offices in Amiens Street. Many new companies set up during the Lemass boom thought it worthwhile to hire Haughey Boland as their accountants, and throughout the past two decades, the firm has looked after the affairs of a staggering number of companies, many of them in the property field.

But Haughey's links with John Byrne may go much deeper. Byrne's principal property vehicles are Carlisle Trust and Dublin City Estates. One of Haughey's former accountancy partners, Des Traynor - now deputy chairman of merchant bankers Guinness and Mahon - has long been a director of both companies. Traynor is one of the closest members of Haughey's tight inner circle of business friends and he is also Haughey's financial adviser. Byrne's property empire is controlled through an off-shore company, the Guinness and Mahon Cayman Trust, in the British West Indies tax haven of the Cayman Islands, where the relevant documentation on its ownership is not available for public inspection. There have been persistent allegations that Haughey is a sleeping partner, though there is one limited disclaimer on the record. In 1983, at the height of the controversy about the 'Endcamp scheme' - Byrne's plans to build over 2,000 houses in the green belt area between Baldoyle and Portmarnock – his solicitors took the unprecedented step of issuing a statement to the media denying that Haughey was involved. He 'has not and has never had any direct or indirect interest, whether beneficial or otherwise, in Endcamp Ltd', Gore-Grimes declared. During the public inquiry into the scheme in January 1984, several local residents marched up and down outside Liberty Hall. One child had a message for John Byrne. She was carrying a placard which read 'Go and build your houses in the Cayman Islands!'.

The fact that Byrne had never had much problem in finding state tenants for his office blocks seems to bear out his strong political connections with Fianna Fáil. In July 1964, five months before O'Connell Bridge House was completed, it was revealed that the Office of Public Works had agreed to lease all the office space in the building for four different government departments. The lease was for a period of thirty-five years at a rent of just over £1 per square foot subject, of course, to seven-year reviews. The political boss of the OPW at the time was Donogh O'Malley, who is fondly remembered as Ireland's most flamboyant Minister for Education. However, what is often forgotten is the fact that, for five years in the early 1960s, he served his time as Parliamentary Secretary to the Minister for Finance with responsibility for the OPW. Thus, he played a pivotal role in deciding whether the state should rent office space in the new blocks then under construction.

As a true acolyte of the Lemass boom, O'Malley saw it as his function to encourage property development, if only because it meant instant jobs for construction workers. He soon found himself at the centre of a charmed circle of young men on the make, usually in the Russell Hotel restaurant, and several deals were done at his table. He put architects in touch with developers and generally kept things moving at a fast and furious pace. But his most critical contribution to the fortunes of the property developers was the decision to lease many of their new office blocks to provide bright, modern workplaces for the state's growing army of civil servants. For the developers, this removed much of the risk element in what they were doing by virtually guaranteeing a stable supply of 'blue chip' tenants.

To Michael Quinn, *Build* magazine's acerbic commentator, this smacked of scandal. In 1965, he wrote,

> *The government appears to have surrendered itself completely to a policy of indulging the civil service. Gone are the days when they would be satisfied with a Georgian drawing room and a turf fire in Merrion Street. It's squandermania, of course, but don't ask me where they are all coming from. We have the bureaucracy of an empire in the confines of three provinces.*

But the state was hooked and, over the next twenty years, it would gobble up almost three-quarters of all the speculative office space built in the Dublin area. This addiction to renting office blocks, rather than building its own or refurbishing its older property, meant that successive governments would virtually underwrite the entire market for speculative office space in the city. And the first fatal 'fix' was administered by the reverend Donogh O'Malley.

Meanwhile, John Byrne and Desmond Fitzgerald were so encouraged by their success with O'Connell Bridge House that, before it was even finished, they submitted plans to the Corporation for an exact replica - in mirror image - on the site of the Ballast Office, the then princely headquarters of the Dublin Port and Docks Board. Instead of just one colossus mounting guard on O'Connell Bridge, there were to be two. This time, however, Byrne's political muscle was to fail him, and planning permission was refused for what was seen as a thoroughly arrogant scheme. (In 1973, the port board sold the Ballast Office to Royal Liver Insurance for £1/4 million. It was demolished in 1979 and replaced by a poor enough replica of itself, executed by Niall Scott, Michael Scott's son. Now called Ballast House, it has an assortment of unsympathetic shop fronts at ground-floor level while the 15,000 square feet of offices on the upper floors remained substantially vacant for almost four years after the building was completed.)

When O'Connell Bridge House first opened in January 1965, it had a roof restaurant with splendid views over the city. Sadly, the restaurant closed down in July 1966 and Byrne converted the space it occupied into an office for himself. The huge Guinness sign on the front lasted much longer and, at one stage, it was generating almost as much in rent as all the office space in the building; perhaps that is why Uncle Arthur recently yielded this prime advertising site to Sony of Japan. Certainly, Byrne never missed a trick when it came to the business of making money. In 1963, he got planning permission on appeal from Neil Blaney for a large block of luxury flats (also designed by Fitzgerald) at St. Ann's, a substantial house on its own grounds at the junction of Ailesbury Road and Anglesea Road, in Donnybrook. But since 1965, there had been a continuing wrangle with the Corporation over an illegal extension on the roof.

In 1968, Byrne demolished two more old buildings on D'Olier Street to make way for a 20,000 square feet extension to O'Connell Bridge House. And in the same year, he paid £211,000 to the liquidator of T. and C. Martin, the long-established builders' providers, to acquire their old premises at 21-24 D'Olier Street. On the site, four years later, Fitzgerald provided him with another utilitarian office block, D'Olier House, which was also leased in toto by the state. Thus, the art deco headquarters of the Dublin Gas Company is now sandwiched between the two Fitzgerald-designed office blocks. Apart from one very strange case which is dealt with later, the only office block Byrne had any difficulty letting to the state was yet another Fitzgerald production on the site of a coal yard in Townsend Street, beside the railway bridge. This ghastly building remained vacant for a full fifteen months before it was finally let to the Department of Social Welfare.

Sir Thomas Bennett, KBE, was even older than Fitzgerald is now when he designed Hawkins House in 1962. Senior partner in the London firm of T.P. Bennett and Son, his design work spanned the entire spectrum of architectural endeavour in post-war Britain - temporary housing, 'new town' planning, tower blocks of flats, big department stores and, of course, offices, with the enormous headquarters of New Scotland Yard as his major memorial. At the ripe old age of 75, this veteran was hired by the Rank Organisation to design the huge office development that they were planning for the site of the Theatre Royal. The *Irish Builder* found the news reassuring and commented that Bennett would find great scope to demonstrate his 'genius in the manipulation of such complex and varied elements as this unit will comprise.' If the beloved Theatre Royal was to be replaced, at least there was some hope that an experienced English architect might prove 'a very good tutor for our native office designers', who were then very much feeling their way in the dark.

Everybody in Dublin over the age of thirty remembers the Theatre Royal; it is part of the folk memory of the city. Modelled on Radio City Music Hall in New York's Rockefeller Centre, which is now a thriving historic monument, the Royal was a huge art deco-style building with a vast auditorium decorated in the Moorish manner. Like Radio City, it was a 'cine-variety-theatre', with movies and a stage show in a unique double-bill. And while its New York counterpart had a troupe of leggy dancers called the Rockettes, the Royal had the equally leggy Royalettes as well as Tommy Dando on the Compton organ that used to rise magically out of the floor, all lit up, with Dando already at the key-board. Other Royal favourites included Eddie Byrne and his 'Double Your Money' quiz, Jimmy O'Dea, Josef Locke, Mickser Reid, Peggy Dell and Noel Purcell as well as visiting stars like Danny Kaye, Vic Oliver and Gracie Fields. But for us, as kids, the greatest treat was to be allowed to run up to the very back row of the Grand Circle, from where the stage seemed as small as a television screen.

In March 1962, the Rank Organisation - masquerading as Irish Cinemas Ltd - announced that the Theatre Royal and the adjoining Regal Cinema were to close down. People said that television had killed them off, but this couldn't have been true, as Telefis Eireann was then just fifteen months old. Cecil Sheridan, one of the Royal's old troupers, was not conned by this nonsense. He saw all too clearly why J. Arthur Rank was planning to destroy Dublin's last great variety theatre. Interviewed in his dressing-room on the night of the last show on 30 June 1962, he said, 'It's not television that's done it, you know. It's a matter of how much money you can make out of a square foot of property.'

The Royal got an emotional send-off. As Rank's auctioneers were preparing to sell off the theatre's fittings, even its ticket kiosks and safety curtain, ordinary Dubliners filled every one of its 2,500 seats for the last time. The 'Royale Finale' featured a host of stars associated with the theatre since it first opened in 1935. Jimmy Campbell and his orchestra played 'There's No Business Like Show Business' towards the end and the huge audience joined the cast in singing 'Auld Lang Syne'. There were half a dozen curtain calls, a little rock 'n roll in Hawkins Street as crowds filed out and tears at the staff party afterwards. Within a matter of weeks, everyone knew the demolition men would be on the job. If only the Royal had survived for a few more years, it would have made a most splendid venue for rock concerts...

But the grisly business of maximising the site value got under way almost immediately and, by November 1962, the Royal and Regal had been obliterated. Rank had already got planning permission for a massive office development on the site; after giving way to John Byrne over O'Connell Bridge House, the Corporation was hardly in a position to refuse, no matter how appalling the design produced by Sir Thomas Bennett. And it really was appalling. With 122,000 square feet of office space encased in a formless twelve-storey slab block and a curtain-walled biscuit tin on each side, Hawkins House is easily the most monstrous pile of architectural rubbish ever built in Dublin. Not surprisingly, when faced with the finished product, those who had held out such high hopes for Bennett were sheepishly silent. For not only was the building a horror in itself, it also ruined several vistas - notably the view of Trinity College from the top of Dawson Street. Along with O'Connell Bridge House, it led to a re-examination of the whole question of height in the city. Thus, in February 1965, the Corporation announced that it would permit further high buildings only in 'exceptional circumstances'. Things had been getting out of hand, with a proliferation of proposals for 18-storey tower blocks in places like Grafton Street and Merrion Row. But the planners had belatedly discovered a new weapon to combat this craze - the 'plot ratio'. In future, the sky would no longer be the limit. Instead, a plot ratio of 2½ - 1 would apply throughout the city. This meant that if a site had an area of 4,000 square feet, the maximum amount of office space which could be built on it would not be allowed to exceed 10,000 square feet.

However, this didn't prevent Rank expanding their office empire into Townsend Street where, along with the New Metropole cinema, they built College House, a loathsome eight-storey block designed - if that's the right word - by Bennett in collaboration with Dublin architects Henry J. Lyons and Partners. This block, along with Hawkins House, was sold in October 1984 as part of a major deal between Rank and British Land, one of the largest property investment companies in the UK. The two blocks netted Rank almost £12 million, a very high price indeed for such architectural scrap. Why? Because most of the office space is leased to the state, which can always be counted on to pay the rent.

Another dreadful development that slipped through the net was Apollo House, in Tara Street, on the other side of Hawkins House. This vulgar pre-cast concrete block, with its street-level showrooms, car park and petrol station, occupies the site of seven old buildings, cruelly breaking the continuity of the streetscape. Nine storeys high and almost full of civil servants, it was developed for Norwich Union in the late 1960s by a British company called B.O.S. (Block Office and Shop) Investments and the architects included David Keane, who had recently been at the centre of the controversy over Irish Life's plans for nearby Georges Quay. Keane, a brother of Judge Ronan Keane, was also the architect for another dreary landmark, the 100-ft high Phibsboro' Tower, with its attendant retinue of single-storey shops covered by a large open car park. Also in pre-cast concrete and quite similar in style to Apollo House, this development by Canadian millionaire Galen Weston replaced a harmless terrace of eighteen cottages, mostly occupied by elderly tenants, who were given their marching orders after the freehold titles had been bought out over their heads.

B.O.S. Investments first cropped up as one of the groups of faceless speculators who would prey on the Gaiety Theatre over the years. In the summer of 1965, during a lengthy national newspaper strike, they put a small advertisement in *Business and Finance* indicating that they were applying for planning permission for a mammoth office development on the Gaiety site. Amid widespread protests, the Corporation rejected the scheme - but merely on the grounds that it would lead to traffic congestion in the area. However, in February 1967 - under pressure from the Arts Council, Actor's Equity and conservative interests - the City Council passed a resolution declaring that both the Gaiety and Olympia theatres must be preserved as places of social and cultural amenity for the people of Dublin. Eamonn Andrews Productions then secured a lease on the South King Street Theatre, and Andrews himself pledged that the Gaiety 'is here to stay'.

Sixteen years later, after the Andrews organisation had failed to keep the building in good repair, they were served with a 'schedule of dilapidations' and ordered to surrender their lease. It transpired that the Gaiety's landlord was Joe Murphy, an Irish-born building contractor and millionaire recluse, who had unwittingly bought the theatre in 1968 as part of a parcel of property extending back to Chatham Street. There were deep suspicions about his intentions but, when the Gaiety closed in January 1984, it turned out to be a temporary measure: Murphy's organisation spent over £750,000 on a thorough restoration and the theatre re-opened with joy unconfined just nine months later. But Murphy had not become a sentimental old fool and he hoped to make a tidy sum by selling off the adjoining site - with planning permission offices, flats and shops - to London and Leeds, the property arm of the Ladbroke group. In July 1984, they sold the completed office block to Telecom Eireann for £7 million, and it is a safe bet that Ladbroke's made as much as £2 million on the deal.

Inevitably, the Olympia Theatre also became a target for speculation. In 1974, it was bought for £70,000 by a London-Irish firm of ballroom proprietors, controlled by Tom O'Gorman and the Gallen brothers. They wanted to turn the theatre into a ballroom, but this was rejected by Dublin Corporation. Trading as Olympia Theatre Ltd, with registered offices at Haughey Boland and Co, they sought planning permission in 1970 to demolish the theatre, which was already leased to Brendan Smith's Olympia Productions Ltd. Despite the City Council's 1967 resolution calling for the preservation of the theatre, the owners wanted to replace it with an office block, a multi-storey car park and a much smaller new theatre. The scheme was drawn up by Cork architect Brian Wain and the required planning notice was inserted only in the *Cork Evening Echo*. This was rightly characterised by *Plan* magazine as a 'backroom attempt' to demolish the Olympia' to make way for a 'manifestly speculative scheme'.

The Corporation again refused permission, citing eight different reasons, none of which, curiously enough, made any reference to the need to preserve the existing building. But what really saved the Olympia, ironically, was the dramatic collapse of its proscenium arch during rehearsals for a loud musical on 5 November 1974. A major campaign was launched to raise funds for the restoration of the theatre and the Corporation itself contributed a 'loan' of £100,000, which it still faintly hopes will be repaid. The Olympia re-opened in March 1977 and, though its fortunes since then have been somewhat mixed, at least it is still there.

The old Queen's Theatre in Pearse Street was not so lucky, however. Founded in 1829 and much-altered over the years, it was arguably Ireland's first 'national theatre', staging patriotic plays which often incurred the wrath of Dublin Castle. Jimmy O'Dea and Harry O'Donovan first got together at the Queen's in 1928 and, for many years, it was the home of the Happy Gang. For the last fifteen years of its life, the rather dingy old playhouse served as a 'temporary' base for the Abbey company until their new theatre in Abbey Street opened in July 1966. Two months later, Lisney's put the lease of the Queen's on the market for just £25,000. Trinity College were the ground landlords and they wanted to acquire the building, but the Department of Education refused to advance the piddling sum they needed. Instead, the theatre was snapped up by Hubert McNally, who had interests in the cinema business. It soon became clear, however, that he was determined to get rid of it. After getting outline planning permission for an office block, he sold out to solicitor Gerry Hickey, one-time legal partner of George Colley and a leading member of Fianna Fáil's fund-raising committee until Charles J. Haughey came to power. Hickey, who dabbled in property development throughout the 1970s, brought in New Ireland Assurance and, through a company called Pearse Estates, they demolished the Queen's Theatre and built an office block on the site.

Five storeys high, with a bricked-in car park at street level, Aras an Phiarsaigh (as it's called) was designed by W.M. O'Dwyer and Associates and it must surely rate as one of Dublin's most ugly modern buildings - though the Corporation is entirely to blame for the fact that it is set at an angle to the street; the demented road engineers have plans to sweep away the entire south side of Pearse Street. Now part of Friends Provident's extensive property portfolio, the block has been occupied by the Revenue Commissioners since it was finished in 1971. At the time, *Plan* mourned the loss of the old Queen's and the tenth-rate quality of what replaced it. '*Private greed has always been given precedence in Dublin, especially in these last ten years of the Faith and Fatherland Party,*' it said.

Meanwhile, serious questions had been raised when the new Abbey Theatre was completed in 1966. Contrary to popular myth, the old Abbey was not 'destroyed by fire' in July 1951. Though damaged by the blaze, the building continued to be used for meetings of the Irish Academy of Letters until its demolition in 1960. '*It would have been better to have reconstructed the old rather than build a new theatre*', said the *Irish Builder* in an editorial. 'The Abbey has won for itself a worldwide reputation and...we feel that the tourists who come here would prefer to see the old Abbey, the Abbey of Yeats and Synge, rather than the Abbey of Scott.'

As far back as 1959, however, Michael Scott and Partners had prepared their plans for a new theatre on the Abbey site. The cost was originally estimated at £235,000, but seven years and six hundred drawings later, the figure had shot up to £725,000 and the Dáil Committee of Public Accounts was calling for a 'thorough investigation' of the matter. It appears that little, if any, consideration was given to the possibility of restoring the historic old building, though this would have been much cheaper. In the end, the Abbey got a very dated modern theatre in a blank-walled building which some felt looked like a huge public convenience.

The new Abbey had seating for only one hundred more people than the old, and one is left with the question: Was it all really worth it?

Eleven.
Seamus Heaney
From Maecenas to MacAlpine, 1986

Lecture delivered at Royal Institute of Architects of Ireland (RIAI) Annual Conference, 1986; reprinted in John Graby (ed.), *150 Years of Architecture in Ireland, RIAI 1839 – 1989* (Dublin: RIAI and Eblana Editions, 1990)

What I propose here is a meditation upon the relations between architectural images and the collective unconscious (consciousness). Basically, I'll be presenting a reverie on what we might call the poetics of architecture in this country at this time.

Buildings and monuments constitute a system of signs which we read and construe into a system of attachments and relationships. What we used to say about the lessons in infant-school reading books can be said equally about the buildings and monuments, streets and squares, churches and factories which constitute our horizon of vision: we read them into ourselves. As we con them, they are conning us – sometimes in the good original sense of that verb, sometimes in its less flattering, more contemporary sense. They take us in and we take them in, first as imprints on the retina, then as known dwellings, then as remembered form. They begin to insist themselves into our consciousness as a kind of language which, like any language, embodies certain values and enforces certain ways of knowing reality.

Like any other language, the language of forms can be understood in terms of its roots, or its borrowings, or its clichés, or its creative action. It can be spoken mechanically or originally, coarsely or elegantly; and just how it is spoken by individual buildings is going to affect its efficacy as an instrument for humanizing and refining consciousness. The formal solutions and imprintings of a building, in other words, serve some function and responsibility beyond the pure utilitarian and aesthetic. They become a human statement and give new emphasis – or express fresh resistance – to values and attitudes already embodied in the existing forms.

The politics of buildings may be mute but they are potent. They supply some of the dream images by which the polis, the group, identify themselves and therefore they cannot be innocent of their own force as political, in the widest, non-partisan sense of the term. Nor can the designers of buildings claim artistic quarantine and say they are dealing only in *techne* or know-how. What they design becomes (by the process which I have tried to outline above) symbolic, and once we enter the realm of the symbolic, we have crossed the threshold of human mind and feeling.

But now cross Ireland, and enter the *hortus conclusus* of Coole Park estate in Ballylee in Co. Galway, former site of the house where the Gregory family resided. This large enclosed space, surrounded by the woods and lakes of Coole Demesne, disposed at different levels, traversed by walks, artfully planted with trees and shrubs, this area is not uniquely an Irish phenomenon. This garden is an image of the achieved life of civilisation. Mythically, it is endorsed of the garden, harmony and fulfilment and a radiant consonance between desire and reality were constantly afforded to the human inhabitants. Outside was the unformed, the inchoate, the unspeakable, the unknown. Inside was the defined, the illuminated, the elect, the fully empowered human life and even when the story proceeds to its great crisis, and man and woman have been cast out into a thorn-world of sweat and tears, the Garden remains as a dream of a possible redeemed life. It becomes a social and architectural form. The leisure and pleasure it affords become intellectually significant, insofar as the Garden now represents a repossession of the order of Eden, a human triumph, a restitution in the sphere of fallen nature of prelapsian harmonies. Romans, Arabs, medieval monastics, Elizabethan courtiers, French aristocrats, Anglo-Irish landlords and English suburbanites all attest, in an unbroken line, to the potency of that designed and planted ground, at once the product of art and nature. Andrew Marvell's famous seventeenth-century poem rehearses all of the common themes:

> Fair Quiet, have I found thee here,
> And innocence, thy sister dear!
> Mistaken long, I sought you then
> In busy Companies of Men,
> Your sacred Plants, if here below,
> Only among the Plants will grow;
> Society is all but rude
> To this delicious solitude.

Society was indeed to prove very rude to the system of values and manners which sustained Coole Park in its prime, but more of that in a moment. Just now I want to come in close-up on one feature of the Coole Garden. This is a neo-classical bust, a white cropped head of carved marble, drawn from Italy by wagon and boat in the nineteenth century, to be planted in the rough Atlantic weather of Co. Galway. This bust represents the Roman aristocrat, Maecenas. Friend of the Emperor Augustus and patron of the arts, Maecenas stands in the European mind for the possibility of a benevolent link between power and art, between imperium and imagination, and as such, he was the proper guardian spirit within a good landlord's garden. He also represented a vital link between the Protestant north of Europe and the warm south, insofar as humanist, post-Reformation Europe has substituted classical Rome for Papal Rome as its sponsoring archetype.

Maecenas in Coole Park. The classical head in the *hortus conclusus*. The image of the patron in the demesne of the landlord. This whole set of correspondences and associations is one which may well have become eroded in the Ireland of the 1980s, but it remains as an enduring emblem of the covenant which architects must surely still observe, a covenant with classical achievements, with powerful patrons, with images of order, with projects of salutary beauty and force.

But if we take things one step further, we can see that Maecenas stands for more than possibility of a disinterested and paternalistic sponsorship of the arts, architecture included. He also stands for a hierarchical system of privilege, of haves and have-nots. He stands for that pre-democratic world where power and arbitration, in matters of taste as well as in matters of state, are kept in the hands of what the Romans called the *optima*, the best people, the privileged oligarchy.

Nobody is going to deny that this system – call it feudal, imperial, aristocratic or whatever – has produced some of the greatest works of architectural magnificence we are likely to know. Versailles, Chartres, St Basil's Cathedral, the Kremlin Palace, Aztec Pyramids, Boyne Valley tumuli, all depended upon a centralised and secure elite to ensure that they were carried through to their imposing completion. That much is self-evident.

Nor is anybody going to claim at this stage that our insular inheritance from this system is anything but enhancing. From the Rock of Cashel to Castletown House, from Jerpoint Abbey to the Custom House and the Four Courts, the contribution of the Norman ecclesiastical power and the Anglo-Irish ascendancy has been assumed into our heritage and our consciousness. We can stand before these monuments and not feel oppressed, politically or aesthetically. If they affirm a sense of possession, they do so by now without any intent to affront. If they symbolise their original proprietors' place at the top of the power structure, they also display an awareness of knowing their place topographically, culturally and – by now – historically. If the scale of Castletown is grandiose, that need bespeak no more than the grandiose ego of Mr. Connolly who had built it for him. It is, after all, something of an exception in being such a big Big House. The post-Williamite flowering of mansion and rectory generally produced houses of less expansive proportions, houses like Coole Park itself which is, of course, no longer with us.

Unlike many of the landlord establishments gutted by fire during the War of Independence, Coole Park stood until after Lady Gregory's death. Then it was bought by a local builder and was demolished. Whatever the motives for this act of vandalism, whether to ransack the existing structure for building materials or to satisfy some half-conscious post-colonial vengefulness, it represents a definite assault upon the covenant between power and aesthetics. That deliberate wrecking of a mature and culturally significant site gave notice of another social reality that was and is still in the ascendant. For want of a better word, I'll call it the MacAlpine principle, since 'MacAlpine' is a word that has almost caricature force in signifying building as a secular, economic, democratic, utilitarian, wellington-booted, hard-hatted enterprise, opportunistic rather than paternalistic, a matter of planning permission and public funds rather than of private patronage, an aspect of the flow of money rather than the fortification of a ruling caste.

MacAlpine builders are sappers. Sappers start in at the bottom, they work from beneath. They demolish in order to clear the way for a new dispensation. They are the workers rather than the visionaries. They are blistered and bloody-minded. They operate on the short term without much self-consciousness about their historical function or the ultimate effect of their labours. And they represent a constant aspect of the social conditions within which architects, as the makers and breakers of form, must also work.

So in contrasting MacAlpine with Maecenas, I do not wish to indulge in any smiling superiority, any implied snobbism. On the contrary, I wish to extend the MacAlpine factor to include much that is admirable in our inheritance, because insofar as it stands for buildings and architectural forms that arise out of the operation of actual ground-level forces, it encompasses much of the vernacular and mercantile and civic architecture which constitutes our given (and more or less cherished) environment.

To go back for a moment to the Garden. A Marxist would maintain that the walled enclosure as an image of the good place where high civilisation is in flower is nothing but a mystification of the facts. This unworked decorative space depended, after all, upon the labour of fieldhands and tenants. The high mode and the high walls were maintained at the expense of the low roofs and the low expectations of the peasantry, the serfs, the labour force. Meanwhile, the expression of their culture was occurring in a less self-conscious way in what we now call a vernacular architecture and all of us are sufficiently sensitised nowadays to identify the vernacular idiom as an important, intricate and indigenous strand in our inheritance, something to be attended to and estimated with the same piety and scholarship once reserved for the high style.

Allied, however, to the original folk vernacular and emerging from it are other forms, ungenteel and mercantile, which reminds us that man earns his living outside the garden by the sweat of his brow and the products of his labour. Thus I would be inclined to co-opt certain forms evolved during the industrial-bourgeois era along with other much older, rural-based styles and think of them all as examples of the MacAlpine factor in our tradition. For it is not just the thatch and the whitewash and the cylindrical gate-post which speak of our unofficial, workaday selves; there are scutch-mills, linen factories, warehouses, hotels, bridges and chimneys, railway stations, breweries and distilleries, convents and colleges, nineteenth-century Catholic churches, twentieth-century parochial halls, mill towns, music halls, opera houses, workers' houses, schoolhouses. We have inherited all these and more as an influential part of our environment also, and it would be effete even if it were physically and psychologically possible to deny them a real place in that formal architectural language which, I suggested, is being spleen to us all the time.

If these buildings and others like them did not originate like the Big House or the Four Courts in the desire for beauty as the end of building, if they do not represent architecture's purely artistic destiny to be a celebration of its own technical possibilities and to be an expression of the common hankering after definitive and symbolically pregnant forms; if instead, their construction was a matter of urgency and utilitarian purpose, they nevertheless, by virtue of their age and their naturalisation within landscapes and townscapes, have by now become objects with emotional, historical and cultural force. They have moved from a first life where they fulfilled a secular purpose and an immediate social need to a second life where they fulfil a need that is psychological and spiritual. Now they provide a locus where human affections can attach themselves; they provide contours for the inner landscapes as well as the outer one. These buildings, whose original status was profane and innocent of any aspiration towards symbolic status, have not only developed that symbolic status but have even, we might say, gradually removed themselves from the realm of the profane into the realm of the sacred. That may sound a bit of an overstatement, so let me expand it. I use the term sacred and profane as they are glossed by the Romanian anthropologist, Mircea Eliade. Eliade (1957, pp. 23-24) writes:

> For religious man, space is not homogenous; he experiences interruptions, breaks in it; some parts of space are qualitatively different from others. 'Draws not nigh higher,' says the Lord to Moses, 'put off thy shoes from off thy feet, for the place is whereon thou standest is holy ground.' (Exodus, 3.5). There is, then, a sacred space, and hence a strong, significant space; there are other spaces that are not sacred and so are without structure or consistency, amorphous...

Revelation of a sacred space makes it possible to obtain a fixed point and hence to acquire orientation in the chaos of homogeneity, to 'found the world' and to live in a real sense. The profane experience, on the contrary, maintains the homogeneity and hence the relativity of space. No true orientation is now possible, for the fixed point no longer enjoys a unique ontological status; it appears and disappears in accordance with the needs of the day. Properly speaking, there is no longer any world, there are only fragments of a shattered universe, an amorphous mass consisting of any number of more or less neutral places in which man moves, governed and driven by the obligations of an existence incorporated into an industrial society.

These perceptions – admittedly analytical of primitive man's world-view – lead to what I would finally want to say about Irish architecture. Ireland itself has for long been an arena where a sacred sense of the world has been under pressure and a sense of the profanity of space has been gaining ground. In this country, for example, we are still near enough the memory of the fire blazing on the open hearth to know instinctively what Eliade means about founding the world around a sacred centre and to know that his notion of a space such as the family hearth being ontologically privileged is no mere abstraction but a true perception of how the personal world is indeed founded. We are still sufficiently emotionally and psychically attuned to that old dispensation to recognise the profanation which occurs in a living area when central heating uncentres it, when the hearth (for which the Latin word was *focus*) disappears, and the room becomes an area of neuter disposition, dependent for its now insignificant definition upon the layout of the furniture. This familiar and unmysterious sensation of displacement from the original, coherent and founded microcosm of the hearth-world represents in miniature the larger displacement which our culture has suffered.

It also seems to me that what I have been calling the Maecenas tradition of architecture, that is architecture which comes into being in order to found or to affirm an order of reality, whether the reality be that of the Boyne tomb builders or of the Norman Cistercians or the Anglo-Irish landlords, it seems to me that in Eliade's terms, such an architecture is basically sacred. While,

for example, the round tower of the Celtic monastery may indeed have had a defensive purpose, and the Irish Houses of Parliament in College Green did indeed function as an assembly place, it is clear that these utilitarian functions derive from and are probably ancillary to their symbolic functions as foundations, sitings, proclamations of a centre.

By contrast, the erection of a factory or a hotel or an office block, while it may intend to establish a centre of efficiency, is an operation of a fundamentally different kind. The architect of such a building will (if we are lucky) feel a need to keep faith with his artistic responsibility to create an aesthetically and ontologically significant structure, but he will necessarily be bound by other more empirically arrived at requirements. The MacAlpine world is one we inhabit and it is a profane one. We need only think of an oratory at an airport to sense how far the

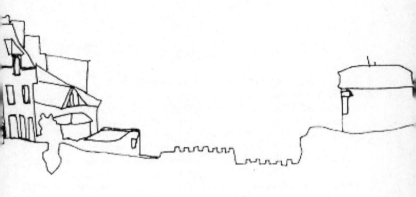

potency of that officially religious area has been overcome by the airport's primary secular reality. The archaic, religious, centred and focused world vision which could once be refracted and concentrated in the very structure of a church has been much debilitated. We have arrived, in fact, at a point where many new churches resemble more and more the insides of airport lounges.

And yet it is still the architect's responsibility to bear witness to space as a human home rather than space as geometric dimension. It is up to the architect to keep faith with human scale, to remember that the spirit and the unconscious need caring for, need to dwell in amity inside a building. Obviously, we do not want the sort of kitsch nostalgia prevalent in the USA where you can have your prefabbed period building at the drop of a dollar; nor do I want to imply that architecture, to be conservative of the nesting instinct in human beings, has to be reactionary in style or technique. But I do suggest that each architect could do well to remind himself or herself that each new structure involves, in a deep metaphorical sense, a re-creation of the world, and so contributes towards the bringing into being of a certain kind of world. What William Blake said of the act of poetic imagination is equally true of architecture: it is a repetition within the finite mind of the eternal I AM. And in this respect, even in the world of the profane space, the architect cannot escape from casting a vote, as it were, in favour of that profanity or against it; a vote which assents or withholds assent to it. The assent or dissent will, of course, be expressed formally, but it will be no less potent and influential for being implicit rather than explicit.

In Ireland, local mana still emanates from much of our environment. Space is not as yet neutral as it is on Manhattan Island. And while it may not have remained as pristine as it has remained in Iceland, for example, space here is still imprinted with indigenous forms and is pervious to domestic human affections. So the Irish architect has indeed one precious advantage over his colleagues in Europe or America. His space is still more than vestigially sacred, and it is both his privilege and his responsibility to be its custodian. What is improvised upon the drawing board today will be impressed upon the consciousness of the future; the writing, so to speak, is in the wall.

References

M. Eliade, *The Sacred and the Profane* (New York: Harvest Books, 1957)

Twelve.

John Olley

The Language of Representation & Thought in Design Drawing, 1989

From Shane O'Toole (ed.), *The Architect & the Drawing* (Dublin: Royal Institute of Architects of Ireland, 1989)

1 - For the artist, drawing is discovery [1]

If he wants to balance his compositions and to arrange his various inventions well, the painter must first do various sketches on paper to see how everything goes together. The idea which the artist has in his mind must be translated into what the eyes can see, and only then, with the assistance of his eyes, can the artist form a sound judgement concerning the inventions he has conceived.

– Vasari [2]

The importance of drawing for the process of design in painting, sculpture and architecture has continually been stressed by critics and artists alike from Vasari to Ruskin, from Michelangelo to Le Corbusier. There is a need to give some external expression to ideas or their fragments so that they can be combined or rejected, composed and developed through a dialogue between mind and representation. The writing down, '*the translation into what the eyes can see*', is also felt to be necessary in other art forms, in poetry and music. 'Beethoven wrote fragments of themes in notebooks which he kept beside him, working on them and developing them over years. Often his first ideas were of a clumsiness which makes scholars marvel how he could, at the end, have developed from them such miraculous results.'[3]

How are the 'miraculous results' achieved, what are the prerequisites and how best can they be assembled? If drawing is the medium, the catalyst and vehicle for the evolution of a design, what makes it so powerful and how can one prepare for its potency?

The relationship between idea and representation has been a preoccupation in philosophy and psychology when debating the descent from thought to language. Vygotsky has examined the thought/speech connection. He suggested a difference in nature between thought and words, and *'because a direct transition from thought to words is impossible, there have always been laments about the inexpressibility of thought...Thought is not merely expressed in words; it comes into existence through words...a thought unembodied in words remains a shadow.'*[4]

Likewise, in his essay, 'The Making of a Poem', Stephen Spender suggests that a first draft of a poem is an attempt *'to sketch out an idea which exists clearly enough on some level of the mind where it yet eludes the attempt to state it. At this stage, a poem is like a face which no one seems to be able to visualise clearly in the eye of memory, but when one examines it mentally or tries to think it out, feature by feature, it seems to fade.'*[5]

A thought or an idea may find expression in a non-linguistic representation, a visual image or an artifact; to prevent the image from being elusive or fading, it must be externalised in some way. Drawing, like speech, is an immediate method for capturing an idea in an external form. However, the production of a more finished and permanent artifact, even if possible at this stage, would be inappropriate and indeed inhibiting, as Leonardo believes:

> *Now, have you never thought about how poets compose their verses? They do not trouble to trace beautiful letters, nor do they mind crossing out several lines so as to make them better. So, painter, rough out the arrangement of the limbs of your figures and first attend to the movements appropriate to the mental state of the creatures that make up your picture, rather than to the beauty and perfection of their parts.*[6]

The writing of a first draft or the drawing of a first image fixes the idea, however inadequately. This embodiment in words or lines can be assessed and then modified to bring about a coincidence of thought and its representation. However, there is much more potential here than matching the idea with its presentation. For Henry Moore, 'Drawing is a means of finding (our) way about things, and a way of experiencing, more quickly than sculpture (building or painting) allows, certain tryouts and attempts.'[7]

More still, more than running through a set of ideas to select the best, a single idea, perhaps ill-defined or inadequate, can be developed or unrecognisably transformed. It is the development and metamorphosis that reinterpreted Beethoven's clumsy fragments to uncover the miraculous results.

Let us return to Leonardo for further advice on the evolution of an idea:

> You who compose subject pictures, do not articulate the individual parts of those pictures with determined outlines, or else there will happen to you what usually happens to many and different painters who want every, even the slightest, trace of charcoal to remain valid; this sort of person may well earn a fortune but no praise with his art, for it frequently happens that the creature fails to move its limbs in accordance with the movements of the mind: and once such a painter has given a beautiful and graceful finish to the articulated limbs, he will think it damaging to shift these limbs higher or lower or forward or backward.[8]

The drawing itself becomes animated, the limbs begin to move, to suggest ways forward to a better composition. The power lies in the imprecision of the drawing, its virtue is its sketchiness. We can see in it things other than the original image - with the body that way we see the arm there, not where we have indicated it with the scribble. The drawing has represented the image. And so the process of development and metamorphosis can continue, through a dialogue between mind and drawing. We discover potential in the original idea, or even new ideas that would never have occurred if we sat thinking in front of a blank sheet of paper. Stephen Spender also identifies this process of reperception in the writing in poetry:

> The work on a line of poetry may take the form of putting a version aside for a few days, weeks or years, and then taking it up again, when it may be found that the line has, in the interval of time, almost rewritten itself.[9]

Furthermore, in order to initiate the process of evolution and transformation, we may not even require an idea. Leonardo tells us how in 'How to increase your talent and stimulate various inventions':

Do not despise my opinion, when I remind you that it should not be hard for you to stop sometimes, and look into the stains of your walls, or ashes of a fire, or clouds, or mud, or like places, in which, if you consider them well, you may find really marvelous ideas. The mind of the painter is stimulated to new discoveries, the composition of battles of animals and men, various compositions of landscapes and monstrous things, such as devils and similar things, which may bring you honour, because by indistinct things the mind is stimulated to new inventions[10]

'By indistinct things the mind is stimulated to new inventions', an echo of his advice for the design of paintings, and surely likewise of sculpture and buildings, Leonardo seems to be conscious of possible disbelief amongst his audience when he entreats them: 'do not despise my opinion'; perhaps there is something dishonest, immoral, artless about the process! But as Leonardo warns: 'though they give you inventions, they do not teach you to finish any detail.'[11]

Intellect and experience are essential.

For Henry Moore, ideas arise:

... in various ways. One doesn't know really how any ideas come. But you can induce them by starting in the far little studio with looking at a box of pebbles. Sometimes I may scribble some doodles... in a notebook: within my mind they may be a reclining figure, or perhaps a particular subject. Then with those pebbles, or the sketches in the notebook, I sit down and something begins.[12]

Moore charts the process of metamorphosis through drawing, through a dialogue between mind and representation, of a bone, the source of the idea, to the human form, a project for a sculpture - a transformation much more efficient through drawing than the medium of sculpture.

2 - The Innocent Eye Is Blind, & the Virgin Mind Empty

- Kant

Experience is necessary for initiating the process of evolution from first draft to final polished work of art, whatever the medium. Acquired knowledge is essential for recognising possibilities in phrases that have been laid aside for a day, months or years, to see wonderful images in the stains on walls, or for the reclining figure to arise from a flint or bone. For Stephen Spender:

> It is perhaps true to say that memory is the faculty of poetry, because the imagination itself is an exercise of memory. There is nothing we imagine which we do not already know. And our ability to remember what we have already once experienced and to apply it to some different situation. Thus the greatest poets are those with memories so great that they extend beyond their strongest experiences to their minutest observations.[13]

But this memory is as much in the realm of the subconscious, it needs a prompt to come forward, it needs a cue for retrieval to aid the perception of images in 'indistinct things'. This experience is in part the faculty of visual perception.

> ...information already acquired determines what will be picked up next. But although perception is directed by expectations, it is not controlled by them. The perceiver has become what he is by virtue of what he has perceived (and done) in the present ... Only through perceptual learning do we become able to perceive progressively more subtle aspects of the environment.[14]

Sir Joshua Reynolds put this in the context of creativity long before the advent of the science of psychology:

> A mind enriched by the assemblage of all the treasures of ancient and modern art, will be more elevated and fruitful in resources in proportion to the number of ideas which have been carefully collected and thoroughly digested. There can be no doubt but that he who has the most materials has the greatest means of invention; and if he has not the power of using them, it must proceed from a feebleness of intellect; or from the confused manner in which these

collections have been laid up in his mind.[15]

With this visual experience stored in our subconscious, and the natural driving force of perception being the search for meaning, we are able to make perceptions with the scantest of data. Drawing is necessarily a substantial attraction and, as a method of pictorial representation, is highly selective and often a brief notation for the visual data that would be available from the actual object or scene it represents. Our visual experience and the need to overlay meaning on the images the retina receives allowed Matisse, Giacometti and Ingres their economical drawings, where a single or interrupted line fills out the volume and imparts a tactile sensation of the flesh portrayed.

So powerful is the pull of experience and the quest for meaning, that not only is it possible to identify a very economical drawing as the object intended, but we can recognise objects and vistas within unintended or random patterns of line or light and shade.

> *Sometimes we see a cloud that's dragonish;*
> *A vapour sometime like a bear or lion,*
> *A towered citadel, a pendant rock,*
> *A forked mountain, or blue promontory*
> *With trees upon't, that unto the world,*
> *And mock our eyes with air...*

- Shakespeare [16]

It is knowledge embedded in the structures of our subconscious that allows us to see things in the clouds or on crumbling walls, and to perceive the unintended in a first draft. The early drawings of a design became catalysts to unearth and combine elements of experience and knowledge, and lead us to further discoveries and inventions. If these drawings, as Leonardo recommends, are imprecise, ambiguous, fluid, they facilitate the exercise of our acquired wisdom. A drawing with 'a beautiful and graceful finish' makes no further appeal to our experience, it locks our perception and thought and inhibits the process of development. The ability to have ideas, to invent and perfect them, is the exercise of past visual experience fired by the agency of making drawings.

Experience and knowledge are indispensable prerequisites for design; a necessary but not sufficient condition. Just as greater perceptual acumen leads to being able to perceive more subtle aspects of the environment, so greater experience of form and elements of the visual world facilitates the process of creation and invention in design. *'For confused things rouse the mind to new inventions, but see to it that you first know all the parts of the things you want to represent, be it those of animals, of landscape, or rocks, plants or others'.*[17] As Gombrich points out, *'Leonardo knew that the fantasies he discovered in the indeterminate could only be made to spring to life by lucid knowledge.'*[18] Leonardo could have made little progress in his composition of subject pictures if he did not have that intimate knowledge of the human form and its movements won by his intense observations and exhaustive analysis of anatomy.

We can now allow Reynolds to recap:

> *It is indisputably evident that a great part of every man's life must be employed in collecting materials for the exercise of genius. Invention, strictly speaking, is little more than a new combination of those images which have been previously gathered and deposited in the memory; nothing can come of nothing; he who has laid up no materials, can produce no combinations.* [19]

3 - Much Drawing

But how are these materials for the exercise of genius to be collected, how are the memories to be lodged in the structures of our subconscious? Again the words of the artist reply:

> *...secret collected treasure of my heart that comes into existence only if the artist has filled his mind by much drawing and out of whose fullness he can create in his heart a new being...*

> - Durer [20]

And for Le Corbusier:

> When one travels and works with visual things - architecture,
> painting or sculpture - one uses one's eyes and draws, so as to fix
> deep down in one's experience what is seen. Once the impression has
> been recorded by the pencil, it stays for good, entered, registered,
> inscribed...To draw oneself, to trace the lines, handle the volumes,
> organise the surface...all this means first to look and then to observe
> and finally perhaps to discover and it is then that inspiration may
> come.[21]

Such is the advice of one of the giants of twentieth-century
architecture. Le Corbusier spent much of his early twenties
travelling and drawing. He drew from paintings, sculpture and
the decorative arts, as well as from architecture and from nature.
This activity was to be an essential part of his education for,
not only did drawing fix his visual experience, but, because of
the intense observation required in drawing, it led to discovery.
Drawing is a path to knowledge and understanding of the world,
a powerful method of self-education, a point Reynolds was to
bring to his students' attention: 'He who endeavours to copy nicely
the figure before him, not only acquires a habit of exactness and
precision but is constantly advancing in his knowledge of the human
figure.' [22]

Leonardo was more demonstrably active in his search for
knowledge through drawing, through his analytical, anatomical
drawings, he sought to understand comprehensively the structure
and action of the human body. Looking at these drawings, one is
reminded of Constable's claim that 'painting is a science, and should
be pursued as an inquiry into the laws of nature.' [23]

Although drawing was universally declared the foundation stone
of any artist's training, opinions differed on the appropriate
methods of drawing appropriate and the legitimate objects for
attention. Approaches varied from slavish copying out of the
master's model or pattern book to the careful observation and
analysis of nature through drawing. Model and pattern books
were used in architecture and painting alike, both for training
of apprentices and as sources of ready-made components.
Within a workshop or strict stylistic tradition, their use ensured

homogeneity amongst a disparate collection of talents by providing a carefully controlled communal form repertoire. Such customs, universal in cathedral lodges and pre-*quatrrocento* workshops, extended well into the Renaissance, especially outside the influence of Florence. Analogous practices were still common in the offices of eighteenth- and nineteenth-century architects, although, of course, the nature of the portfolio of forms was by then much altered.[24]

In the early Renaissance, the model and pattern books continued to contain images which were usually copies of existing works of art, often at second- or third-hand; a state of affairs that Leonardo complained could only lead to the decline of art.[25] However, in periods of stylistic change and reaction there was a recourse to the fountainhead: nature or the antique classical past.[26]

In his *Il Libro dell' Arte*, Cennini, recording workshop practice in the trecento, warns apprentices that:

> ...if you undertake to copy after one master today and another tomorrow, you will not acquire the style of either one or the other and you will inevitably, through enthusiasm, become capricious, because each style will be distracting your mind. ... If you follow the course of one man through constant practice, your intelligence would have to be crude indeed for you not to get some nourishment from it.[27]

In more liberal times, the sources of an artist's repertoire of forms have been allowed to be more eclectic, when works by a larger number of recognised masters have no longer been out of bounds and have instead become fair game for plunder by the eye and pencil. Although Leonardo permits this for the young painter directed 'to train his own hand by copying drawings from the hands of good masters', he thinks it better to return to the objects of nature to avoid being infected by bad habits: 'for he who can go to the fountain does not go to the water jar'[28] However, this did not prevent him from taking a furtive sip from Michelangelo's jar. Normally so disparaging of the youngster's work, he had made a surreptitious sketch of David to recast as Neptune in his own repertory.[29]

In architecture, more abstract and utilitarian than the mimetic arts of painting and sculpture, the need for recourse to nature may not be immediately obvious. Consequently, architects in search of materials for the exercise of their genius have depended more heavily upon the works of their predecessors. Although less explicitly necessary in architectural training, nature has often been considered the essential source of fundamental and universal truths and of inspiration as well as the ultimate root of all architectural styles.[30] Michelangelo insisted that no-one should contemplate designing buildings until they had thoroughly acquainted themselves with the human form.[31] And Le Corbusier, well taught by the writings of Ruskin, tells of the benefits of studying nature:

> *Nature is order and law, unity and diversity without end, subtlety, harmony and strength: that is the lesson (Jeanneret) learnt between the ages of fifteen and twenty.*[32]

> *If you have a pencil in your hand, look at (natural objects) and you will understand ... a storehouse of inspiration to draw upon, the lessons taught by natural phenomena ... have riches to offer which the mind cannot conceive.*[33]

The eighteenth century saw the consolidation of Rome and Naples as the main collecting grounds for the form repertoire of any architect who was to succeed. Architects followed in the wake of the Grand Tourists not only to woo their future patrons but to enlarge their storehouse of forms by harvesting the fertile remains of ancient Rome. Often they carried out measured drawings and speculative reconstructions of the ruins which could be published in portfolio form on their return. Such publications, whilst serving as a kind of external form repertoire for the architectural community as a whole, combined with their sketchbooks and inlayed visual experiences to form the materials for the travelled architects' professional lives.

Not always did the visual horizon stop at the antique; buildings of the Renaissance and Mannerist architects were also to be admired and plundered, although Baroque was to remain suspicious, or simply unacceptable.[34] Earlier, Inigo Jones had awakened Britain to the artistic developments in Italy. He returned from his travels not only with his own sketchbooks and an annotated copy of Palladio's *Quattro Libri* but with a collection of drawings by the Italian master and others. This collection, along with Jones' own drawings and those of Webb, was in part purchased by Lord Burlington and was augmented by his own collection of Palladio's drawings acquired in Italy.[35]

This impressive collection became an exclusive source of forms for Burlington and his inner circle. Yet, because Burlington did not acquire the potentially rich library of images through the process of drawing, either as an apprentice constantly tracing and transposing the collection, or by himself drawing from life the buildings it portrayed, it could not be absorbed into his subconscious thereby providing him with a sure base for creative design. Without the thorough inculcation of the forms from his collection, which he sought to recombine in the making of his architecture, his mind would have been hopelessly mute in that dialogue between mind and representation so important and powerful in the process of design. So it is we find Wittkower refers to the *staccato* nature of Burlington's designs, the simple tacking together of fragments cut from his collection.[36] Nay, at times, he did not even resort to collage, but produced his design for General Wade by a verbatim transcription of the facade of Palladio's unbuilt project for a town house. This was then to arrive in Ireland as the Provost's Lodge at Trinity College Dublin by way of its appearance in Volume Three of Colen Campbell's *Vitruvius Britannicus*.

Travel in the search for visual knowledge was not the intention of the eighteenth-century English gentleman. The medieval mason, after completing his apprenticeship in a cathedral lodge, would be expected to travel and work as a journeyman, studying and recording state of the art building elsewhere. The experience gained and inscribed in a pattern book could be brought back to his lodge to update and develop its practices. Therefore, travelling and keeping a visual notebook played a vital role in the dissemination of ideas and techniques throughout Gothic Europe.[37] The famous sketchbook of Villard de Honnecourt may, at least in part, be such a document.

In spite of the decline of the Grand Tour for the youth of the

European aristocracy brought on by changing fashion and rising political unrest, travel continued to be considered an expected part of an architect's education. Sir William Chambers, who studied in Paris and Rome, was to write: 'travelling to an artist is what the University is to a man of letters.'[38] The visual diet was to become increasingly eclectic. Le Corbusier, travelling extensively not only in his youth but throughout his life, drew avidly to discover and understand. He cast his net wide searching for the universals hidden in the different styles of all the visual arts as well as in landscape and nature. Such was the approach recommended in the eighteenth century by Reynolds:

> *To find excellencies, however dispersed, to discover beauties, however concealed by the multitude of defects with which they are surrounded, can be the work only of him who, having a mind always alive to his art, has extended his views to all ages and to all schools: and has acquired from that comprehensive mass which he has thus gathered to himself, a well-digested and perfect idea of his art, to which everything is referred. Like a sovereign judge and arbiter of art, he is possessed of that residing power which separates and attracts every excellence from every school; selects both from what is great, and what is little; brings home knowledge from the East and from the West; making the universe tributary towards furnishing his mind and enriching his works with originality, and variety of intentions.*[39]

4 - Analysis Through Creation

Just as Leonardo dissected the human body with his eye and pen in order to understand more deeply the body's form, it is possible to subject culture's artifacts, its paintings, sculpture and buildings, to the same exacting analysis. In his series of *L'Art de Bâtir*, Auguste Choisy sought to reveal the buildings' structural and constructional systems. Reynolds also argues that an incisive analysis of a painting can be achieved through sagacious imitation whereby one would discover and enter into the principles residing in the work.[40] Through using drawing to investigate nature or culture's artifacts, one is drawn into intense observation coupled with the search for the means of transcribing what is seen. '*It is the actual drawing that forces the artist to look at* the object in front of him, to dissect in his mind's eye and put it together again... A line, an area of tone, is not really important because it records what you have seen, but because what it will lead you on to see.'[41] As we perform the activity of making a drawing, our thought towards it changes and this changes our activity.

Henry Moore performed an exploration into the sculptural qualities of the three figures and their compositional relationship within a small oil sketch by Cézanne. He made maquettes of the figures and disposed them in space to recreate the grouping depicted. Moore then produced a series of three drawings of the group viewed from various directions. Having completed the study, he commented:

> I enjoyed the whole of this experiment. I had thought I knew our 'Bathers' picture completely, having lived with it for twenty years. But the exercise - modeling the figures and drawing them from different views has taught me more than any amount of just looking at the picture. This example shows that working from the object - modeling or drawing it, makes you look much more intensely than ever you do if you just look at something for pleasure.[42]

Although this again reinforces a point made earlier on the authority of both Reynolds and Le Corbusier, there is something more here. The analysis, the extraction of knowledge from Cézanne's work, involves a process of making, of creation; the maquette and the drawings become works of art in their own right that can stand independent from their source. Furthermore, the analysis is unmistakably that of Moore, but at the same time it induces a resonance between the work of the sculptor and Cézanne. To a certain degree the analysis has become an assessment, an interpretation of Cézanne using Moore's language.

Picasso painted many interpretations of works of past masters: Poussin, Delacroix, Velázquez, Manet, etc. Of Manet's Le Déjeuner sur l'Herbe, Picasso made 138 drawings, 23 paintings and 5 linocuts, an exhaustive dissection, analysis and reconstruction through the production of interpretations, laying bare the full range of knowledge and potential embraced by Manet's painting. Picasso translated and updated it. Indeed, the nineteenth-century painting itself could be seen to be an interpretation in the same way. In the much quoted passage, Proust recalls:

> Some women were bathing. Manet had his eye fixed on the flesh of those coming out of the water. 'It appears' he said 'that I must do a nude. Very well, I'll do one. When we were at Couture's I copied Giorgione's 'Concert Champetre'. It is black, the picture; the dark priming has come through. I want to do that over again in terms of transparent light and with people like these.[43]

However, the main compositional element of Manet's painting, the group of three figures in the foreground, was transplanted from elsewhere, from the bottom right hand corner of a now lost painting by Raphael, *The Judgement of Paris*.[44] In its turn, the composition of Raphael's work comes substantially from an early imperial Roman sarcophagus.[45] The pedigree stretches from antiquity to the twentieth century.

The procedure adopted by Picasso is a potent method for gaining access to Manet's stock of forms. For Reynolds, *'what is learnt in this manner from the works of others becomes really our own, sinks deep, and is never forgotten; it is by seizing on this clue that we proceed forward, and get further and further in enlarging the principles and improving the practice of our art.'*[46] Merleau-Ponty provides the words to sum up and put into context the long ancestry of *Le Déjeuner sur l'Herbe*.

> The productions of the past, which are the data of our time, themselves once went beyond anterior productions towards a future. [...] It is always only a question of advancing the line of the already opened furrow and of recapturing and generalising an accent which has already appeared in the corner of a previous painting or in some instant of his experience, without the painter himself ever being able to say (since the distinction has no meaning) what comes from him and what comes from things, what the new work adds to the old ones, or what it has taken from the others and what is its own.[47]

Architecture also abounds in examples of implicit and explicit interpretations and adaptations of works of the past. At times we find crude literal quotations, at others such total assimilation of a catholic range of precedents that it is difficult to unravel the dependence on the past. Among the drawings now in the Soane Museum by the Elizabethan architect, John Thorpe, we find as well as surveys of existing buildings, some designs of his own. One is du Cerceau's *Plus Excellent Bâtiments de France* of 1576.[48] In other drawings we find plans traced from the 1601 edition of Palladio's *Quattro Libri* which are then adapted and dressed with stylistically very different façades.[49] Other works by Palladio appearing in his *Four Books* have been the subject of emulation and interpretation, none more than his Villa Rotunda.

If Burlington, to create a house for General Wade, was content to put a plan, and not a very distinguished one at that, behind Palladio's drawing, he was to be more adventurous in the variation on the rotunda theme for his very own villa in Chiswick. The plan embodying the exemplar's character sought its divergence in the introduction of the enfilade sequence along the garden front of circular, double-apsed rectangular and octagonal spaces. To transform the exterior he had only to make a selection from his collection of Palladio's drawings. And on the sheet that provided the garden front can be found the trio of Serlian windows looking into an enfilade sequence that provided the inspiration for Burlington's 'novelty'.

To suggest William Chambers' Casino at Marino as Ireland's version of Villa Rotunda may at first seem surprising. This is because the Vicenzine model was thoroughly assimilated and combined with other completely digested non-Palladian precedents. The Casino's four vestigial porticoes that direct the gaze to command the surrounding landscape bears comparison with the original. From here the complexity of the invention begins. Defined by pairs of columns, the porticoes viewed in plan disappear into the conceit of a Greek cross inscribed within a circle of columns. This would have delighted the Elizabethan architects in Britain with their appetite for geometric devices and mazes. All trace of Palladio disappears as the interior disengages from the exterior to deceive the latter's expression. Such discontinuity between façade and plan was a leitmotif of the Parisian *hôtel* of the eighteenth century. It can be clearly seen in the work of J-F. Blondel, in whose school of architecture, in Paris, Chambers was sucked into the vortex of Piranesi's energy and imagination. From the hand of this Venetian eccentric came a multitude of architectural interventions in graphic form. The excesses of these megalomaniacal extravaganzas seem far removed from the miniature architectural gem overlooking Dublin Bay. However, the smoking urns that added drama to the creations of Piranesi lead directly to Chambers' invention for disguising the chimneys as vases. Chambers had practiced the advice he was to give to one of his students studying in Rome:

> Seek for those who have most reputation, young or old, amongst which forget not Piranesi, who you may see in my name: he is full of matter, extravagant 'tis true, often absurd, but from his overflowings you may gather much information.[50]

The synthesis of the Casino confirmed his colleague, Reynolds' description of the great artist: he *'has extended his views to all ages and to all schools: and he has acquired from that comprehensive mass which he has thus gathered to himself, a well-digested and perfect idea of his art, to which everything is referred. ... The more extensive your acquaintance with the works of those who have excelled, the more extensive will be your powers of invention.'* [51] With his powerful draughtsmanship, Chambers gathered and fused the images of the past. This skill and accomplishment in drawing was the centre of the young Robert Adam's jealousy of his future rival. Just as Chambers was leaving Rome, the ambitious Scot arrived and immediately set about closing the ability gap. He took Pécheux as instructor in anatomical drawing to provide for what Adam was to believe to be 'absolutely requisite' for the architect. But it was Clérisseau that led him towards the fluid graphic style that so clearly served the imagination and ambitions of his hero, Piranesi. Adam performed many a fanciful composition to emulate the extravagances of his idol. In this he was not alone. The eighteenth century saw amongst the French and British the design of triumphal bridges, monuments and mausolea of megalomaniacal scale to be submitted to academies in pursuit of prizes and publicity. The expansion of the imagination required to conceive one of these designs forced the natural reticence of the northern Europeans to be pushed to the limits of fantasy, and the experience instilled a firmer assurity in subsequent more modest work. Such explorations, such flights of fancy, return to influence the reality of subsequent built architecture. They are works of research.

For the artist, a new work is born of his previous knowledge. It is a progeny of his existing stock and can go forward to contribute to the production of the next generation. A new work, whether on paper or built, can both influence its artist's future productions and that of others. But for the individual, there are the dangers of inbreeding and stagnation, especially where the existing personal stock of forms is limited. So, for Reynolds:

> *The greatest natural genius cannot subsist on his own stock: he who resolves never to ransack any mind but his own, will be soon reduced, from mere barrenness, the poorest of all imitations: he will be obliged to imitate himself, and to repeat what he has before often repeated.*[52]

The architect, too, must seek to replenish and expand his stock of forms. Le Corbusier was a painter and sculptor as well as an architect, yet he saw architecture as his primary artistic endeavour. He considered the other arts as an expansion of his horizons, a process of pure research, discovery through doing, but without any particular project or immediate application in mind.

> *Each day of my life has been dedicated in part to drawing and painting, searching for the secrets of form wherever I could find them. [...] I believe that if people are going to see something in my work, it is to those private labours that one should attribute the deepest qualities.*[53]

5 – From Sublime Dreams to Reality

For Horace Walpole:

> *The sublime dreams of Piranesi, who seems to have conceived visions of Rome beyond what is boasted even in the meridian of its splendour. Savage as Salvator Rosa, fierce as Michael Angelo, and exuberant as Rubens, he has imagined scenes that would startle geometry, and exhaust the Indies to realise. He piles palaces on bridges, and temples on palaces, and scales Heaven with mountains of edifices. Yet what boldness! What grandeur in his wildness! What labour and thought both in his rashness and details.*[54]

Piranesi is but one of a long line of speculator-draughtsmen whose pens make proposals beyond the realm of possibility, but whose influence on the built environments becomes prodigious. Drawings are speculation without hindrance, invention without limits. Flights of fancy and polemical statements can be realised as graphic images, and then be disseminated to become inspiration for the faint hearted.

For Piranesi, drawing became a powerful argument to confirm the grandeur of ancient Rome. By exaggeration, he sought to readjust the perception of antiquity. So successful were Piranesi's publications, that, drawn to Rome by the engravings, Goethe at first expressed dismay to discover the smallness of the monuments. In more general terms, drawings, through their necessary abstraction and their immediacy, can reveal new and surprising aspects of the visual world, altering our perception of the environment. Often, at the boundaries of stylistic change, new ways of drawing are developed to aid the creation of a style and to facilitate thinking about new preoccupations. These conventions provide new metaphors. Evolved to enable thinking, they become determinants of thought. Perspective, reinvented by Brunelleschi to provide new insights and ensure spatial order, entered Western sensibility to dictate further perception. It is a process with an analogy in language. For the philosopher, Whorf: *'the background linguistic system of each language is not merely a reproducing system for voicing ideas, but rather is itself a shaper of ideas: the users of markedly different grammars are pointed by their grammars towards different types of observations.'*[55]

For the architect, drawing is seeing and discovering; it sharpens perception and educates. It is a means of speculating and both an aid to, and controller of, thought. Drawing is design.

Design, known also by the other name of drawing, constitutes the source and body of painting, sculpture (and) architecture. It is the root of all sciences. Let him who has attained a mastery of it know that he holds a great treasure in his power. He will be able to create figures more lofty than any tower, either out of colours or carved from the block, and will never find a wall or screen which will not prove narrow and small for his sublime imaginings.'

- Michelangelo

Footnotes

1 - John Berger, 'Drawing in Permanent Red', in *Essays in Seeing* (London: 1960), p. 23

2 - Giorgio Vasari, *Lives of the Artists* (Harmondsworth: 1965), p. 443

3 - Stephen Spender, 'The Making of a Poem' reprinted in P E Vernon (ed.), *Creativity* (Harmondsworth: 1970), p.64

4 - L S Vygotsky, *Thought and Language* (trans. E Hanfmann and G Vakar, Cambridge Mass: 1962)

5 - Spender, op cit, p.65

6 - Leonardo da Vinci, *Treatise on Painting*, (ed. A P McMahon, Princeton: 1956), no. 261. I have used Gombrich's translation in Leonardo's 'Method for Working Out Compositions' in Norm and Form (Oxford: 1966), p.59

7 - Henry Moore in P James (ed.) *Henry Moore on Sculpture* (London, 1966), p. 146

8 - Leonardo da Vinci, op cit (see note # 6)

9 - Spender, op cit, p. 68

10 - Leonardo da Vinci, 'Treatise on Painting' in I A Richter (ed.), *Selections from the Notebooks of Leonardo da Vinci* (Oxford, 1977), p. 182

11 - Leonardo da Vinci, in McMahon (ed.), op cit (see note #6), no. 93

12 - Henry Moore, op cit, p. 141

13 - Spender, op cit, p. 72

14 - U Neisser, *Cognition and Reality: Principles and Implications in Cognitive Psychology* (San Francisco, 1976)

15 - Sir Joshua Reynolds, *Discourses on Art* (ed. R R Wark, New Haven and London: 1975), p.99

16 - From *Anthony and Cleopatra*

17 - Leonardo da Vinci, ed. McMahon, op cit, No. 76

18 - Gombrich, op cit, (see note #6), p. 62

19 - Reynolds, op cit, p. 27

20 - Albrecht Durer, *The Writings of Albrecht Durer* (trans. W M Conway, New York: 1958)

21 - Le Corbusier, *My Work* (trans. J Palmes, London: 1960), p. 37

22 - Reynolds, op cit, pp. 19 -20

23 - John Constable, *Discourses* (ed. R B Beckett, Ipswich, 1970), p. 69

24 - For an excellent account of drawing practices in the early Renaissance and their development from medieval times, see F Ames-Lewis, *Drawings in Early Renaissance Italy* (New Haven and London: 1981); also, F Ames-Lewis and J Wright, *Drawing and the Italian Workshop* (London: 1983). Among the drawings of Sir Charles Barry in the British Architectural Library, Drawings Collection, there are several copies of drawings he did in Italy. These are probably done later by his pupils. In 'The Making of an Architect: the travels of Sir Charles Barry' in *Country Life* (28 August 1969), p. 495, Marcus Binney suggests that one of the methods by which Barry trained his pupils was by their tracing and copying of his own drawings. Sir John Soane, on his own, traced decorative details from drawings of his employer, Henry Holland. From these he formed a scrapbook which acted as an archive of ornaments for his future use (P. de la Ruffinere Du Prey, *John Soane, the Making of an Architect* (Chicago, 1982), p.32)

25 - Leonardo da Vinci, op cit (see note # 10) pp. 226-7. See his note headed 'That painting declines and deteriorates from age to age, when painters have no other standard than paintings already done.'

26 - The Renaissance and the eighteenth century saw much archaeological study of the art and architecture of ancient Greek and Roman cultures. Also, today, eyes are again turning towards the images of classical architecture.

27 - Cennino Cennini, *The Craftsman's Handbook: Il Libro dell'Arte* (trans. D V Thompson Jr, New York: 1954)

28 - Leonardo da Vinci, ed. McMahon, op cit, No. 61. Leonardo da Vinci, ed. Richter, op cit, p. 179. See also Leonardo da Vinci, ed. McMahon, op cit, No. 59: '...next, copy work after the hand of a good master, to gain the habit of drawing parts of the body well; and then work from nature to confirm the lessons learned.'

29 - Sir Kenneth Clark argues that the Leonardo drawing No. 12591 verso in the Royal Collection at Windsor is after Michelangelo's *David* and then incorporated into an idea for *Neptune (with sea-horses around his feet)*. K Clark and C Pedretti, *Leonardo da Vinci Drawings* in the Royal Library at Windsor Castle (London, 1968), p. 118

30 - See Joseph Rykwert, *On Adam's House in Paradise (the Idea of the Primitive Hut in Architectural History)* (New York: 1972). Ruskin, in *The Seven Lamps of Architecture* (London, 1880), discusses the relationship between forms found in nature and those of the styles of architecture and its decoration, and also his Aphorism 19 reads: 'All beauty is founded on the laws of natural forms'

31 - '...there is no question but that architectural members reflect the members of Man, and whoever has not been or is not a good master of the figure and likewise of anatomy cannot understand anything of them...' G Milanesi, *Le Lettere di Michelangelo Buonarroti* (Florence, 1983) p. 554, quoted in J S Ackerman, 'Architectural Practice in the Italian Renaissance' in JSAH (13, 1954), p. 4

32 - Le Corbusier, *The Modulor* (trans. P de Francia and A Bostock, London: 1961), p.2533 Le Corbusier, op cit (see note # 21), p. 209

34 - 'How affected and licentious are the works of Bernini and Fontana? How wildly extravagant are the Designs of Boromini (sic), who has endeavoured to debauch mankind with his odd and Chimerical Beauties, where the Parts are without Proportion, Solids without their True Bearing, Heaps of Materials without Strength, excessive Ornaments without Grace, and the whole without Symmetry? And what can be a Stronger Argument, that this excellent Art is now lost in that Country, where such Absurdities meet with Applause?' Colen Campbell, *Vitruvius Britannicus* (London: 1715), p.1

35 -

1613-15 – Inigo Jones acquired about 250 of Palladio's designs and drawings during his second Italian tour.

1653 – All Jones' collection and his own drawings and his library inherited by John Webb.

1672 – Webb's will left his library and 'prints and cutts etc.' to his son, William.

c1692 – John Oliver (Master Mason in the Works 1685/6 – 1701, City Surveyor) possessed most of Jones-Webb and Palladio drawings.

C1699 – c1701 – Oliver's collection passed to William Talman.

Before 1713 – Some of what is now the Burlington-Devonshire Collection still in the possession of Mrs William Webb.

1719 – Burlington's second Italian visit; purchase from Monsignor Trevisani, Bishop of Verona, of about 60 Palladian antique restorations and a few designs.

1720 – Burlington acquired Jones-Webb drawings from John Talman.

1721 - Burlington acquired Palladio drawings in Jones-Webb collection from John Talman.

1724 – Dr G. Clarke acquired from Mrs William Webb some of Whitehall drawings and Inigo Jones' library.

1730 – Burlington published Palladian Therme restorations as Fabriche Antiche.

1753 – Burlington Collection passed to 4th Duke of Devonshire.

1894 – Burlington-Devonshire Collection divided by Trust Deed between Chatsworth and RIBA Library.

36 - Adapted from H E Stutchbury, *The Architecture of Colen Campbell* (Manchester, 1967), Appendix III 36 R Wittkower, Palladio and English Palladianism (London: 1974), ch. 8

37 - John Harvey, *The Medieval Architect* (London, 1972), p.90

38 - From Sir William Chambers' 'Royal Academy Lecture Notes' quoted in J Harris, *Sir William Chambers, Knight of the Polar Star* (London: 1970)

39 - Reynolds, op cit, p.110

40 - Ibid, p.101

41 - Berger, op cit, p. 23

42 - Henry Moore, *Henry Moore Drawings 1969 – 79*, (Exhibition Catalogue, New York: 1980), p. 74

43 - Quoted in J Richardson, *E Manet* (London, 1958), p. 84

44 - Raphael's *Judgement of Paris* is known through a drawing and two engravings by Marcantonio and Marco Dente.

45 - R Jones and N Penny, *Raphael* (New Haven and London: 1983), p. 174

46 - Reynolds, op cit, p. 102

47 - M Merleau-Ponty, *Signs* (trans. R C McCleary, New York: 1964), pp.58-9

48 - The drawings of John Thorpe (c1563 – 1655) comprising *The Book of Architecture of John Thorpe* are reproduced with commentary by John Summerson as volume XL of the Walpole Society (1966). As well as J

Androuet du Cerceau's *Le Premier Volume des Plus Excellent Batiments de France*, publications of Palladio, Serlio and J Vredeman de Vries were used as sources for Thorpe's drawings. Among the drawings of Robert Smythson (c1536 – 1614) there are copies of, or adaptations from, the designs in the published works of Serlio, Dietterlin and de Vries M Girouard, *The Smythson Collection of the Royal Institute of British Architects (vol 5, Architectural History*, 1962)

49 - Summerson, Ibid, pp. 69, 83

50 - A letter from Sir William Chambers to M Edward Stevens in Rome dated 5th August 1774. Chambers also gave this letter to Soane when he, too, was setting out for Rome. See John Harris, op cit.

51 - Reynolds, op cit, pp. 110, 28

52 - Ibid, p. 99

53 - Le Corbusier wrote many variations on this passage; here the first part is from *L'Architecture d'Aujourd'hui* (1948), p.39, and the second form Petit, Le Corbusier, Dessin.

54 - Horace Walpole, *Anecdotes of Painting in England* (Vol 4, 1765)

55 - B L Whorf, *Language, Thought and Reality* (ed. John B Carroll, Cambridge, Mass, 1

Thirteen.
Raymund Ryan
Dublin 1991

Unpublished article, originally for John O'Regan
(ed.) _Portfolio_, proposed issue IV, 1991

Design continues to be excluded from the inner sanctum of Irish culture. But then culture, that "C word" that both induces yawns and has Nazis reaching for their revolvers, has – in this the wannabe *annus mirabilis* of 1991 – received little critique. A random cull of postcards from Grafton or O'Connell Streets will invariably highlight Dublin's Georgian inheritance, icons of our own civic image. Yet today the Custom House, in all its splendid restoration, risks being stranded as a traffic island.

Culture, if it is to be vital, must have something of the organic, of the messy and probably unpredictable context of life. Similarly, at the interface between appreciation of the past and application for the future, design exists not just in the boutique as 'something different' but in all of our everyday existences. Whereas civilization has do to with functional ease (plumbing, teller machines, the DART), culture goes beyond that to where, as Mara's boss said to *The Irish Times*, 'we see ourselves reflected'.

Dubliners often consider architecture as a sidekick to property speculation, a tacky exploitation of the urban fabric. Such alienation should be addressed with informed discussion of building as a positive act. The City of Culture officials have been criticized for poor liaison with local communities. Correspondingly, architects need to engage their fellow citizens – their potential clients – to help maintain the environment and, where necessary, make vigorous intervention for change.

Thus the Royal Institute of the Architects of Ireland (RIAI) organized, with Power's Whiskey, an Architectural Ideas Competition for the market square and vicinity of Smithfield. Their invitation captured, in its very first line, the competition's *raison d'être*: its search for 'new perspectives on Living and Working in the City.' The participants exerted themselves with little prospect of real jobs but rich potential for debate; concepts (temporarily) overrode fiscal censorship. After all, since the Renaissance, the most inventive Western architects have hustled Ideas.

Idea is connected to the Ideal, and architectural culture exists in a dialectic between pragmatism and imagery that is grand, Utopian and sometimes propagandistic. Dublin-born Reginald Malcolmson – whose lectures at Michigan are a passionate espousal of a vanguard from [Claude Nicolas] Ledoux to [Ludwig] Hilberseimer – believes that 'projects point the way towards the future.' Emphasizing our human need for visionary architecture, Malcolmson has stressed how 'the primary concern, that which over-rides in importance the incidental circumstances of its realization, is the architectural idea.'

This momentum of pure Idea has, in European theoretical discourse, fused with a re-thinking of the city, its meaning and potential, with the amelioration of the *res publica*. In describing and prescribing the communal character of block and place, the work of Italian rationalist Aldo Rossi has been paradigmatic. The influence of his 1966 book *The Architecture of the City* has seeped so profoundly into the thought processes of younger Irish designers as to be almost subliminal and runs, inevitably, through many laudable responses to the Smithfield Competition.

I

The architectural ideas of the two joint first prize winners are operative at two agreeably different scales. The members of d-Compass – a band of recent graduates from the College of Technology, Bolton Street – applied themselves to an entire quarter stretching out from Smithfield into the surrounding matrix of the city. The other laureates, Benedetti McDowell Woolf from London, proposed, as almost surgical insertions, a series of precise moves within the space itself, including the introduction of freestanding objects.

Smithfield is not yet a feature of Bord Fáilte publicity. In the 1960s its raw dilapidation was able to masquerade, in *The Spy Who Came In From The Cold*, as war-torn Berlin. Without the softening of vegetation or Georgian filigree, it's an elongated sea of cobble open to the skies and the silhouette of a totemic brick stack. The alternate names, Smith-field and *Margadh na Feirme*, assert a lingering agrarian mercantilism. In very ancient times, the *Slighe Cualain* ran through Stoneybatter, en route from Tara to Glendalough via the Liffey ford. With this history, and with the ongoing Chaucerian Horse Fair, Smithfield has within it primal essences of settlement.

The 1980s' image of designer chic, the bestubbled Fountainhead, is debunked in the team spirit of d-Compass. Their exposition of an 'Urban Maze' is a rich banquet of proposals to fortify a transportation policy for the city centre with a central focus on form and programme for the revitalization of the square. They propose a 'machine for information and entertainment', an infiltration into those blocks facing onto Smithfield of a Media Centre, Public Gallery, Industrial Museum and Technology Information Centre. They further envisage a processional route with museological exhibits ramping down and under the Square to reappear on the river.

The graphic techniques of d-Compass allow the layperson comprehend a cluster of building types. By setting their extensive and vibrant vision within a clearly discernible one of Dublin, they reach back through Rossi to Enlightenment typologists who saw the city as a totality. The constituent proposals are however imbued with a non-Classical flux. The plans suggest a Small Is Beautiful, ergonomic and ecological view of the world. The machine is described as a 'morphic flexible zone' with the catalytic potential of Paris's Beaubourg.

From the City of Light itself came a viscerally red board emblazoned 'This Is Not Architecture.' The astute pundit – remembering Magritte's *Ceci n'est pas une Pipe* – should suspect otherwise. Sam Mays with John Coyle gained joint second prize with this ostensibly anarchical proclamation, a menu of issues or a manifesto that recalls those of the early Russian avant-gardes.

Indeed it comes as no surprise to discover, as 'anchor' in Blackhall Street, the insertion of a slender 'constructivist cage.' Differing from today's voguish if often powerless Deconstructivism, this new Town Hall is intended to provide a political base in juxtaposition to the legal establishment on Blackhall Place. As Mays and Coyle state: 'We reject mega-development as INAPPROPRIATE & IRRELEVANT...We suggest a FRAMEWORK that accepts & affects the REALITIES of Dublin's ways & Dublin's life...A QUARTER is also a political entity.'

This cult(ure) of democracy is shared in d-Compass's concern with collective gathering. Their metaphor of Flea Market conjures up those chance encounters so characteristic of organic urbanity. Their subterranean passage into the floor of Smithfield – a sculpture of absence – suggests however a linear historicity at odds with the analogous souk above, its myriad yards and fragmental relationships. [1]

II

Rossi writes of a City of Parts divided into dwelling areas and primary elements that accelerate urbanization. Benedetti McDowell Woolf supply the latter in answering the RIAI/Powers call 'to make the first move, to show how it will begin the process of transformation.' They make four elemental interventions towards the creation of the Rossian 'locus', an eventful nucleus in an undifferentiated terrain.

Benedetti McDowell Woolf plug the northern end of Smithfield with an exposed peristyle hall. They call this 'The Roof: a permanent shelter for market' that, with its spindly steel columns and rippling translucent roof-fabric, 'will provide a strong identity...without disrupting the singular spatial unity of the square.' Against the boundary of [the] Distillers' [Building] car park, they propose 'The Wall: private workspaces edging the square', a frame with tiny shops below to set perimeters of the block. At the river end, they bring on 'The Box: a temporary public room' which slides and pivots to allow performances animate and unexpectedly charge the space.

The fourth move by Benedetti McDowell Woolf is to connect this arrangement of objects by homogenising 'The Square: reconditioning the surface itself.' By removing vehicles – potentially parked underneath – and 'simplifying the landscape, the surface of cobbles is freed (and) re-established as a field to support overlapping levels of activity.' Such minimalist clarification has affinities with the other second-placed scheme, by David McNulty and Kittery Verdier.

Exhibiting a filmic disposition, this second Paris-based duo seizes the linear strip of square and principal flanks. They affirm *en deux langues* that Smithfield 'must remain closed in order to retain its character,' that they wish to 'accentuate its boundaries yet create links with the surrounding area.' Freestanding containers (hotel, museum, library) take up position along the eastern edge with more massive structures towards housing in the west. The prediction is for the filtration of people through these zones and across the open space.

McNulty/Verdier are stylish, their reverse-reading site plan an exquisite hieroglyphic x-ray. Its notational rhythm is tuned by an array of lampposts leading back from a folly of interlocking digits poking out onto the Quays. These lights are an installation in the planar vacuum of the square and perforate the western and eastern precincts. This is not a master plan. As with the very feasible assemblage of Benedetti McDowell Woolf, the emphasis is on aesthetic precision, not social planning. [2]

III

Jonesy, Gary and Ken have been at the Children's Court again. Perhaps the aerosol gangs target this adornment to Smithfield due to its good manners, its acknowledgment of the line and mass of its neighbours. Yet future archaeologists may find John Tuomey's urbane composition as a relic, marooned from surrounding decay. The word 're-construction' normally implies the artificial. The new office building at Arran Quay, for example, pretends to be more complex, more meaningful than it actually is. Its empty campanile awaits...an enormous cuckoo?

The RIAI/Powers call for ideas emphasised employment and economic improvement. Cathal O'Neill's commended re-presentation of the traditional Dublin Shop House evokes a Zolaesque intensification of the food and beverage business. McNulty/Verdier have the gumption to propose a hypermarket – with tilted roof and oval satellite – of a size usually found, far from the city centre, off some far suburban ring road.

How to get to and from Smithfield? d-Compass plan pan-urban arterial strategies. Commended like O'Neill, Kelvin Campbell puts trams running up and down the Quays. Smithfield's peripheral location may in fact be beneficial to traffic flow, to light industry and sporting facilities. Thus Linders is almost alright! And thus the third commended project, by Gerard Carty, Eva Byrne and Helen Thomas, with its supermarkets and grand typological modelling, submitted not by chance from Spain. Their gym and swimming pool are reminiscent, in function and civic spirit, of the shamefully neglected Iveagh Baths.

The admission by a distiller's executive that that company's imaginative foray into Smithfield has failed, as a catalyst to subsequent development, begs consideration. It suggests that the metropolitan *grand projet*, where one isolated masterpiece supports a trendified quarter, is an inappropriate model. Such Parisian examples raise dubious expectations and invariably expel poorer residents. The Smithfield responses lean more towards Barcelona where functional behemoths such as railroad stations and marinas are grafted to a network of pedestrian-friendly plazas.

What has the Smithfield Competition revealed of contemporary Dublin's architectural thinking? The mostly younger participants assume that the heritage of this city is of value. The common attitude is to enrich what already exists, to intensify the city's subtle weave. After the Americanisation of the 1960s, and the academic study of urbanism in the 1980s, there now appears to be an informed freedom to invent and dream.

Projects like these *do* point to the future. They broaden the design *status quo* through innovation and dissemination. They may have the pleasantly nagging ability to reappear, in the future, to shadow architectural discussions. The architects, however, cannot expect too much. For all their colonnaded markets, public tearooms, and performance tents in a re-animated Smithfield, no contender seems to have included a local architecture studio. [3]

Footnotes

1 - d-Compass comprised Ralph Bingham, Tom Creed, Michelle Fagan, Paul Kelly, Gary Lysaght and Cliona White. In 1998, Fagan, Kelly and Lysaght formed FKL architects.

2 - This trio of architects subsequently practiced, in London, as McDowell+Benedetti architects and Jonathan Woolf architects.

3 - Soon after the Smithfield results were announced in October 1991, Group 91 won the Framework Plan competition for Temple Bar.

Fourteen.
Edward McParland
Edward Lovett Pearce & the
Deanery of Christ Church Dublin, 1992

From Agnes Bernelle (ed.), *Decantations. A Tribute to Maurice Craig* (Dublin: Lilliput Press, 1992)

I am grateful to Dr R. Refaussé, Librarian and Archivist of the Representative Church Body Library, for his help with the preparation of this paper.

- Edward McParland

The story begins with a letter from John Harris asking if I could tell him anything interesting about the Deanery of Christ Church in Dublin. His suggestive question really amounted to this: the Deanery looks as if it could be by Pearce, is it?

The long-demolished Deanery stood beside the church of St. John, on the west side of Fishamble Street. It is best known from the photograph of the facade in vol. 4 of *The Georgian Society Records* of 1912. This shows a distinguished, three-storey, five-bay, brick facade with a forecourt in front: its distinction derives from its full crowning entablature (with pulvinated frieze), and the eventful way in which it opens are dressed. The house would look perfectly at home in Old Burlington Street in London, or engraved in *Vitruvius Britannicus* and attributed, perhaps, to Colen Campbell. In other words, in the context of early eighteenth-century Dublin, it looks as if it could be by Pearce. It is.

One oddity of the building suggested a possible link with a plan found among the drawings of Pearce and Vanburgh in Elton Hall, Peterborough: instead of a front door, the Deanery shows a central passage, leading into the building as if it were the androne of an Italian palazzo. The plan in Elton Hall, also for a five-bayed structure, with forecourt in front, has a central vaulted passage: it leads to a little vestibule, apparently in the heart of the plan.

The drawing is catalogued in Howard Colvin and Maurice Craig, *Architectural Drawings in the Library of Elton Hall* (Oxford 1964) as being a plan for a house, perhaps in the hand of Vanbrugh. It is, however, an ingenious plan for three separate houses, all entered from the centrally-placed domed vestibule. Facing down the vaulted passage is the door into the house at the back of the plan. This door leads into a hall and staircase similar to that in No. 9 Henrietta Street, Dublin, a house designed by Pearce for

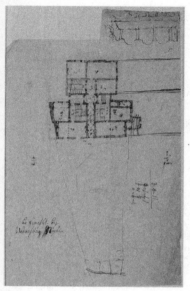

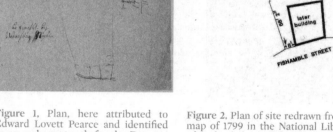

Figure 1, Plan, here attributed to Edward Lovett Pearce and identified as an early proposal for the Deanery (courtesy Victoria and Albert Museum)

Figure 2, Plan of site redrawn from a map of 1799 in the National Library of Ireland (maps of Christ Church estate, MS 2789, folio 12

Thomas Carter, Master of the Rolls. The other two houses are also entered from the domed vestibule. In each case, the door leads into an entrance hall, with a short flight of steps. From this the visitor enters the main staircase hall. None of the three houses has a secondary staircase. (We may note in passing that the domed vestibule approached by a vaulted passage is a domestic version of the grotto Pearce built for Viscount Allen at Stillorgan, for which there are also drawings in Elton Hall.)

The link between this plan in Elton Hall and the Deanery is established by a map of the site in Fishamble Street among the Christ Church maps in the National Library of Ireland, and by the chapter acts of Christ Church which shows that Edward Lovett Pearce designed and built the Deanery between 1731 and 1733. The map 'of the old Deanery House on the North West side of Fishamble Street... Survey'd by Jno. Brownrigg 1799' shows three houses, disposed as in the plan in Elton Hall, at the back of Deanery Court, one house for the dean, one for the chancellor, and one for the chanter.[1] It gives no details of internal arrangement, and no other plan of the houses has been found. Brownrigg's map differs, in dimensions and proportions, from the Elton Hall plan, but the similarities are sufficient to allow us to identify the Elton Hall drawing as a plan for the Christ Church Deanery.

The chapter acts fill in the details.[2] On 21 November 1716, the chapter decided to build houses for themselves and their successors in Fishamble Street. The dean was Welbore Ellis, Bishop of Kildare (the two posts were always held together); strangely, the matter did not resurface until 1731, just before Ellis was translated to Meath. On 12 August 1731 'A Plan drawn by Capt. Edward Pearce Surveyor General of three Houses ordered to be built for the Habitation and residence of the Dean Chanter and the Chancellor' was approved. The houses were finished within two years: on 15 November 1733, the proctor was ordered to pay fifty guineas to Pearce 'for his trouble and Care about the buildings in Fishamble Street...'

The chapter acts give a little more information than this. They throw light on how Pearce conducted such a commission. On the day his plan was approved, 12 August 1731, it was agreed that he be

'Impowered to agree with and Employ Artificers and Workmen for the carrying on and finishing the said Buildings and to buy necessary materials for the same, and that the Proctor shall sign Articles with the respective undertakers and pay the Workmen from time to time according to Capt. Pearce's Directions, and also that the Proctor shall Employ a person to look after and take care of the Materials which shall be laid in for the carrying on of the said Work'.

Pearce's role, therefore, was somewhere between that of modern building contractor and modern architect: he arranged the supply of materials, and engaged workmen, but was not responsible for the security of the materials on the site, and left payment - probably for materials and certainly for labour - to his clients. On completion of the work, his client paid him a gratuity (fifty guineas); it is probable that the eighteenth century considered it proper for him to receive considerations from the firms of craftsmen and suppliers he engaged (though did not pay). Such professional practice left one interest unprotected: that of the client - the cathedral chapter - who needed to know that their architect had not instructed them to pay for more materials than were actually needed for the erection of their building. In cases of dispute they would call in other builders for an opinion. It is also quite possible that a client would forgo a system of checking, particularly if their architect was Captain Pearce, surveyor general.

The procedures seem to be the same as those involved in 1716 in the employment on a non-governmental commission of Pearce's predecessor as surveyor-general, Thomas Burgh.[3]

Welbore Ellis was translated to the See of Meath before his new Deanery was complete. Charles Cobbe, the builder of Newbridge, was therefore the first occupant. One of his neighbours was Patrick Delany, chancellor from 1728 to 1744. Early in 1743 Cobbe became Archbishop of Dublin and his successor in the Deanery was George Stone. Stone immediately decided the Deanery was inconvenient.[4] He moved to Derry in 1745 where he stayed for an equally short time, settling into the Primacy early in 1747. His successor at Christ Church, Thomas Fletcher, also found the Deanery inconvenient 'on account of his bad state of health':

like Stone, he settled for an allowance of £60 a year in lieu of occupying the house. By 1765, we hear of Thomas Johnson, apothecary, already in arrears of rent for the Deanery, taking a lease of the three houses for forty years at an annual rent of £103.

And so John Harris's question is answered, if only in part. What of the final shape of Pearce's plan? What of the interiors? When was it demolished? Were records made of it other than the single photograph published in 1912 by the Georgian Society? Let us hope so, now that we know, at least, that it was an ingeniously planned building by the greatest resident architect of eighteenth-century Ireland.

Footnotes

1 - National Library of Ireland, 'A book of maps of the several estates of the...Dean and Chapter of Christ Church Dublin, partly survey, & partly copied by Brownrigg, Longfield & Murray 1800', Ms 2789, fol. 12.

2 - Representative Church Body, Dublin, copy character acts of Christ Church Cathedral, vol. iv., 21 Nov. 1716; vol. v, 12 Aug. 1731 and 15 Nov. 1733.

3 - Patric Judge, 'The state of architecture in Ireland, 1716', *Irish Arts Review*, vol. iii, no. 4 (winter 1986), p. 63.

4 - For details in the rest of the paragraph see Representative Church Cathedral, Dublin, copy chapter acts of Christ Church Cathedral, vol. vi, 17 Oct. 1743, 25 June 1748 and 12 Nov. 1765.

Fifteen.
Shane O'Toole
A Pavilion for Paintings of Brian Maguire: Sheila O'Donnell & John Tuomey, 1992

From Rosamund Diamond + Wilfried Wang (eds.),
9H No. 9: On Continuity (Cambridge, MA/ Oxford:
9H Publications, 1995)

I have been sitting at my table for days on end, engulfed in a haze of emotion, troubled by the memory of this little red tin shed. Such a little thing! And so familiar, too: at first glance recalling so many casual images of farm buildings in the countryside of my youth. But there is also a sense of unease, a certain disquiet, at the prospect of re-entering that hermetic world, that psychological space.

I return again and again to the scale drawings. There the pavilion is pinned down and may be measured out, described, controlled. Rationality dissects the dry structure, the taut order of the plan, the undulating volumes, the clanking outer shell. I note with reassurance the blank rectangles – empty canvases! – on the walls. It seems to me now that only the planimetric projection betrays the ritualistic intent of the project, reveals the secrets of this prison house.

In an early attempt to describe the background and sources of inspiration for his own work and that of some colleagues, John Tuomey focused on the urbanity of the Irish rural building tradition, denied by modern architects. He wrote of disparate buildings from different periods, built for diverse purposes, but which share an architectural presence transcending time or function. They have the same elemental character, given by prismatic and cubic forms, and a power that has to do with the archaic simplicity of those forms seen in relation to the landscape. The apparently contrasting buildings and land are each enhanced, merging to form a desolate and poetic proto-architectural image that seems specifically Irish. 'If we could develop a way of seeing that indigenous architecture as an inspiration to work,' he concluded, 'then we could build with certainty and imagination in a spirit of contribution to the continuum of architectural culture.' [1]

That description of one of the primary components of the Irish architectural project of the past decade provides a clue as to the many readings of the pavilion's form: border post or handball alley; temple, ark, or boat house; farmyard shed or stable. I recall a visit one summer's evening to the courtyard at Kilmainham. A warm breeze was blowing through the pavilion – there were no doors – and the suspended lights were swaying like lanterns in a barn. There were pigeons among the rafters and droppings around the entrances. *Rus in urbe?*

The pavilion stood in the courtyard of the 17th-century Royal Hospital at Kilmainham for its re-opening as the Irish Museum of Modern Art in summer, 1991. The Museum occupies the first classical building in Ireland, a building so charged with historical and ideological ghosts that it was untouchable for many decades following independence. In a sense, the opening of the Museum was to have been part of the moral process of acknowledging our broader heritage, of defining a more inclusive Irish culture and identity, of taking possession of the past.

It was ironic, then, to be confronted at the opening ceremony, not with an 'alien' patrimony to be embraced, but with that other Ireland, the 'real' Ireland, in all its red corrugated glory. The architects had always hoped that the pavilion would be subversive of the institutional character they had expected to find in the new Museum. They wanted visitors to walk in and think: what is that barn doing in the middle of Ireland's Museum of Modern Art? [2] The response was both immediate and emotional, embarrassed and affronted at the connotations of the farmyard. The Irish, it appears, want to get away from all that. Initial popular reaction was shocked, even hostile, but there have been encouraging signs recently of critical revisionism. [3]

The Irish Pavilion was originally commissioned for the '11 Cities, 11 Nations: Contemporary Nordic Art and Architecture' exhibition, organised by Dries Wiecherink in 1990 for the Frieslandhal, Leeuwarden, The Netherlands.[4] Leeuwarden's main claim to fame is as the starting and finishing point for the renowned *'Elfstedentocht'*, a 140-mile, ice-skating marathon of very hard winters, which describes a circuit linking the eleven cities of the northern Dutch province of Friesland.

Naturally, then, the exhibition took the form of 11 pavilions representing 11 northern European cities – Reykjavik, Dublin, Edinburgh, Oslo, Stockholm, Helsinki, Tallinn, Gdansk, Copenhagen, Hamburg and Leeuwarden – their disposition within the vast exhibition hall approximating to their relative geographical locations. In this configuration the Irish pavilion read as an island to the West, from which direction visitors were intended to enter. That had a critical bearing on the design of the pavilion: it was to have been the gateway to the exhibition, through which visitors would pass. However, the original idea was overtaken by the dramatic events of 1989, which led the organisers to adopt a more political symbolism: the exhibition layout was reversed, with the eastern European city-pavilions located next to the entrance. That had the regrettable side-effect of utterly distorting the reading of the Irish Pavilion, a situation which unfortunately recurred in Dublin.

The architects have said that, in some ways, the pavilion was designed for Kilmainham; that in that setting, 'it is like a theatrical thing, a momentary thing. You blink and you wonder: is it really there?' Like a piece of theatre, it needed that setting: that permanent, repetitious, dignified, historical, institutional, stone background. Skewed at an angle, it appeared temporary, as if it had simply been carried in and left there in the corner. This is as the architects wanted it: a building within a little building within a larger building; a gallery within a gallery set askew within the symmetry of the courtyard, or first room, of the Museum. Nevertheless, it must be said that the desire to read the pavilion as object, as a magnificent play of forms in light, literally cast all else into the shade – most notably the only meaningful approach to the pavilion, relegated to a cramped and quiet corner of the courtyard.

That enigmatic facade, with its twin doors of differing scales, was the most durable remnant of the initial ideas for the project. There, in the very first sketches, we sense that the carnival is coming to town: we see a box on wheels, a box with a funny hat, a circus trailer built astride a spindly, jaunty truss on wheels, a moving house. Suddenly, before our very eyes, the wheels come off, the cube inflects about the crown of the ramp and two alternative routes appear: one elevated and ramped, the other level, earthbound. It is entirely rational that each should demand its own specific representation on the facade. Yet the duality heightens anthropomorphic associations: we are looking, perhaps, at a child's drawing of a face, with its one big eye and one little eye. We sense a magical innocence, a protective naïvety, a seeking to come to terms with all the strangeness of adulthood – to understand the incomprehensible, pathological world behind the mask.

Brian Maguire's paintings already existed before this collaborative project got underway. Thematically, two kinds of scenes dominate his imagery: public violence and domestic unhappiness. Donald Kuspit has noted that his paintings reveal the despair of everyday life, that they are an emotional exposure of the misery of the *status quo*: 'Maguire's angry Expressionist paintings give the lie to the happiness of Irish life, betray the fabled Irish romanticism. In this, they are violently adversarial.'[5] Maguire himself remarked in Leeuwarden: 'I actually believe it doesn't matter whether you choose to paint a rose or a hanged man. But I haven't painted many roses.'

O'Donnell and Tuomey chose to adopt one extreme of the collaborative possibilities, by creating a pavilion whose spaces deliberately heighten and intensify the experience of viewing Maguire's paintings. The design of the building is a direct response to the content, meaning and formal properties of the paintings. It derives its final form from a deep understanding of the psychological space of Maguire's work: the architects have treated the artist's psyche as the site, immersing themselves fully in the world of the paintings, with their dual themes of the despair and isolation of prison and the fierce loneliness of sexual love.

They have described how they took photographs of his work and pinned them up in their office, of how they spent a long time trying to learn how to look at them. Not superficially, but to look at them for what they meant, and then to try to derive grist out of them. They found two ways into the work. One lay in its formal structure in relation to buildings and ways of viewing architectural space, with simultaneously varying points of view: looking up, looking down, looking across, looking through. Their other insight was that the geometrically framed figures were somehow like icons: 'If you took those two ideas, the architectural space of the prison and the iconic status of the figure, those were two touchstones for us that we gained through looking at Brian's work.'

Ascending three shallow steps, we enter through either portal into a great double-height volume, a gallery space for the prison paintings. The large works are bleak and oppressive, a battleground 'of violent emotion and angry intimacy,' to use Kuspit's phrase. Over and over again we see bodies that seem trapped in some involuntary agony – bodies that seem pure emotion. They are uncontrollably anxious, even when erotically vivid. We cannot avert our eyes; the windows are placed high up on the wall, permitting no view out.

This discordant room, with its architecture of pain, is dominated by an imposing, silent sentinel. That single refined element, an enigmatic cube suspended above this Babel, might, at first, be a watchtower. But no, its solitary window is blind. Here, suspended between heaven and hell, is the prisoner's cell, a cerebral cell. A passage, beneath, is signalled by a gridded window redolent of subterranean entombment. Balanced precariously on a narrow plank, constricted by the oppressive walls, I am alone, looking through the open door of a prison cell. A young man is hanging by a rope from the bars of the window, his cell mate pulling on his ankles, hastening the end. The very painting itself has burst outwards through the side of the pavilion, just as the painted window is punched deeply into the massive prison wall.

There seems to be no escape from this labyrinth. I will not cross the sandy depression (of the execution yard?) beneath the open, gridded floor. Nor do I wish to climb the rough-hewn ladder, built as a scaffold. I choose the external stairs. I see, but cannot reach, the outside world, and am delivered instead onto an open, timber-and-metal, lattice floor: the upper galleries of prisons are always full of light and air. There is a small room to one side. It is the cell. A hole in the floor ensures one person fills the room. There is no window. There are three small love drawings, one on each wall: we are alone during the sexual act, at breakfast, in death.

The door behind me is open. A large portrait faces me, across the gallery. The door in Peter Pringle's cell is open, too, and he is standing in the doorway. There are photographs fixed to the canvas, old images of Peter, taken outside. In the murderer's bloody hand is a paintbrush. He has become an artist while in prison, and has, in some way, been liberated. There is suddenly a welcome air of redemption about this bright, tall, tapering, top-lit gallery. At the end of the nave, I emerge, blinking, into the sunlight at the top of the ramp.

I believe it was John Hejduk who, thinking about another recent pavilion, was moved to write: 'We cannot enter a building without a heart.' Sometimes our hearts are put to the test.

Footnotes

1 - Tuomey, John. 'Images of the Past', in Annexe 4, John O'Regan (ed.),
Studio 6, Dublin, 1982, p 51. This essay is reprinted in this book, see essay
9. The compilers are grateful to Shane O'Toole for this direction - ER.

2 - O'Toole, Shane. 'Conversation with Brian Maguire, Sheila O'Donnell
and John Tuomey', in *Works 8: The Irish Pavilion*, John O'Regan (ed.),
Gandon Editions, Dublin, 1992, pp 17-26. All quotes are taken from this
source, unless otherwise attributed.

3 - MacGonigal, Ciarán. 'The Opulent Eye', in *The Irish Times*, 29 August
1992: 'I miss the pavilion when I go to IMMA and it's not there; it was
such an impressive presence. Even if at the time I wasn't madly keen on
the piece, it remains an important memory both for its own sake and for
the works of Brian Maguire which were its internal focus.' See also Patrick
Gallagher, 'Fine Art', in *The Sunday Independent*, 30 August 1992: 'Maybe
like O'Connor's Dun Laoghaire monument or Clarke's fugitive window it is
destined to become a legendary icon of Irish art, an object of rumour and
conjecture, half-remembered and half-understood.'

4 - Vegter-Kubic, Erica (ed.). 11 STEDEN, 11 Landen: Hedendaagse
Noordeuropese kunst en architectuur / 11 CITIES, 11 Nations: Contemporary
Nordic Art and Architecture, Frieslandhal Leeuwarden, 1990. For an
illustration of each pavilion, see 'Reclaiming the Nordic Heritage', in
Architecture Today, no. 9, June 1990, pp 26-27. For a review of the exhibition,
see Shane O'Toole, 'A Devourer of Lives', in *The Architects' Journal*, vol. 192,
nos. 7 & 8, 22 & 29 August 1990, pp 70-71.

5 - Kuspit, Donald. *Brian Maguire*. The Douglas Hyde Gallery, Dublin and
The Orchard Gallery, Derry, 1988.

Sixteen.
Tim Robinson
Residence, 1995

From *Stones of Aran: Labyrinth* (Dublin: Lilliput
Press 1995/ second edition: New York Review of
Books Classics Series, 2009)

The weed-grown path, north-south, bisects the rectangle of
our garden. The house is symmetrical about the same axis, and
at times the solar system nods to this fact. At six o'clock of an
equinoctial evening the half-moon, seen from the gate, stands
just above the chimney-pot, its diameter exactly vertical. A long
braid of starlight and dark matter divides the glamorous night
of Aran above the garden: the Milky Way, the home-galaxy
seen from within. As the earth rotates, this vast pointer swings
across the dial of the sky at half the rate of an hour-hand; twice
a day, therefore once a night, it is aligned with the garden path.
Life is repetitious enough for us to rehearse tomorrow's words,
it provides respites in which one can try to make sense of
unrepeatable acts like our coming to Aran; it suggests that a book
is a compilation of sentences. I think much about these things,
thinking nothing of them. Once, chatting with a passing islander
at the gate on a summer evening, I aired my knowledge of the
constellations (which in fact does not extend much beyond the
two Bears and the Seven Sisters), and he said 'I suppose now, if
you were put down in the middle of the Mediterranean' - that
being the most impressive-sounding sea he had to hand - 'you
could find your way to shore, on the strength of your education!'
But education assumes that yesterday's lesson is valid today, and
as a might-have-been mathematician whose thumbs ache from
milking a cow, I know that nothing happens twice, that if today
you find the right words to greet your beloved or the passer-by,
it does not mean you will do so tomorrow; nor does a surplus of
meaning in one sentence stand to the credit of the next. At six
o'clock of a midwinter evening the half-moon is high in the sky
above the chimney, and tilted; the slant of its flat side, according
to a little diagram I have drawn in the margin of my manuscript,
represents the inclination of the earth's axis to the plane of its
orbit about the sun. So the midwinter moon says Here we go,
spinning through space like a stone skipped on water; if we slow,
we sink - but we will never slow. And why should I accept even

that assurance from the backslider of the heavens, every evening a little later, a little older? However I do not envy those with a southern hemisphere to their minds, whose night skies are certified with the Cross. Mine are queried constantly by those three constellations, the Greater, Lesser and Least Question-marks, and I like it so.

The garden wraps around the house like an old coat, out at elbows, suitable only for gardening in, pockets full of seeds and string. Moloney built high walls to temper the wind to his shrubs, and put windows in the walls to sun them; the glass is long gone and blackbirds can fly through their panes of air. The garden is neither battlefield nor neutral ground between nature and the domestic, but a bazaar of exchanges and thefts. As I tug out yards of goosegrass and bindweed, the guardian robin watches me from the bushes, its eye glinting through first one triangle of twigs and then another. Donkeys wandering the road make a note of what they see, and come back by night to nose the gate open and rip the young carrots out of my neat ridges. The white stonecrop does not grow in our garden, but it must have done so once and been thrown out of one of the windows with garden rubbish, for it flowers on a heap of stones outside and has crept along the grykes to the east and to the south for a hundred yards or more. When I wanted a rockery (a curious wish, on Aran!) and brought in stones from the crag with interesting saxifrages and cranesbills, various grasses came too, and soon all I had was a grassy mound.

To the left of the house, where the cyprus lifts its derelict limbs into the windy spaces above the walls, there is a gateway which once had a high wooden gate in it, leading to the back yard and a stone outhouse, its doors, windows and corrugated iron roof half wrecked by storms. Gusts funnelling through the gap between this store and the house are to be respected; in squally weather when we have to run out for a bucket of coal or to disentangle the sheets on the clothes-line strumming across the yard, we find ourselves adopting the crouched, hen-like scuttle we have noted in certain village housewives on their rare sallies into the open. The floor of the yard is a single huge flag of the limestone bedrock, the two or three fissures across it filled in with concrete. We often dine there, moving cushions around to catch the last of the sun. In high summer we sunbathe with our backs to the back of the house, naked as the rock, melting into a drowse but keeping an eye awake for the horsefly that materialises out of a tiny crescendo whine into sudden immobility beside us on the baking stone, and an ear for the click of the front gate or the tactful whistling with which the postman always announces his approach. Sometimes the small stone enclosure is too intense with life for comfort. One spring there was an exceptional emergence of six-spot ladybirds; the split husks of their larvae were everywhere on the whitewashed rear wall of the house, with the adult beetles oozing out as glossy as fresh drops of blood. Every summer there comes a humid day on which the ants take their mating flight, and by sunset the yard is littered with fallen wings and spent bodies.

The thick, solid, chin-high wall closing the yard off from *An Chreig Mhór*, the great crag, is of big blockish stones mortared together, with alternate stones of the topmost course set on end as a rough castellation. It is inhabited by little ferns - wall-rue, common spleenwort, the rusty-back, which is rather an Aran speciality - and is knobbly enough to be climbed with ease; I once scrambled over it from the other side holding a butterfly in my cupped hands, an unfamiliar moth-like one I'd caught on the crag and was bringing home to identify (a dingy skipper, it turned out to be). It is a good wall to lean against with one's morning coffee and look over at the level acres of rock stretching southwards to the Atlantic. If the ocean is still and grey it is hard to make out in this low perspective where stone ends and water begins, somewhere beyond the rooftops of *Gort na gCapall* half a mile away. But further to the right of the view the edge of the land rises, and *Dún Aonghasa* is profiled against the sky. I had not realized how much the daily sight of that fold of mysteries, in uninterrupted co-presence with my own home, meant to me, until we returned from a brief absence to find that an electricity-pole had been erected exactly on that line of vision. I have no belief in the flow of Celtic energies and the psychic virtues of ancient stone, no respect for the theory of ley-lines, based as it is on the fusty paradigms of Victorian physics - but some communication was broken by that damned pole. On seeing it for the first time I felt that my presence in Aran was unsettled, that the idea of leaving Aran could be explored, as one's tongue worries at a tooth that has been loosened by a blow.

The front door of the Residence is difficult to open; it has sagged
on its hinges and drags on the tiled floor within. Now and then I
rasp a bit of rotten wood off the lower edge with whatever tools
I can find, but it soon lapses a bit further and jams again. The
hallway is just space enough to turn around in and hang up a
coat. And there is sometimes another obstacle to getting through
it, an image that fills it completely with horror. A very old lady
I met on the road one day told me about the death of David
Callaghan's wife, whom she could remember. Mrs Callaghan, she
said, was very fat and heavy, and she liked a drop of drink. One
day she staggered against the kitchen range and set herself on
fire. She tried to run out of the house to scream for help from
anyone passing the gate, and she died in that little box of a hall
- perhaps the door jammed even then. But we pass through
the hall so often that the idea of Mrs Callaghan's death there is
fading, like linoleum due for renewal.

Two doors open off the hall, the living-room to the left and the
kitchen to the right. The living-room has a little hearth, and a
sash window at either end. When we moved in, it was papered in
a curious pattern of seaweed-coloured bricks which undulated
subliminally because the wallpaper was half detached from the
damp plaster, and the yellowish net curtains had tattered hems
because, as Mícheál explained, his dog Oscar had once been
locked in here accidentally and had clawed at them in jumping
up to the windows. But once we had scraped down and whitened
the walls and filled an alcove with bookshelves, it became a
charming room. Its front window faces into the lower boughs of
the cyprus; once during a sudden battering downpour I looked
out to see a sparrowhawk perched within a few feet of me, as
impatiently self-contained as a clenched fist. The back window
faces onto the yard and the great crag beyond. I used to write
up my diary at a table before this window. Some days rave on
for pages, others expire in a phrase. One entry, I see, reads in its
entirety:

*September 24th, the Light Arches, dullest of moths, dead
on the windowledge this morning.*

I have no memory of this unmemorable September 24th, on which I must have allieviated my boredom by leafing through the pictures of dozens of species of dull, ochreous, brindled moths in my childhood copy of Richard South's *The Moths of the British Isles*, and savouring the names of the Light Arches, the Reddish Light Arches, the Dark Arches, the Cloud-Bordered Brindle, the Clouded Brindle, the Brindled Ochre - a nomenclature which I take it was the great achievement of rural Anglicanism in its early nineteenth-century torpor, a state I thoroughly understand. Too many days I have sat at this table, staring vacantly at the view over the back wall of the dozen roofs of *Gort na gCapall*, which looked smaller than the cauliflowers of spray slowly burgeoning from the rim of the land behind them and apparently hanging above them for moments before subsiding. I was supposed to be writing, or researching, or thinking. Oscar would come rattling in and hop up to lie in the sunlight on the table-top; sometimes it hardly seemed worth disturbing him by lifting his paw aside to put another word on my paper. Or the chorus-line of M's slips and nighties belly-dancing in the breeze on the rope outside would lure me from my withered plant specimens into erotic reveries. Later I made myself a study out of a room with only a tiny window, upstairs.

The kitchen, with its concrete floor, its ceiling of mahogany-painted board that Mícheál thought was real mahogany and would not let us repaint, its rudimentary furnishings that had suffered many a summer letting and winter mouldering, and the scullery and bathroom in the dank little back-extension opening off it, were the most intractable parts of the Residence. During our first brief summer visit to Aran, lodging at Gilbert Cottage, we had noted the engaging expression of the frontage of the house, but had not seen the interior. Mícheál, whom we happened to meet at its gate, had mentioned that he sometimes let the place to visitors 'for seven pounds a week; that's a hundred and forty shillings'; and later on in London, faced with a sudden bifurcation of life's paths, we had recalled that modest and comfortable-sounding arithmetic, and wrote to book the house for an indefinite period from the middle of November. My diary of our arrival:

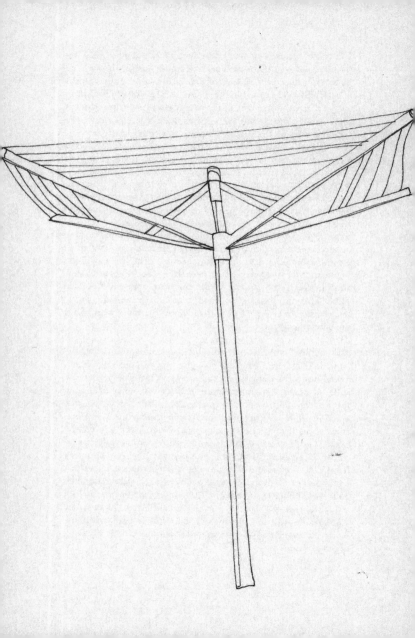

Mr King was at home, by chance, as he hadn't got our last card, so I collected the key and ran down from his gate to ours because I was too excited to get into the taxi again. The house was just what I had hoped for, bare and a little bleak inside, with potato ridges in the garden, and the wind blowing through the empty window-frames in the high walls round it. We were soon alone in it, and began making it liveable. I tried to make a fire in the living-room but it wouldn't go. The kitchen stove, a little Jubilee range, burned well enough though. Mr. King ran down with a craggy lump of home-made soda bread and a whiskey bottle full of milk, though milk is scarce on the island at this time, he says. We had nothing to make tea with so we walked a mile back to the shop at Eochaill, which was shut, and then another couple of miles to Kilronan. A vicious hail driven into our faces by the wind forced us to hide behind a gate-post. I enquired at the post office about our trunk, but it hadn't arrived. In the shop M learned that the hens weren't laying in this weather, that no meat was to be had, that we could order bacon after tomorrow's boat from Galway had delivered it, and that yesterday's storm had cut the telephone link. When she said 'I hope we survive the winter!', the lady of the shop looked amazed, and said 'With the help of God and His Blessed Mother, you'll survive!' She gave her some salted rockfish. The shopkeeper's van brought us back with our load, a few cans of stew and spaghetti etc. We had tea and arrowroot biscuits, and rearranged the furniture. We put the settee in front of the range, with a little form as a table. Through the kitchen is a scullery with a sink and a back door and a window giving onto the yard, a level area of shiny wet rock between the outhouses and their spouting gutters, and to the right out of that the bathroom, both damp and draughty, but Mr. King has pointed out the big keyholes we can stuff up in the back door, and the lump of stone for holding the sacking in place under the door, so no doubt we will get used to it. A short walk later; the sun had a halo round it, and we had to shelter from a couple of showers. We ate fried cornbeef on toast and bread and marmalade, read by the range, then up the narrow staircase in procession with candlestick and chamberpot. Once the candle was out the darkness was perfect. I woke once or twice, almost terrified by the roaring of the wind and the rattling of hail in the fireplace, and this solid alien presence of darkness. 'Tiefe schauervolle Nacht' - I don't know where I got the phrase but it was in my mind all night. M had a bad night too, and was chilled at first, and apparently had a little cry later on.

But M is courageous and resourceful, and soon took the place in hand, gradually bearing down my feeling that every ridiculous derelict detail of it, such as the lump of stone holding the wet sacks in position against the gale under the back door (which Mícheál had pointed out with the air of a landlord showing a prospective tenant the controls of the central heating) was more respectable than all the comforts we had abandoned in London and should not be changed. We scraped the fungus from under the leaky stone sink in the scullery, we got tea-chests and covered them with plastic tablecloths from Evelyn's shop to make working surfaces and storage places. We survived the winter. One morning I found that the sun, striking obliquely through a knot-hole in the back door, had left a golden guinea on the floor; I put my hand down to it, and called M to admire it glowing in my palm. As I lifted it towards the knot-hole it fluttered and dwindled, until I had it dancing like an angel on the tip of my finger. When I poked it back into the hole and took away my hand, it flitted instantly back to the same spot on the floor. Despite all our improvements the Residence, a jackdaw-nest among the stars, never ceased to be subject to drips, draughts, cosmic conjurings, elemental percolations.

The stairs begin in the back right-hand corner of the kitchen, where a fan of three wedge-shaped, hollow-trodden, steps leads up to what looks like a cupboard door; inside, they turn left and climb the narrow stairwell unsteadily, creaking like an old man going off to bed. At the top is a small landing with three low doors of flimsy tongue-and-groove, an old wooden chest full of bedclothes and the smell of mothballs, and a knee-high window looking out to the rear of the house. With the door of my writing-room open I can look across the landing and out of this window at the great crag beyond the back wall of the yard; in fact *An Chreig Mhór* is for me an adjunct to that cramped little study and in some ways the most familiar room of the house. I have botanized so intensively on it that most of Aran's extremest rarities have turned up there, and I watch over their welfare as if they were part of the family circle: for example, *Calamagrostis* (Praeger: '... that very rare Irish grass, the Wood Rush'), waving a fine foxy whisk out of a deep crevice; the unobtrusive *Neotinea* or dense-flowered orchid, rare in the Burren and practically unknown elsewhere (Praeger: 'It is strange that it does not occur on the

Aran Islands'); the common butterwort that catches flies on its sticky leaves and is so well-adapted to life on the unnourishing bogs of Connemara that it is an ecological scandal here, where it clings to the bare sides of two or three tussocks of black bog rush in a watery little gully. Plant-hunting is a relief and distraction from writing, but that too happens on the crag. If I cannot lay my hand on the phrase I am searching for in my room, I stroll out, scramble over the back wall and go rooting for words among the crevices of the rock. The crag is my testing-ground for the aerodynamics of sentences, a rebounding-place to prance upon when a chapter comes to its own conclusions and sets me free. Since we look down into it every time we go up or down stairs, the crag, even in its most unhomely aspects - by moonlight for example, astir with rabbits like splatters of ink on a silver tray - is not impossibly remote from domesticity. I have even gone down there for reassurance when time seemed to have got lost in the darkness of the night. I remember one starless three-o'clock vigil, crouched in the lea of a granite boulder under steadily drifting drizzle, unable to make out anything of the world but a wavering layer of dim ellipses floating a foot above the ground, the flowers of hundreds of moon-daisies, forming a false bottom to all appearances.

Of the landing's three doors the first, on the left, with a dented brass knob like an unripe fig, is the bedroom door. The room is small, an attic with sloping ceiling. The high ends of the black wrought-iron bedsteads we found there on our arrival seemed almost to bar entry; later we tackled the rusty bolts and dismantled the bedframes, and replaced them with floor-hugging bed-ends made out of planks from an old crate. M dispelled the morosity of the damp-stained walls and impending ceiling with avocado-green, flower-sprigged, wallpaper and billowing lace curtains that trawled the skies from the tiny dormer window and came back full of light and fragrance; there seemed no reason why we should not enjoy a Laura Ashley fantasy of nineteenth-century country living just because we were living in the country and indeed in the nineteenth century. The small tortoiseshell butterflies that besiege the house on hot days, looking for a dark corner that will become their winter quarters, come in at this window and congregate on the opposite corner of the ceiling, where they hang like the faded standards of their glorious summer campaigns. The bedroom has become our secret retreat too, from both nature and society. With the wooden shutters on the inside of the window closed and a blanket stuffed into the crack between them, our Tilly-lamp can tell no-one we are at home, and even when the wind gets one fist down the chimney and the other somehow into the wall-cupboard, it cannot buffet us here, while the oil-heater toasts the dampness into a cosy fug and we lie on the floor examining with voluptuous lingerings a newly-arrived parcel of books. Concerned friends now and then post us a few cassettes of music, which fall into our hands like messages whirled up by storms raging very far away, and which become through repeated hearings as spent as old pennies or else so overcharged with meaning as to be unbearable. Monteverdi's Tancred and Clorinda mutually unrecognized in their armour, hacking at each other in the dark with the intimacy of lovers quarrelling in bed - but I close the door on this. So much has happened in that room, of which I shall never write.

The next room, straight ahead at the top of the stairs, about eight feet square, with a hard chair by a postage-stamp of a window dedicated to bare rock, was at first a common boxroom and sulking-room. Then one day the ceiling collapsed because of the unstaunchable leaks in the roof, and some plaster fell off its interior walls, revealing that they were built of ancient sods of turf, grey and twisted like senile bricks, which came tumbling round our ankles when we tried to patch the holes. We had to get a local workman to help me wrestle bulging sheets of hardboard into position and nail them to the joists, and then, having the hammer in my hand, I went on to build a desk-like construction under the window out of plastic-coated chipboard delivered from Galway by the cargo boat, and proudly presented the room to M as her study or boudoir. Occasionally My Lady of Silent Reservations withdraws herself into it, leaving me nervously dislocated. What is she doing in there, hour after hour? - weeping herself to death? - writing that feminist thesis we used to joke about, entitled 'Derrida, I married him'? - or is she savouring her solitude like a cat grooming its fur?

My own room, apart from its little window looking onto the front garden, was initially a void, the interior of some lop-sidedly truncated Platonic polyhedron. I installed a peculiarly tall table made by Mícheál's father, and a chair that to match it had to be supplemented by several cushions. The room is so small that from my perch I can reach almost all the shelves I have contrived around the walls. Over the years these have filled up with specimens of rocks and fossils, files of correspondence with the botanists, geologists and archaeologists from whom I extort knowledge, drafts of stories, volumes of diary, record-cards of place-names, and parcels of copies of my first map of Aran. One of the functions of a publisher is to protect the author from the physical reality of the book, its weight and volume multiplied by the print-run. Only the self-published know the sudden condensation of the ideal into inert mass, upon the printers' delivering. By the time I had lugged the boxes of the Burren map upstairs, the joists of the ceiling below were sagging under the product of that initially empty room.

Stones of Aran was begun here too; the lumpy stuff of fact and feeling was excogitated through a machinery of emptiness and silence into something that would lie on a page. The pain of that process! How can it be, that a contrivance of 'negative capability' is sometimes blocked for days or weeks at a time, jammed, seized up? Research is easy; however severely it taxes the eyes in libraries or the body in the field, it is a distraction and a relief. Remembering, noting, filing, identifying, querying, confirming - one has resources that can be squandered on such preliminaries. But for the finding of a form of words, there are no resources. Education, vocabulary, information, even wit, imagination, sensibility - these are teeth tensed to snap together, pressing out too-ready formulations; the mind aches with the stress of holding them apart, preserving the space in which words can think themselves into shape. Somehow this is not so bad on winter days, with the rain splattering on the window and the oil-heater singeing my shins, but on a still, hot afternoon it is sometimes unbearable. The intensely alert silence of the garden, the white emptiness of the road going by the gate, the wide amnesia of the world towards me - and then the sudden fidget of a blackbird in the shadow under a bush, exactly 'the sound of the clapping of one hand'. Turns of words cunningly composed to disorientate the mind reveal their banality. A linguistic philosopher, I forget who, put together as a specimen of a meaningless sentence, 'Colourless green ideas sleep furiously.' Seeing the invisible flickering of the air above the hot stone of the garden path, I know exactly what he did not mean to mean. Hopelessly sensible nonsense! I give up. I go downstairs.

The house is empty; M must be sunbathing. I make two mugs of coffee, carry them through the silent inferno of Mrs Callaghan in the hall and round to the back of the house. 'Did you write a sentence?' asks M who really believes that I can write sentences. 'Bits of one,' I reply, eyes and voice uncertain, dazzled, after the deep shift in the word-mine. I strip off and lie beside her. The light is enprismed between the whitewashed south-facing wall of the house, the grey limestone so hot we have to lie on rugs, and the black shadow-side of Moloney's back wall. Butterflies are dithering between the stone-hard sky and the chinks in the masonry of the outhouse, entering crouched like pot-holers, backing out, unfurling themselves again. The hour ripens for another heat of the undecidable beauty competition between left breast and right breast. There is no more than a grain of salt between them, but it soon becomes the centre of gravity of the cosmos. The garden sleeps furiously, the road passes by, the world is unmindful, as we mould each other's bodies into their brief perfections.

Afterwards, lapsing back into ourselves, we drift into half-imagined conversations. 'Did you notice how at that moment the Milky Way swung into alignment with my spine?' 'In broad daylight? It was merely that we happened to be lying north-south, as recommended by Marie Stopes.' 'Well, did you hear the sun pounding the stone on either side of us with the flats of its hands?' 'I did not. And you didn't notice that the postman called, and left a parcel of books on your rump.'

Remembering such times, I am moved to a declaration: that making love with Máiréad has been the sustaining joy of my life. There's a certainty! And where else but in the secret heart of my book could I dare such simplicity? From where, proclaim it to so wide a world?

Seventeen.
Fintan O'Toole
Ireland, 1999

From Declan McGonagle (ed.), *Irish Art Now: From the Poetic to the Political* (London/Dublin: Merrell Holberton and Irish Museum of Modern Art, 1999)

In May 1897, an Irish Fair was held at the Grand Central Palace on Lexington Avenue, New York. The most popular exhibit was a giant topographical map of Ireland. In a long, rectangular room, surmounted by a huge green shamrock and surrounded by five columned archways, the map was spread across the floor. It was divided into thirty-two parts, representing the exact contours of the island's thirty-two counties. But the special attraction of the map was that each of these 'counties' had been filled with 'the veritable Irish soil of the county... duly attested as truly genuine.' For ten cents, the visitor to the fair could walk the length and breadth of the island. The nostalgic Irish immigrant could feel under foot the land itself, could lean down and touch his native soil. As the New York *Irish World* newspaper reported, 'many a pathetic scene is witnessed daily.'

One day an eighty-year-old woman called Kate Murphy paid her ten cents, stepped across the coastline and made for her native county, Fermanagh. She knelt down and kissed the soil,

> then, crossing herself, proceeded to say her prayers, unmindful of the crowd around her. While thus kneeling, a photographer took a flashlight picture of her. The flash was a revelation to the simple-hearted creature, who seemed to think it a light from heaven, and was awed into reverential silence. When she finally stepped off the Irish soil, she sighed sadly and clung to the fence, still gazing at 'Old Ireland'. She kept looking backward as she walked away, as if bidding a long farewell.

This event has a strange, haunting quality, for although it happened a century ago, it seems to belong so obviously to the beginning of the twenty-first century: to the era of virtual reality (the real soil 'duly attested as truly genuine'), of nature turned into culture (an exhibit framed, packaged, and sold to paying customers), of intense personal experiences played out in the artificial glow of camera flashes. Even stranger is the fact that the event anticipates by a full century the preoccupations of many Irish artists now as they grapple with images of a packaged culture, a landscape shaped by human intervention, a people at home in a displaced world but yet haunted by memories, gazing back at 'Old Ireland' as they walk away.

2

The Irish have always wanted to be as well-off as anyone else. The things that outsiders tended to admire about the place - its empty spaces, its vestiges of an older culture, its apparent simplicity - were also the things that Irish people wanted to escape. They were marks of failure.

If the landscape was empty, it was because famine and emigration had, uniquely in Europe, led to a drastic decline in the population, from eight million in the 1840s to five million in the 1990s. If an older culture survived, it was because the place had been left behind in a double sense, abandoned by the immigrants who could not make a decent living in the country, and bypassed by the Industrial Revolution. If the way of life was simple, it was because poverty leaves people with little room for variety and complexity. Far from shunning the modern world, as romantics fondly imagined, the Irish traveled great distances to get into it. At the beginning of the twentieth century, there were more Irish-born people in New York than in Dublin. There were large, and growing, Irish communities in London, Liverpool, Glasgow, Boston, Philadelphia, Sydney, and almost every other English-speaking city in the industrialized world. Irish people have, therefore, been modern city-dwellers for over a century. They just didn't dwell in Irish cities.

The emigrants sent letters and photographs to the folks back home. Images of modern luxury, of modern success, flooded the country in a peculiarly intimate way. Children in small and relatively remote villages wore American clothes sent by their aunts in Brooklyn and Springfield. Women in dingy cottages in Ireland knew all about suburban living in 1950s America because their sisters sent them pictures of their cars, fridges, and televisions. Modern consumerism was not just an abstract force, out there somewhere on the fringes of consciousness; it was a part of the family. It was at once utterly familiar and completely out of reach. And the Irish were desperate to close the gap.

What has happened in Ireland in the past decade is that, in a sense, everyone has become an emigrant, even without leaving home. The entire society has left the old country of traditional Ireland and migrated into the strange, exhilarating, and confusing surroundings of the globalized, post-industrial, post-modern world. Ireland has ceased to be an island off Britain and become a place that seems, culturally speaking, to be in the middle of the Atlantic, halfway between Europe and America. Its relationship to both of those continents has become much closer and, at the same time, much more contradictory.

For a long time, to those continental Europeans who thought about the place at all, Ireland had the magic of an endzone, the mystery of things at the very edge. A long European history of romantic longing for the Celtic fringes encouraged the idea that Ireland's real place in Europe was as an antithesis, as the opposite of Europe, the wild, rugged, noble alternative to Europe's urban and industrial heartland. Yet Ireland did not want to be wild, rugged or noble. It wanted to be part of post-war, industrial, prosperous Europe. European affection for Ireland, based partly on the notion that Ireland was none of these things, encouraged the European Union to give it generous assistance towards its transformation. By now, Ireland has achieved its aim of becoming, in economic and political terms at least, a fairly typical European country, untypical only in the sheer pace with which it has pursued prosperity. In fact, membership of the European Community has transformed Ireland from an economic backwater to the 'Celtic Tiger,' the fastest-growing economy in Europe, with annual growth rates in the late 1990s of over 10 per cent.

If Ireland's relationship to Europe was changing profoundly, so was Ireland's relationship to America. Whereas, until very recently, Irish labour went to American capital in the form of mass emigration to the United States, now American capital is going to Irish labour. The direction of the flow, at least for now, has been reversed: Ireland is not migrating to America; America, in the shape of IBM, Intel, Gateway 2000, and many other US-based multinational corporations, is migrating to Ireland. The Irish economy is, in many respects, a branch of the American economy. Two-thirds of its booming exports come from foreign-owned firms. Almost one-sixth of its gross national product disappears every year as those companies send their profits back home, usually to America.

In the course of all the change, Ireland has taken displacement to new levels, becoming so dislocated that it is hard to say even to what continent it belongs. There has been a kind of divide in the way the Irish have encountered modernity. Institutionally and economically, they deal with the modern world through Europe. Culturally, they deal with it through America and, to a lesser extent, through Britain. If you think of the best-known imaginative expressions of modern Ireland, the movies of Neil Jordan and Jim Sheridan, the songs of U2, the novels of Roddy Doyle, the dance show Riverdance, it is immediately clear that the dominant influences they are dealing with come from the West, not the East.

It is no easier to say what epoch Ireland currently inhabits. For what is peculiar about Ireland is that it has become a post-modern society without ever fully having become a modern one. It went from being conservative and rural to being high-tech and global; from scratching a living on a few acres of rocky soil to working in Dublin's gleaming new Financial Services Centre; from excessive religiosity to wild hedonism; from a slow pace of life to a fast, trendy culture; from the pre-modern to the post-modern with only a half-finished project of modernity in between. Ireland is, arguably, the most globalized society in the world. Its economy is almost completely dependent on transnational corporations. Its population is a diaspora spread throughout the English-speaking world. Its political institutions are increasingly integrated with Europe. Yet, even twenty years ago, it stood out for its parochialism, its inward-looking nature, its relative innocence.

And nothing dies. New things arrive; massive changes happen.

But what was there before does not really disappear; it just sinks down a little further beneath the surface. Irish culture is sedimentary, with layers of experience and emotion folded on top of each other. Christianity, for example, succeeded in Ireland by adapting itself to the pagan nature religion that was already there, so that holy wells and holy mountains have survived, even to this day, as an integral part of Irish Catholic practice. Likewise, the new secular culture that has arrived in recent years is being grafted on to a religious tradition. And often, change itself seems merely to remove a recent accretion and to allow buried memories to come to the surface. The looser, more tolerant Irish Catholicism that is emerging now turns out to look very like the kind of Catholicism that was prevalent two hundred years ago.

The arrival of an urban way of life allows contemporary Irish people to connect in a way that was not previously possible with the experiences of their ancestors who emigrated to the great cities of America and Britain. The American popular culture that is washing over Ireland itself contains memories of the Irish emigrants who helped to shape it. It is not at all accidental that the work of the artists in this exhibition is so full of layers, so utterly concerned with the way meanings gather and accumulate, so deeply interested in delving beneath surfaces.

3

The most important thing to understand about Ireland, then, is that the Irish have left it behind, that they are trying to find a stable place from which they can glance back and take it all in. Over sixty years ago, when the Irish state was still young and fragile, one of its most important ideologues, the writer Daniel Corkery, tried to define what made Ireland Irish. He came up with three things that were so obvious and solid that no one could dispute their overwhelming presence: '(1) The Religious Consciousness of the People; (2) Irish Nationalism; and (3) The Land'. No one could have disputed the inescapable power of these great forces. The political partition of the island of Ireland in the early 1920s had left, in effect, a Protestant British province in the North, and in the South, the larger part of the island that became the Republic of Ireland, a Catholic Irish state. In the South, religion, in the shape of the Catholic Church, was so pervasive that Ireland supplied not just its own church but much

of American, African, Australian, and British Catholicism with priests and nuns.

The importance of Irish nationalism was equally self-evident. The State itself had emerged from a violent struggle for independence from Britain, fuelled by a deep belief that Ireland was a place apart, with its own history, language, culture, and destiny. Nationalism was so powerful that the major political disputes were not between nationalists and others, but between fervent nationalists and even more fervent nationalists.

The land, the soil that Kate Murphy venerated in New York, was an object of both religious devotion and national pride. The Catholic peasantry had wrenched it from the grasp of the old Protestant landlords, creating in the process a society of smallholders fiercely protective of their few acres. Ireland was essentially a rural society, and its towns and cities were regarded with contempt and suspicion. The economy was utterly dependent on agriculture.

Roughly until the early 1970s, Corkery's three pillars of Irish identity were still standing. Ireland was still so Catholic, so saturated with religion, that it seemed closer to Africa or Asia than to Europe. With the outbreak of civil conflict in Northern Ireland, nationalism was, if anything, resurgent. And the Republic was still a largely rural society: it was only in 1971 that a census showed that, for the first time in Irish history, a majority of the population of the Republic was living in towns and cities.

Yet now, facing into the new millennium, that Ireland is completely gone. Irish Catholics are, as Bishop William Walsh put it recently, 'hurt, sad, angered, frustrated, fearful and insecure,' shocked by child-abuse scandals within the Church and dazed by the pace of change beyond it. The Church's political influence, once overwhelming, is now minimal. In 1998, for the first time ever, the main Catholic seminary in Dublin got no new recruits at all. The Irish still attend church services in unusually high numbers, but their sexual mores and attitudes are now the same as those of other Europeans.

Nationalism is dead. In a referendum in 1998 on the Northern

Ireland peace agreement, 94 per cent of voters in the Republic of Ireland and 71 per cent in Northern Ireland approved of the deal. In the process, they dropped the main demand of Irish nationalism - that Northern Ireland be recognized as an integral part of the Irish state. The old nationalist orthodoxy had become by then the domain of a few cranks. And the land has lost its grip. Ireland is primarily an urban society now. Just 10 per cent of the workforce is employed in agriculture. Those who remain are not romantic peasants, but business people who spend much of their time filling out forms for European Union subsidies.

So the essential Ireland, as any intelligent observer would have understood it when most of the current generation of artists was growing up, has disappeared. What remains is something rather like that giant map in the Irish Fair in New York a century ago: the image of a place that is no less resonant, no less capable of inspiring deep emotions, for the fact that it is just the memory of an old world artificially constructed in the middle of a new one.

And those images do resonate. What has happened is that religion, nationality, and land have become languages. Because the Irish no longer live within their embrace, they no longer take them for granted. They have become aware of them as symbols that can be interrogated, manipulated, taken apart, and put back together. They carry great weight, and even great danger, but no fixed meaning. Artists can find the deep grammar that makes these symbols articulate. They can find a fluid syntax within which these categories of Irishness can be made to say new things. Land can be fused with nationality to create a politicized landscape. Religious ritual can be made intimate and sexual, so that it ceases to be the domain of celibate men. Contested places can become imaginative spaces. Traditions can be re-invented.

All that is left of Ireland is an extraordinary openness. Ireland now is not at a crossroads, it is a crossroads, a spot where different kinds of journey converge and collide for an instant, where ideas and experiences resolve themselves for a moment in a certain pattern and then dissolve again, to be replaced a moment later by a different pattern. And yet this is not, for the Irish, quite as disconcerting as it might seem. For it is in some respects a more benign version of something that they have long suffered in a malign way. For most of its history, Ireland has been a contested space, fought over not just with arms, but also with ideas and symbols. It has always been possible to imagine it in different, sometimes opposite, ways. Often the ways of imagining it - language, symbol, frame of reference, point of view - have become more important than the place itself. And for most of its history, the presence of opposing imaginations has been a source of conflict and cruelty, as well as of richness and complexity.

Now, finally, Ireland may be reaching a point at which it is comfortable with the knowledge that its distinctiveness does not lie in any one way of imagining itself, but in the fact that it is a place forced from moment to moment to imagine itself. It is beginning to understand that movement itself, and not anything fixed or intact, is its identity. It is beginning to enjoy the freedom of knowing that what is important is not the triumph of any one way of imagining the country, but of the imagination itself.

Irish artists in particular are revelling in that freedom. For them, the collapse of old certainties - of political orthodoxies, religious restrictions, tribal loyalties - has been perplexing and liberating. They find themselves no longer having to define their culture in opposition to Britain, but facing all ways at once - toward a Europe in which Ireland is finding a place, toward the United States with its huge Irish population and its dominant popular culture, and toward the wider developing world with which Irish history has odd and interesting connections. As they move through the labyrinths of the wide world they are bringing a ball of Irish thread with which to find their way back home.

Eighteen.

Roger Stalley

Sex, Symbol & Myth:

Some Observations on the

Irish Round Towers, 1999

From Colum Hourihane (ed.), *From Ireland Coming* (Princeton: Index of Christian Art/ Princeton University Press, 2001 - originally presented as a conference paper 1999)

The round towers of Ireland have been the focus of more speculation and eccentric theorising than any other class of medieval monument. The arguments reached an intense pitch in the early years of the nineteenth century, when there was no shortage of fabulous ideas about the function and origin of these remarkable structures.[1] According to one popular view, they were fire temples, the idea being that they were designed for sun worship, with a fire kept perpetually burning at the summit. Then there was the notion that they were intended for celestial observations by the Druids, functioning, it was supposed, as primitive astronomical observatories. Given their distinctive form, it was perhaps inevitable that some would see them as monuments to Priapus, a triumphant assertion of masculine virility. A certain Henry O'Brien, who was active in the middle years of the nineteenth century, had no doubt that they were relics of phallus worship, a cult supposedly brought to Ireland by Buddhist emigrés from India, who, he claimed, colonised the country in the pre-Christian era. In 1832, this gentleman was awarded a prize of £20 for his work by no lesser body than the Royal Irish Academy, paid not to reward his endeavours but as an attempt to keep him quiet.[2] Already in the eighteenth century, many antiquaries had come to appreciate that the round towers were Christian buildings, though there was much dispute about their precise purpose. For some it was self evident that they were built by Irish followers of Symeon Stylites, the dwellings of devout anchorites imprisoned a hundred feet above the ground.[3] A variant of this interpretation was the penitential tower, the theory being that miscreants were sent to the top storey and allowed to descend floor by floor as they gradually fulfilled their penance. Others saw them as gnomons, with the towers functioning as the centre of giant sun dials.[4] With the publication of George Petrie's book in 1845, most of these bizarre and splendid theories were, it is sad to relate, banished to the footnotes.[5]

By establishing the historical context of the towers, and by confirming their religious and moral respectability, Petrie helped to give the towers a new lease of life as symbol of Irish nationalism. During the second half of the nineteenth century, the round tower joined the wolfhound, the shamrock, and the Irish harp as a national emblem, a context in which it appeared in some very strange locations. It found favour with a number of publicans and there was a famous pub in Dublin, now destroyed, in which a line of six round towers was silhouetted on the skyline, advertising alcohol and Ireland, rather than the Christian faith. At Listowel in County Kerry, a round tower, painted appropriately in green, takes it place alongside a buxom Érin over the doorway to the Central Hotel.[6] With only a slight shift in meaning, the round tower came to be exploited as a memorial for heroes. Thus a massive tower was one of the buildings constructed to celebrate the achievements of Daniel O'Connell in Glasnevin cemetery. This was a truly heroic version of the ancient form, over fifty feet higher than any of its medieval predecessors. Another tower was erected at Ferrycarrig (Wexford) as a memorial to those who died in the Crimean war. Even today, the round tower still retains an association with fallen heroes. Within the last twelve months, a new round tower has been constructed at Messines in Belgium to commemorate Irish soldiers who died during the First World War.[7] In the nineteenth century, many antiquaries were convinced that round towers had once functioned as giant mausolea, an interpretation which has now, belatedly, been fulfilled by Irish builders in Belgium.[8]

Despite the symbolism, myth and speculation that has encompassed the study of round towers, there is a mistaken belief that scholars have established a clear view of their function and meaning. While most of the more bizarre theories have been cast aside, the twentieth century has managed to create a few myths of its own.

In recent years I have heard it suggested that the towers provided high-level chapels, on the lines of those depicted in the St Gall plan. This was a red herring started by Walter Horn, who somewhat mischievously reconstructed the St Gall towers on the basis of the Irish round towers.[9] As the plan gives no indication of the height or design of the towers at St Gall, this is a circular argument in every sense of the phrase. The Carolingian drawing has an inscription with the word 'clocleam', indicating that spiral staircases were projected for the interior of the towers, not wooden ladders as was the case in Ireland.[10] Struggling up a network of ladders might have been a useful penitential exercise, but it was scarcely a convenient means of access for regular worship.[11] This suggestion has at least some historical credibility when compared to a theory which emanated from Kansas in 1982. Thanks to the research of a professor of entomology, we have been informed that the position, and alignment, of the sixty odd remaining towers is related to the position of the stars in the map of the northern sky at the time of the December solstice: the towers we are told are in fact 'magnetic antennae used for concentrating paramagnetic energy' for eco-agricultural purposes.[12] It is good to know that the speculative endeavours of Vallancey and the other eighteenth-century antiquaries is still alive.

Anyone who has listened to the local guides in Ireland will be well aware of the popular view of round towers: that in times of danger everyone in the monastery dashed for the tower and climbed up a ladder. When all were safely inside, the ladder was pulled up behind and the door firmly locked. Not long ago I heard one of the guides at Clonmacnois recounting this very tale to a group of impassive tourists.[13] It does not seem to have occurred to most people that, in many cases, pulling up a ladder would have been a physical impossibility. At Kilmacduagh the door is so high that an external ladder would have been over 30 feet long; only if it had been made of rubber or some other flexible material could it have been manipulated into the tower. Lennox Barrow in his 1976 book on round towers was well aware of this, and, not to be defeated, came up with an imaginative solution, namely rope ladders. This conjures up a rather extraordinary picture of life in the early Irish monastery, with elderly monks scrambling up rope ladders at the first sign of danger, books and reliquaries under their arms. And the *aistreoir* - or bell ringer - who sounded the regular offices would presumably have been selected for his physical prowess on the ropes. It does not seem a very plausible scenario. The external ladder or steps must I think have been semi-permanent structures, probably with a platform outside the door.[14] There is some confirmation of this at Iniscealtra, where excavations have uncovered post holes outside the base of the tower.[15] In fact the occasional burning of towers suggests that an aggressor with enough determination could reach the first floor without too much difficulty. If defenders managed to raise a ladder to protect themselves, it was more likely to be that between the first and second floors.

There are six references in the annals to people being killed in the towers at times when they were being used as places of protection and escape.[16] Together with the raised doorways, this has encouraged the almost unstoppable belief that the towers were designed, at least in part, as places of refuge. While George Petrie saw this as very much a secondary function,[17] Margaret Stokes gave it far more emphasis, valiantly trying to link the towers with areas of known Viking activity.[18] It is very unlikely that the design of the towers had anything to do with defence. If monastic communities seriously regarded them as some sort of proto-keep, it would have been logical to install stone vaults to guard against fire; there are only three cases where this happened.[19] It is an interesting coincidence too, that the monastery at Kilmacduagh, the tower with the highest doorway, was, as far as we know, never attacked. This makes an interesting contrast to that on Scattery Island, where the door is at ground level.[20] Scattery was a sitting target, exposed to every band of marauders sailing up the Shannon estuary, and it is no surprise to learn that it was ransacked at least five times in the two hundred years between 972 and 1176.[21] Here is one case where a raised doorway would have made good sense. While round towers were certainly regarded as a suitable place to hide, it is unlikely that defence was uppermost in the minds of the first builders.[22] The raised doorway certainly made access more difficult, which meant that the chambers within the tower could function as secure places for storing valuables, but this was very much a secondary purpose, as Petrie argued.[23]

When erecting circular towers, there may have been structural advantages in lifting the doorway well above the level of the foundations. A large opening in the main wall at ground level was a potential weakness and this is the belief of experts on castle design, who have argued that the elevated entrance served a structural as well as a defensive purpose. It is particularly relevant in the context of the tall cylindrical towers which became fashionable in France during the second half of the twelfth century. In some instances, as at Piégut-Pluviers (Dordogne), the visual parallels with the Irish towers are surprisingly close.

For much of this century, there has been a broad consensus about the date and purpose of the round towers. It is generally accepted that they were designed primarily as belfries, and that they were constructed from sometime shortly before 950 until 1238, the latter being the last recorded date we have for the building of a (medieval) round tower, that at Annaghdown.[24] There is also general agreement that the prototypes must be associated in some way with the campaniles of Italy, where the detached circular belfry found its ultimate expression in the twelfth century tower at Pisa.[25] There is also general agreement that a high proportion of the surviving towers belong to the twelfth century.[26] The discovery of the foundations of an earlier tower at Devenish twenty years ago underlined the fact that in many cases we are looking at a second generation of towers.

There are, however, at least four other questions which are not so easy to answer:

1 - Why are the towers so remarkably consistent in design and why was there so little change over a period of almost three hundred years? There are of course variations, like those in the quality of masonry noted by Margaret Stokes or the addition of Romanesque ornament. But the general form shows remarkably little alteration, especially when seen in the context of the changes that occurred in European architecture between 900 and 1200.

2 - Where was the first round tower erected in Ireland and in what circumstances? Why were they deemed to be such an essential feature of the monastic environment?

3 - What determined their dimensions, in particular their height? It has often been observed that they are out of all proportion to the neighbouring churches. Was it really necessary to build them so high? Kilmacduagh, the tallest, rises over 34 metres (111 feet) above the surrounding graveyard.[27]

4 - What sort of bells were used in the towers and how were they rung?

When considering these questions, it is very easy to take the form of the towers for granted, not least the gradual taper, the raised doorways and the conical roofs of stone. The corbelled roofs are particularly curious.[28] Constructed 100 feet above the ground, these roofs were no mean feats of engineering. Masonry caps were virtually unknown in Europe before the development of the stone spire in the twelfth century. Early Romanesque towers usually had roofs of lead, tiles or stone slates, built over a wooden frame. So what was the advantage of the stone roof? Presumably it had something to do with the fact they were less vulnerable to lightning, a regular cause of fire in medieval churches. The annals contain six references to towers being damaged by lightning or thunderbolts, a danger to which, in an age before lightning conductors, the towers were exceedingly vulnerable.

Examples include Tullerherin (Tullamaine) and Clonmacnois, both of which survive today.[29] Tullerherin was struck in 1121, and it resulted in the death of a student who was killed by falling masonry. In 1134 the annals report that *'lightning knocked off the head of the steeple of Cluain-muc-Nois'*, the head presumably referring to the capstone of the fine tower which had been completed only eleven years before. More interesting, however, are two earlier references in the annals, in 995 and 1015, which relate to Armagh and Down. Here the entries record towers which were burned by lightning, whereas all subsequent references are to caps being split or knocked off.[30] In other words fire seems to have been a factor only in the early cases. From this one must deduce that the first towers had wooden roofs, and that the introduction of the stone roof was an attempt to reduce the dangers. It is possible that the stone roof also offered some acoustic advantages, providing added resonance to the sound of the bell. [31]

Another intriguing feature of the towers is the tapering profile, which varies quite considerably from tower to tower. At Rattoo, for example, the batter follows an almost straight line, and the diameter of the tower is reduced by almost a quarter, from 4.60 metres at the base to 3.50 metres at the cap, a reduction of 1.10 metres. At Glendalough the reduction is far more gentle - a mere 34 cm - though it is still sufficient to give the tower a certain life and elasticity.[32] In both these cases, the reduction follows a straight line from base to summit, but this is not always the case. At Clonmacnois, for example, the batter on the west side of the tower is quite acute until the level of the doorway, at which point there appears to have been some change in design or construction. Although the batter usually improves the look of the buildings, it is quite rare to find diminution of this sort elsewhere in early medieval Europe. Most circular towers on the continent are constructed as cylinders, and, if they were narrowed, this was achieved in a regular manner by the introduction of offsets. This is very obvious in the brick towers at Ravenna, as in the churches of Santa Apollinare Nuovo and Santa Apollinare in Classe.[33]

In Romanesque architecture, such offsets were often marked by decorated string courses, which were introduced in some of the Irish 12th-century towers. Diminution and offsets were really alternatives, but at Ardmore the builders tried to get the best of both worlds, with string courses and an element of batter. In this case, the narrowing is pronounced and irregular: indeed the tower is almost two metres narrower at the top than at the bottom, with the diameter diminishing from 5.0 metres to 3.05 metres.[34] The gradual reduction in width must have been quite difficult to control and it meant that the Irish builders would not have found it easy to use plumb lines to test the verticality of the towers. Clearly diminution mattered, but what was its purpose? While it has been regarded as an architectural refinement, akin to the entasis on Greek columns, it is more likely that it was felt to have some structural value, an equivalent to the inclined jambs found on so many lintelled doorways. As such, it may have been founded on constructional beliefs stretching far back into Irish pre-history. The gradual taper may have been regarded as a means of improving stability, a view which could have been reinforced when the corbelled roof was introduced at the top. In other words, diminution was a sign of strength.

The presence of putlog holes at several towers show that they were erected with external scaffolding, perhaps not dissimilar to that used by the Board of Works when repairing the tower on

Scattery island in the years around 1916.[35] But this raises another interesting point about construction. The lifting of stone to heights in excess of 100 feet was without precedent in Ireland, and must have demanded considerable mechanical expertise in the use of pulleys and hoists. The introduction of the round tower may thus represent a technological, as well as an architectural, milestone in Irish society.

The question of the height of the towers is a further issue that has never been seriously addressed. Why was it thought necessary to build to such a height? It cannot simply be a question of ensuring that the bells were heard by the entire community. Belfries attached to churches, as at St Kevin's church at Glendalough or Temple Finghin at Clonmacnois, were far smaller in scale, and presumably their bells were intended to be heard over a wide area. There are several alternative ways of approaching the issue:

1 - Were the dimensions an arbitrary matter, something that was left to local masons and local clergy? Once the stone or the money ran out, was work brought to a halt?

2 - Were the dimensions related to the size of the adjoining church? This is suggested by the famous commentary on the Laws which attempts to fix the price of churches and round towers; in this, the height of a round tower was related to the length and breadth of a 'domliacc'.[36]

3 - Were the dimensions fixed either by a famous exemplar or by a number with symbolic connotations? In other words, was there a 'correct' height for a round tower?

4 - Was there a proportional relationship between the height and the plan? It has long been established that builders in the later Middle Ages made use of proportional formulae, sometimes in the belief that they helped to ensure the stability of their work.

There are over twenty towers where the original height is more or less known. If one excludes three abnormally low towers (Dromiskin, Castledermot, and Turlough) the average height is 29.53 metres.[37] This of course is only an average and many towers differ quite considerably from this dimension. The tower at Devenish, for example, is only 25 metres (82 feet) high, whereas that at Fertagh must have reached a height of 35 metres (115 feet), the tallest example known.[38] But it is interesting to note that the average of 29.53 metres corresponds to 97 English feet. This brings us to the subject of medieval systems of measurement, a subject which is extremely complex in view of medieval variations in the value of the foot.[39] Although the Irish used feet and inches,[40] the exact length of the Irish foot is unknown; nor is it clear whether the same foot was used consistently throughout the country. If the Irish foot approximated to the English foot, the average height of 29.53 metres for the round towers tends to suggest that on a fair number of occasions the builders were aiming at 100 feet.

The circumference of the towers is also interesting. They vary from 13.10 to 17.86 metres but a high proportion cluster around the average of 15.63 metres, which is 51 feet 3 inches, close to half the average height. Could it be that Irish builders were following a formula which ordained that the height of a round tower should be approximately twice its circumference? While hard to prove, it is at least worth thinking about.[41] Glendalough, incidentally, is the most perfect exemplar of the 1:2 ratio, being 100 feet high (30.48 metres), and 50 feet 2 inches in circumference (15.30 metres) at the base.[42] It is hard to believe this is a coincidence.

What would have been the merit of such a scheme? A relationship between height and circumference may have been regarded as a way of achieving stability or correct proportions, much as Gothic architects built their cathedrals to the square or the triangle. But the 100-foot tower also invites symbolical readings.[43] As a perfect number, one hundred is frequently cited in both the Old and New Testaments, and the same figure is frequently alluded to in Early Christian commentaries. It was used as a sign of the heavenly life and it could also represent the words of the gospels. Bede, in his commentary *De Tabernaculo*, for example, dwells on the heavenly significance of the number 100.[44] Without delving too far into the world of allegory and symbolism, it is not difficult to see why 100 feet would have had its attractions for a Christian community well versed in the scriptures.[45] The fact that the number 100 was associated with the gospels would have had a

particular relevance for towers, from which bells sounded the regular hours of Christian worship. The figure is frequently encountered in early medieval architecture: the cloister at St Gall was intended to have a width of 100 feet and the internal width of Charlemagne's palace chapel at Aachen measures 100 Roman feet.[46]

This brings us to an important historical issue, namely which monastery was responsible for introducing the round tower to the Irish landscape. The evidence is meagre but there are a few pointers. The general consistency of their architectural form suggests that there was a prestigious exemplar, which provided a model for the early builders. If such a model existed, it was presumably to be found at one of the more influential monastic establishments, Kildare, Clonmacnois, Kells or Armagh perhaps. In this context the annals provide a few hints. A majority of the references to round towers in the tenth and eleventh centuries relate to places in the north and east of the country; in fact four of the first five entries are linked to establishments associated with St Patrick or Armagh (Slane, Louth, Armagh twice, and Down).[47] If one was forced to choose, Armagh surely has one of the best claims to be the monastery which introduced the round tower. Armagh was an important centre of ecclesiastical art in the decades around 900, with a climate of patronage that seems to have encouraged both cross carving and the production of illuminated manuscripts, a context in which architectural experiments would not have been out of place.[48] The construction of the first circular belfry, 100 feet high, must have been a momentous occasion, a dramatic innovation which would have accorded well with Armagh's claims to jurisdiction over all the churches of Ireland.[49]

But why did tall belfries acquire so much importance in the years between 900 and 950? It is too simple to assume that they were merely copied from the detached campaniles of the Mediterranean world, as if they spread to Ireland like some sort of virus.[50] They must have had some more specific function or meaning for the Irish clergy, or some important association. In what way did they improve or enhance Irish monastic life? The most obvious advantage is that a bell rung from a high tower could be heard over a much wider distance than a bell rung at ground level. For any well disciplined monastery, the bell had to be audible and we know from the penitentials that those who arrived late at the daily offices were punished. The rule of St Columbanus makes it clear that failure to hear the bell was not accepted as an excuse.[51] Hearing the bell must have become more of a problem as monastic settlements grew larger and the general noise and hubbub increased. A tall campanile was one way of improving discipline.[52] The sound of the monastic bell was however more than just a call to prayer. For everyone living in the neighbourhood, it divided up the day, much as country people fifty years ago could tell the time from the passing of the trains. Bells and belfries were in fact the clocks of the medieval world, a point neatly made in the words of the Tudor poet Stephen Hawes:

> For though the day be never so longe
> At last the belles ryngeth to evensonge. [53]

When public clocks came to be mass produced, it was natural that they were fixed to church belfries. Indeed the importance of church bells in medieval time-keeping suggests a greater social significance for the round towers than is sometimes realised. Almost certainly they are one more reflection of the so-called urbanisation of the Irish monasteries, which was well under way by the tenth century. [54]

It is usually assumed that at appropriate times, the bell ringer climbed up the tower and rang a hand bell out of each of the four windows. While this might be true, it is odd that Irish monasteries put their bell ringer to so much trouble; if a bell was rung from the tower at the start of each of the seven offices, the *aistreoir* would have had to climb almost 700 feet each day, almost 5,000 feet each week. Elsewhere in Europe, everyone else avoided such physical labour by using bell ropes. Notker, for example, tells a story about a craftsman named Tancho from St Gall who cast a bell for the Emperor Charlemagne. He tried to cheat the emperor by substituting tin for silver in the alloy, and when the bell was eventually hung in the bell-tower, nobody could make it ring. Tancho 'seized hold of the rope and tugged at the bell', whereupon it broke free from its frame and crashed to the ground, hitting the unfortunate Tancho en route and 'taking

his bowels and testicles with it'.[55] Notker wrote his *Life* about
883-7 and he writes as if what he says about bells was a perfectly
normal arrangement. Bell ropes were known from at least the
sixth century[56] and there is a famous painting from a Spanish
Apocalypse which shows a multi-storied belfry, with a bell ringer
using ropes to sound the two bells suspended in turrets at the
top.[57] This dates from 970. Why therefore did the Irish not adopt
the same solution? Is it possible that larger bells were hung
permanently at the top of the towers and operated by ropes?

At first sight there seems to be little evidence to support this.
Over seventy Irish bells survive but all are hand-bells and there
is not a single example of a larger bell such as might be hung
in a permanent frame.[58] Early Irish bells have been catalogued
and studied by Dr Cormac Bourke, who divided them into two
classes, those made from sheet iron and those cast in bronze.
The largest examples are 31cm in height.[59] Given the size of
this collection, it is odd that no large bells survive, if indeed
they were manufactured for the early Irish Church. Dr Bourke's
study may provide the answer. The vast majority of the hand-
bells belong to the period 700-900, a period in which they are
occasionally depicted in sculpture, as in one of the famous stelae
on White Island (Fermanagh). There is only one bell that can be
assigned to the twelfth century with any confidence. For some
reason hand-bells seem to have gone out of fashion after 900, at
the very period when the round towers began to appear on the
landscape. Having gone to the trouble and expense of building
huge campaniles, it seems extraordinary that new bells were not
commissioned at the same time. In fact I suspect new and larger
bells were produced.[60] The old hand-bells were retained in the
monastery, but as they became obsolete, they were valued more
as relics than practical items.[61] Yet if this was the case, why do
none of the larger bells survive? The dearth of evidence is not
altogether surprising. Many of the round towers remained in
use as belfries during the later Middle Ages, so their bells never
became redundant like the early hand-bells. When a bell was
cracked or damaged, it was simply recast, especially if it was
made of bronze. Hundreds of large bells occupied the medieval
belfries of Ireland but, with one or two exceptions, they have
vanished without trace. Bell metal was just too valuable to
survive. In 1552, for example, the English garrison of Athlone

seized the 'large bells' from the *cloigtheach* of Clonmacnois, no doubt with an eye on their potential use as gun metal.[62]

There is no doubt that bell ropes were employed in Ireland in the twelfth century, if not before. A rope must have been used at St Kevin's church at Glendalough, for nobody could have been expected to scramble into the turret every time the bell had to be rung. From the outset, the 'pepperpot' tower was designed to hold some form of hanging bell. Moreover, there is documentary evidence for the use of bell ropes in Connacht in the twelfth century. One of the endowments granted by Rory O Conor, King of Connacht (1156-98) to the abbey of Cong included the right to receive a bell rope from every ship coming to the port of Cill Mór from time to time for fishing and trading.[63] Bell ropes were thus familiar items in twelfth-century Ireland; it would be extremely odd if they were not used in the round towers, where their advantages would be most appreciated.

Finally, it is important to remember that the early sources suggest that there were different types of bell. As the Laws explain, when describing the duties of the aistreoir - or bell ringer:

> *Noble his work when the bell is that of a cloictheach,*
> *humble his work when it is hand bell.*[64]

The bells of the *cloigtheach* were clearly different and evidently harder to ring.

To confirm the point, an obvious step would be to search for archaeological evidence of bell frames within the actual towers. This is not as easy as its sounds. There are only a handful of towers with access to the top, and in virtually every case the fabric has been subject to extensive repair and reconstruction. Even if joist holes were found in the right area, there would be no guarantee that they belonged to the early Middle Ages, unless of course a piece of timber had actually been left behind. Several of the surviving towers remained in use as belfries until relatively recent times; at Cloyne a round tower is still in use today. Here the chapter books of the cathedral record the replacement of bells on several occasions. In 1663, for example, there were payments for taking down two old bells, which were then sent to Cork, presumably to be melted down. They were replaced by a new bell, which cost £10 - 12s to cast. At the same time a new bell cage was constructed at a cost of £9.[65] In such contexts, the search for archaeological evidence for ancient bell frames is likely to prove fruitless.

Debates about the nature of the bells or the reasons for the height of the towers may seem rather modest issues compared with the excitement generated long ago by fire temples, anchorite prisons and phallic worship. Although the writings of George Petrie lifted the discussion to a more sober level, he failed to confront a number of fundamental issues. The purpose of this paper is to encourage archaeologists and historians of architecture to question the myths and assumptions of our own era, many of which can be traced back to the days of George Petrie. At the very least I hope I have managed to rescue one of Ireland's most impressive group of monuments from the speculative fringes of academe, without succumbing to the spell of eccentricity which seems to have contaminated so many of those who have studied them in the past.

Acknowledgments

I should like to place on record the help and encouragement I have received from Professor John Scattergood, Professor Liam Breathnach, Professor James Lydon, Professor Etienne Rynne, Dr Ann Hamlin, Dr Peter Harbison, Dr Cormac Bourke, Dr Colum Hourihane, Conleth Manning, Rachel Moss, George Cunningham and the late Liam de Paor. I should stress however that I must take responsibilty for the suggestions and conclusions.

Footnotes

1 - The literature on round towers is extensive. The most recent general survey is by G.L. Barrow, *The Round Towers of Ireland* (Dublin, 1979), a book which has useful descriptions of the towers but is seriously at fault in its interpretations of the historical evidence. It contains a lengthy bibliography. For a recent summary of antiquarian opinions see S. O'Reilly, 'Birth of a Nation's Symbol, The Revival of Ireland's Round Towers', *Irish Arts Review Yearbook* 15 (1999), pp. 27-33. Amongst antiquarian writers, see especially M. Keane, *The towers and temples of ancient Ireland: their origin and history discussed from a new point of view* (Dublin, 1867), R. Gough, *Observations on the round towers in Ireland and Scotland* (London, 1779), H. de Montmorency-Morres, *A historical and critical enquiry into the origin and primitive use of the Irish pillar tower* (London, 1821), H. O'Brien, *The Round Towers of Ireland or the Mysteries of Freemasonry, of Sabaism and of Buddhism for the first time unveiled* (London, 1834, new edition 1898) and republished as *Atlantis in Ireland* (Blaufelt, New York, 1976), R. Smiddy, *The round towers of Ireland: their origin, use and symbolism* (Dublin, 1876), J. H. Rice, *The round towers: their use and origin* (Dublin, c.1920), and C. B. Phipps, *'The Monastic round towers of Ireland'* (unpublished typescript in the Royal Dublin Society Library, Dublin).

2 - O'Brien, *Round Towers*, 91, 101, 176. O'Brien complained bitterly about the failure of the Academy to award him first prize for the best essay on the subject (it went to George Petrie). There was a vitriolic correspondence, with O'Brien complaining that the Academy had even failed to return his essay. Despite the obvious eccentricity of O'Brien's ideas, an American publisher has, within the last few years, been sufficiently impressed by them to produce a complete reprint of his book, see note 1.

3 - One advocate of this view was the Reverend J. Milner, *An Inquiry into certain vulgar opinions concerning the catholic Inhabitants and the Antiquities of Ireland* (London 1808). Milner's opinions are discussed by O'Reilly, 'Birth of a Nation's Symbol', pp. 27-8.

4 - L.C. Beaufort, 'An Essay upon the state of Architecture and Antiquities, previous to the landing of the Anglo-Normans in Ireland,' *Transactions of the*

Royal Irish Academy XV (1828), pp. 210-11.

5 - George Petrie, *The Ecclesiastical Architecture of Ireland. An Essay on the origin and uses of the Round Towers of Ireland*, (Dublin, 1845, reprinted Shannon, 1970).

6 - J. Sheehy, *The Rediscovery of Ireland's past: The Celtic Revival 1830-1930* (London, 1980), 70, 76, 91. The work at Listowel was executed by Pat McAuliffe (1846-1921). The Irish pub was O'Meara's Irish House on Wood Quay in Dublin, designed by Burnet and Comerford, 1870.

7 - It is interesting to observe the coincidence of dates: the first documented reference to an Irish round tower comes in the year 948, the last round tower was built in 1998, an interval of exactly one thousand and fifty years. The tower at Messines is reported to be 120 feet high, nine feet higher than the tallest of the medieval towers, that at Kilmacduagh.

8 - In 1841, for example, 'some gentlemen composing a society of antiquaries' sought permission to excavate within the round tower at Cloyne, and much to their delight discovered human bones. They were unaware that debris from the churchyard had been shovelled into the lowest storey of the tower, R. Caulfield, *Annals of the Cathedral of Cloyne* (Cork, 1882), p. 39.

9 - W. Horn and E. Born, *The Plan of St Gall* (Berkeley, 1979), I, p. 129, p. 166.

10 - Ibid., III, 35: 'ascensus per clocleam ad universa super inspicienda'.

11 - In 1992, a different role for the monuments was suggested by Peter Harbison: He argued that they might have served as focal points of pilgrimage, with relics being displayed from the doorways to crowds assembled below. Given that shrines are known to have been stored in the towers, at least in times of crisis, it is an interesting idea, though it lacks documentary support, Peter Harbison, *Pilgrimage in Ireland, The Monuments and the People*, (London and Syracuse, 1992), pp. 169-174.

12 - Dáibhí Ó Cróinín, *Early Medieval Ireland 400-1200* (London, 1995), 8, citing Philip S. Callahan, *Ancient mysteries, modern visions: the magnetic life of agriculture* (Kansas, Missouri, 1984).

13 - June 6th 1997.

14 - In conversation (7th July 1997) the late Liam de Paor explained that he had come to a similar conclusion, favouring the idea of a wooden

platform in front of the doorways. In such circumstances, the stairs may have descended beside the tower, rather than directly in front.

15 - My information comes from Liam de Paor. The excavation report has still to be published.

16 - The references in the annals are conveniently listed by Ann Hamlin in M. Hare and A. Hamlin, *The study of early church architecture in Ireland: an Anglo-Saxon viewpoint, with an appendix on the documentary evidence for round towers,'* in *The Anglo-Saxon Church, Papers on history, architecture, and archaeology in honour of Dr H. M. Taylor,* ed. L.A.S. Butler and R.K. Morris (Council for British Archaeology, London, 1986), pp. 140-2.

17 - Petrie, *Ecclesiastical Architecture* (1845), 2, felt the towers had a twofold use, 'to serve as belfries, and as keeps, or places of strength'.

18 - Margaret Stokes, *Early Christian Architecture in Ireland* (London, 1878), pp. 77-8, pp.103-9.

19 - At Meelick, Castledermot and Tory Island, *Barrow, Round Towers,* p. 24.

20 - As Peter Harbison pointed out to me, the lost round tower at Downpatrick also appears to have had a doorway at or near ground level, Barrow, Round Towers (1979), p. 80.

21 - A.T. Lucas, 'The Plundering and Burning of Churches in Ireland, 7th to 16th Century,' *North Munster Studies, essays in commemoration of Monsignor Michael Moloney,* ed. E. Rynne (Limerick, 1967), p. 173, p. 209. The years are 972, 977, 1057, 1101, 1176.

22 - It has been suggested that it was structurally more efficient to raise the doorway well above ground, so avoiding a large opening close to the foundations.

23 - It is worth noting that towers with raised doorways are not unique to Ireland. A number of Anglo-Saxon towers have doorways at a high level, as in the distinctive tower at Earls Barton, H.M. and J. Taylor, *Anglo-Saxon Architecture* (Cambridge, 1965/80), pp. 222-6.

24 - J. Mesqui, Châteaux et Enceintes de la France *Médiévale* (Paris, 1991), p. I, p. 103.

25 - Hare and Hamlin, 'The study of early church architecture' (1986), pp. 140-2.

26 - The case for an Italian origin for the round tower has been reviewed

by Hector McDonnell 'Margaret Stokes and the Irish Round Tower: A Reappraisal,' Ulster Journal of Archaeology, 57 (1994), pp. 70-80. Peter Harbison has suggested a specific origin in Rome, on the basis of the circular towers depicted in the Grimaldi drawings of the frescoes inside Old St Peter's, P. Harbison, Pilgrimage in Ireland, The Monuments and the People (Syracuse and London, 1992), p.170. The problem with Rome as a source is that there is no documentary or archaeological record of circular towers having been built within the city, as demonstrated by Priester Ann Edith, The belltowers of Medieval Rome and the Architecture of Renovatio (unpublished PhD thesis, Princeton, 1990), especially chapter IV. The circular towers depicted by Grimaldi recall those found in a number of illuminated manuscripts, especially psalters, as for example in the ninth century Kludov Psalter (Moscow, State Historical Museum, gr. 129), which contains (folio 61v) an image of Sion, depicted as a basilica with a detached circular belfry alongside. Although produced in Constantinople, there are no surviving campaniles of this type in the Byzantine world. As with the frescoes in Old St Peter's, the motif of a detached tower does not appear to have a relationship with contemporary building. The suggested Italian origin for the round towers is thus fraught with difficulties. Detached circular towers appear in a number of contexts in paintings and ivories between the sixth and ninth century: these include an ivory in the Domschatz at Trier depicting the arrival at relics, W.F. Volbach, Elfenbeinarbeiten der Spätantike und des Frühen Mittelalters (Mainz, 3rd edition, 1976), pp. 95-6, pl. 76; the Utrecht psalter, c820, (psalm 26, folio 15r), The Utrecht Psalter in Medieval Art, ed. K. Van der Horst, W. Noel, and W.C.M. Wüstefeld (Utrecht, 1996), p. 144; and the ivory cover of the Prayer Book of Charles the Bald, c860, in Zurich (Schweizerisches Landesmuseum), Ibid., pp. 205-6. Although Ravenna is frequently cited as a source for the Irish examples, the five examples clustered in and around Ravenna (Sant' Apollinare Nuovo, Sant' Apollinare in Classe, the cathedral, Santa Maria Fabriago, and the Pieve Quinta near Forli) are exceptional in an Italian context. Sometimes attributed to the eighth century, they are now thought to date from the eleventh century at the earliest, post-dating the earliest documented dates for towers in

Ireland, Priester, *Bell Towers of Rome*, p. 132, M. Mazzotti, '*I Campinili di Ravenna e del suo territorio*', *Corso di cultura sull'arte ravennata e bizantina*, IV (1958), pp. 85-93, and F.W. Deichmann, *Ravenna, Haupstadt des Spätantiken Abendlandes* (Wiesbaden, 1974), passim.

27 - A point made by E. Rynne, '*The Round Towers of Ireland - a review article*', *North Munster Antiquarian Journal*, XXII (1980), p. 28.

28 - Measurements are all taken from Barrow, *Round Towers* (1979).

29 - It should be noted that most of the existing caps were rebuilt in the nineteenth century. Those at Swords and Dromiskin appear to represent medieval repairs. The cap at Temple Finghin at Clonmacnois was constructed with carefully shaped trapezoid blocks, before being reconstructed in the later years of the nineteenth century. For the original form see the Dunraven photograph reproduced in J. Scarry, '*Early Photographs of Clonmacnoise*', in *Clonmacnoise Studies, volume 1, Seminar papers 1994*, ed. H.A. King (Dublin, 1998), p. 26.

30 - This was presumably the form of the roof of the bell tower at York, for which Alcuin gave 100 pounds of tin in 801, Alcuini Epistola 226 in *Monumenta Germaniae Historiae: Epistolae Karolini Aevi*, II (1895). It is also the type of roof found in the many belfries of Rome between 1100 and 1250, Priester, *Bell Towers of Medieval Rome*, passim.

31 - C. Manning, '*The Date of the Round Tower at Clonmacnoise*', *Archaeology Ireland*, volume 11, number 2 (summer 1997), 12-13; C. Manning, '*Some notes on the early history and archaeology of Tullaherin*', *In the shadow of the steeple*, no 6 (1998), pp. 19- 31. In the latter instance the author demonstrates that references in the annals to Tullymaine in fact relate to the surviving tower at Tullaherin (Kilkenny).

32 - Hare and Hamlin, '*The study of Early Church Architecture*,' (1986), p.140.

33 - This was a point made to me by a number of delegates at the Princeton conference.

34 - The figures come from Barrow, *Round Towers*, p. 110, p.197.

35 - There appears to be a constructional break at the level of the doorway, marked by the change in angle of the batter, a slight change in the colour of the stone, and a change in the size of the masonry blocks.

36 - There is however quite marked diminution in the campanile of the

cathedral at Ravenna.

37 - Barrow, *Round Towers* (1979), p. 193.

38 - Putlogs are most obvious in the tower at Roscam (Galway). It is puzzling that there is no trace of them in many of the towers. Either they have been carefully filled by the Office of Public Works or a different method was employed to support the scaffolds.

39 - The ambiguous passages in the Laws have been discussed on many occasions. Petrie drew attention to their significance, Petrie, *Ecclesiastical Architecture* (1845), 364-6, and for a recent consideration of their meaning see W. H. Long, *Medieval Glendalough, An Inter Disciplinary Study* (unpublished PhD thesis, Trinity College, Dublin, 1997), chapter 5.

40 - Despite Barrow's view to the contrary, Barrow, *Round Towers* (1979), 148-9, I believe the tower at Dromiskin was reduced in height in the later middle ages. On the west side the crude belfry opening almost overlaps a window of much earlier form; it is difficult to believe that the tower was designed in this way.

41 - Barrow, *Round Towers* (1979), p. 92, p. 128.

42 - For the potential pitfalls in this sort of exercise see E. Fernie, '*A Beginner's Guide to the Study of Architectural Proportions and Systems of Length,*' in *Medieval Architecture and its Intellectual Context, Studies in Honour of Peter Kidson*, ed. E. Fernie and P. Crossley (London, 1990), pp. 229-237.

43 - Long, *Medieval Glendalough* (1997), p. 141.

44 - It is interesting to observe that the diameter of a circle with the circumference of 15.63 metres is 4.97 metres or 16 feet 4 inches, which is within two inches of the medieval perch (16 feet 6 inches).

45 - The measurements are taken from Barrow, *Round Towers* (1979), p. 197. The circumference was measured at the top of the two offsets which form the foundation. The height was measured from existing ground level. From the base of the foundations, the tower is 31.40 metres.

46 - I am grateful to Gosia D'Aughton for helping me with symbolical references to the number 100.

47 - *Bede: On the Tabernacle*, translated and introduced by A. Holder, (Liverpool, 1994), pp. 96-7, p. 103. Abraham, for example, was a hundred years old when Isaac was born (Genesis 21.5), and Isaac sowed in Gerar

and in the same year acquired a hundredfold (Genesis 26.12). When the word of the gospels fell on good soil, it gave fruit a hundredfold (Luke 8.8). Bede explains that those who live for Christ will receive a hundredfold reward in this life and everlasting life in the future.

In speaking of the 'harvest of the Lord' the so-called second synod of St Patrick explains that 'the hundredfold are the bishops and teachers, for they are all thing to all men'...'Monks and virgins we may count with the hundredfold', L. Bieler, *The Irish Penitentials* (Dublin, 1975), pp. 191-3. An old Irish metrical rule stipulated that monks were to perform 'one hundred prostrations at the Beat every morning and evening,' J.F. O'Sullivan, 'Old Ireland and Her Monasticism,' *Old Ireland*, ed. R. McNally (Dublin, 1965), p. 113.

48 - O.K. Werckmeister pointed out that there are a hundred dots in the tonsure of the 'imago hominis' in the Echternach Gospels, which he interprets as a sign of perfection in relation to man and monks, *Irische-northumbrische Buchmalerie des 8. Jahrhunderts und monastische Spiritualität* (Berlin, 1967), pp. 35-8.

49 - E. Fernie, 'Historical Metrology and Architectural History,' *Art History I*, (1978), pp. 389-391.

50 - Hare and Hamlin, 'The Study of Early Church Architecture' (1986), 140: Slane (950), Louth (981), Armagh (995-6), Down (1015-6), Armagh (1020). The odd tower is Tuamgraney in county Clare (964). The distribution may of course be explained by the origin of the annals.

51 - Ann Hamlin, 'The Blackwater Group of Crosses,' *From the Isles of the North* ed. C. Bourke (Belfast, 1995), pp. 187-96.

52 - I have not been able to identify any particular event or circumstance which might have led to the building of a round tower at Armagh between 900 and 950. A desire to improve monastic discipline, however, might have coincided with the arrival sometime before 921 of the Céli De, A. Gwyn and R.N. Hadcock, *Medieval Religious Houses, Ireland*, (London, 1970), 29. For the general development of Armagh see N.B. Aitchison, *Armagh and the Royal Centres in Early Medieval Ireland* (1994).

53 - The European background of the towers has been discussed by Stokes, Early Christian Architecture (1878); A. Champneys, *Irish Ecclesiastical*

Architecture (London, 1910), pp. 48-62; F. Henry, *Irish Art during the Viking Invasions* (800-1020AD) (London, 1967), pp. 54-7, Harbison, *Pilgrimage* (1992), pp. 169-174.

The presence of a 'domus clocarum' at York in 801 indicates that detached campaniles were not unknown in Britain.   The fact that the Irish word 'cloigtheach' appears to be a direct translation from the Latin underlines the point that this type of building was introduced to Ireland from abroad.

54 - *'Regula coenobialis S. Columbani Abbatis,'* ed. O. Seebass, *Zeitschrift für Kirchengeschichte*, XVII (1897), part XII, p. 230:   *'Et qui audierit sonitus orationum, XII psalmos'*. For references in the penitentials along the same lines see Bieler, *Irish Penitentials* (1975), pp. 55, 63, 107, 127.

55 - The argument that bell towers were associated with discipline and reform was also invoked by Priester to explain the remarkable flowering of belfry towers in Rome after 1100:   'By providing a monumental framework for bells, belltowers served as architectural symbols for liturgical regularity and reform, a symbol that was all the more apt in the context of the Gregorian reform movement, given Gregory's advocacy of a regular life for secular as well as monastic clergy', Priester, *Belltowers of Medieval Rome*, p. 196.

56 - *The Oxford Book of Late Medieval Verse and Prose*, ed. D. Gray (Oxford, 1985), p. 361; Stephen Hawes, The Pastime of Pleasure, ed. W.E. Mead (London, Early English Text Society, 1509).   For a discussion of time-keeping in the early Irish church see Ann Hamlin, *'Some northern sun-dials and time-keeping in the Early Irish Church'* in E. Rynne (ed.) *Figures from the past: studies on figurative art in Christian Ireland in honour of Helen M Roe*, Dun Laoghaire (1987), pp. 29-42; also Harbison (1992), pp. 211-215.

57 - C. Doherty, *'The Monastic Town in Early Ireland,'* in *The Comparative History of Urban Origins in Non-Roman Europe: Ireland Wales, Denmark, Germany, Poland and Russia from the Ninth to the Thirteenth century*, ed. H.B. Clarke and A. Simms (London, BAR International Series 255, 1985), pp. 45-75.   The utilitarian function of bells and belfries should not obscure the possibility that in the eyes of the monks they had some mystical resonance.   The sound of the bell was not just a summons to the church; in some contexts it was likened to the Holy Spirit spreading its protective

powers around the monastic precinct. There is a tenth-century French prayer which makes these associations in a very explicit way: 'Christ, absolute and all powerful master who calmed the tempest on the sea..., now help your people in their time of need, spread the ringing of this bell like a dew of the Holy Spirit; at its sound the enemy will always flee; that the Christian people should be called to the faith..., that today, every time the sound of this bell traverses the sky, the angels themselves attend with their hands the united assembly of the church, and that eternal protection assures the safety of all the goods of the faithful, of their souls and of their bodies,' C. Voguel and B. Elzé, *Le pontifical romano-germanique du Xe siècle. Le texte I, Studi 226* (Vatican City, 1963), cited by E. Vergnolle, *L'Art Roman en France* (Paris, 1994), 71, 354 n71.

58 - L. Thorpe, *Einhard and Notker the Stammerer, Two Lives of Charlemagne* (Harmondsworth, 1969), pp. 126-7.

59 - Horn and Born, St Gall, I, 129-131, citing Gregory of Tours, *History of the Franks.*

60 - Madrid, Archivo Histórico Nacional, cod. 1097B, folio 167v; Los Beatos, ed. Luis Revenga (Biblioteca Nacional, Madrid, exhibition catalogue, 1986) p. 111, p. 137. The illumination also shows the way in which the different floors within the tower were reached by separate ladders, as must have been the case in the Irish round towers.

61 - Ledwich, citing Smith in his *History of Waterford*, records that 'there was no doubt but the round tower at Ardmore was used for a belfry, there being towards the top not only four opposite windows to let out the sound, but also three pieces of oak still remaining in which the bell was hung; there were also two channels cut in the cill of the door where the rope came out, the ringer standing below the door on the outside', E. Ledwich, *The Antiquities of Ireland* (Dublin, 1790), p. 295.

62 - Cormac Bourke, 'Early Irish Hand-Bells,' *Journal of the Royal Society of Antiquaries of Ireland,* 110 (1980), pp. 52-66.

63 - The size of such bells would have been limited by the width of the doorway, assuming that they were lifted up internally.

64 - One such bell was sent by the doge of Venice c867-886 to the emperor Basil I, the first time a bell suitable for ringing from a belfry had been

encountered in the capital of the Byzantine world, McDonnell, *Margaret Stokes and the Irish Round Tower* (1994), 73, citing G.T. Rivoira, *Lombardic Architecture, its Origin and Development* (Oxford, 1934), pp. 52-3.

65 - *AFM* 1552: 'Clonmacnoise was plundered and devastated by the English of Athlone and the large bells were taken from the Cloigtheach. There was not left, moreover, a bell, small or large, an image, or an altar, or a book, or a gem, or even glass in a window, from the wall of the church out, which was not carried off. Lamentable was this deed, the plundering of the city of Kieran, the holy patron.'

66 - Michael Duignan, *Journal of the Galway Archaeological and Historical Society*, XVIII (1938), 145, 148.

67 - Petrie, *Ecclesiastical Architecture* (1845), 382-3. The word 'aistreoir' is derived from the Latin 'ostiarius', listed seventh in the order of ecclesiastical officials in the Irish canons, H.Wasserschleben, *Die Irische Kanonsammlung* (Leipzig, 1885), 25. Cormac Bourke has pointed out to me that the reference in the Laws is found in a commentary which may be of twelfth-century date. This of course was an era of intensive round tower construction.

68 - Caulfield, *Annals of Cloyne*, 17. A new bell had to be made in 1749 after the tower was struck by lightning, the bell dropping through three of the wooden floors. The present bell at Cloyne dates from 1857, P. Galloway, *The Cathedrals of Ireland* (Belfast, 1992), 54. I am grateful to Rachel Moss for the references to the annals of Cloyne.

NB. - Ringing of Bells - In the sixteenth century, the ringing of bells in the morning and evening at Christ Church Cathedral alerted citizens to the passing of time and was regarded as a civic duty, Raymond Gillespie's two essays "The Shaping of Reform" and "The Crisis of Reform" in Kenneth Milne (ed.), *Christ Church cathedral, Dublin: a history* (Dublin: Four Courts Press, 2000)

Nineteen.
Tom de Paor
N3, 2000

Graphic/flyer from press release for 1st Irish
Pavilion in Venice Architecture Biennale, 2000

"The ground possessed and repossessed"
- Seamus Heaney, from *North*

The making of N³___

the tomb
Corbelled, turfed and chambered
Floored with dry turf-coomb.
-Heaney, from 'Belderg'

The proposal is to construct a sensory pavilion, an intelligent structure, a speculation on land and Santa's grotto.

Contemporary Ireland, as a gesture of solidarity with Venice, donates a section of its landmass to the smaller island. Ireland's gift consists of 22.86 tonnes of compressed peat in the form of 43, 2000 briquettes with polypropylene strapped into 1,800 bales and assembled into a slumped cube of 3.5 metres (3,800 x 3,750 x 3,220 mm).

The method of assembly is of stacking and of corbelling. The extent of the corbel projection of each successive course (23 courses) is the incremental thickness of one briquette (the dimension of each bale is a double row of 12 briquettes).

The structure contains three corbelled chambers interlined as a miniature labyrinth (abstracted confessional). Two dark corbelled voids (earth, smell), unequal in length, lead to an inverted interior corbelled space open to the air (sky, sound). This space is drained by a stainless steel channel laid into the peat. Three steps measure the sequence. In passing, a turf bench and screen allow a momen's contemplation.

The twinned profile of the extruded briquette, when assembled as a bale, results in a grid of voids - these interstices are exploited as conduits of information. The construction is oriented north; its plan is therefore an inhabitable north point. Each briquette is inevitably oriented similarly.

At the close of La Biennale, the construction is demounted and the briquettes, decompressed by soaking in water, become a peat contribution to a public garden in the city.

N³

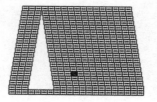

north

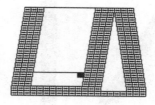

section aa

plan +140mm

east/west

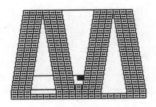

section bb

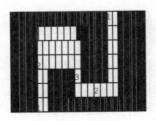

plan   +1600mm

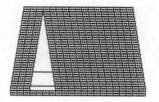

south

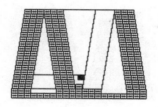

section cc

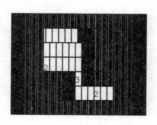

plan +2660mm

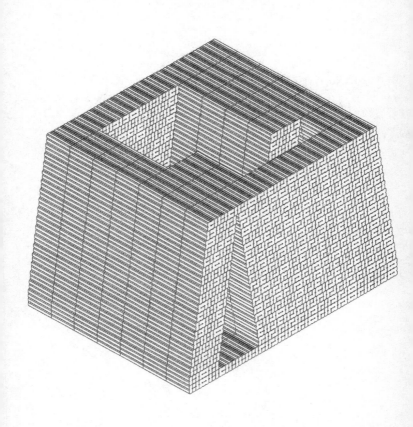

Twenty.
Hugh Campbell

Open up the Window
(and let some air into this room), 2000

Unpublished paper from *UnCommon Senses*
Conference, Concordia University, Montreal,
27-9 April 2000

At the beginning of Charlotte Bronte's *Jane Eyre*, in what is to become a recurring motif in the novel, the young Jane climbs into the breakfast room's window-seat. Here, with the curtain drawn behind her, she is 'shrined in double retirement', dividing her time between staring out at the 'dreary November day' and imagining the 'forlorn regions of dreary space', the 'death-white realms' conjured up in the book she reads. [1] The window for Jane is a way of escaping the pressures of her day-to-day existence. It provides a breathing space, a slice of stolen time. At the window, what is real and what is imagined have equal weight. What is more, they start to intermingle: the weather immediately outside supplies the climate for Jane's imagined far-off lands. The window allows her to daydream, to be simultaneously present and absent. (In the *Poetics of Space*, Gaston Bachelard finds the home to be full of such vehicles for daydreams.)

This is true not only of her conscious state, but also of her physical state. She has withdrawn to the edge of the room and concealed herself from view - so is she now in the room or not? And though she is now at a remove from human society this is where - paradoxically - she gets the clearest sense of her own identity and her relationship to others. At the window, she finds herself.

The phenomenological and psychological richness of this moment of being at the window is reflected in its familiarity as a trope in literature and painting. The image of a figure at the window is capable of conjuring a wide range of associations and meanings. As J.A. Schmoll observes:

> Since the late eighteenth century, homesickness, Wanderlust, longing, secret and indeterminate love, roaming thoughts, the

*attunement to Nature comes to expression par excellence at the
window. It is where the bourgeois and the city dweller is to be found
who, from his window, takes up the relationship to nature and the
desired intimacy. And it is where the solitary is to be found.*[2]

So the window allows the city-dweller to reacquaint themselves
with nature, by which is meant among other things a
reacquaintance with the 'natural self', and also to achieve a
sense of intimacy - of closeness to one's own sensations - and
a solitariness - a temporary removal from the demands of the
social world. All of these qualities become apparent in this
painting *Die Frau am Fenster* - the most famous of a number of
Casper David Friedrich's paintings and etchings which feature
the windows of his studio. The woman stands alone, with her
back to us, looking through the small open light to the river
beyond. She is part of the room and yet also absorbed in what is
going on outside it (she is both present and absent). The painting
speaks of both intimacy and a kind of civic-mindedness. What
is particularly interesting is how the window calibrates and
controls the relationship between interior and exterior. The
upper portion of the window - disappearing out of view - admits
light deep into the space, and permits a view of the sky, its clear
expanse of glass divided by the slender timber mullions. The
whole pane may be lowered to admit air. The lower portion of
the window is within human reach - it invites engagement and
allows change, is capable of being, in whole or in part, shuttered
or transparent, open or closed to the outside air. The interior
is exposed to external sensations - smells and sounds as well as
sights. The world acts on the room, but we can control the extent
to which it does so. In his *Phenomenology of Perception*, Merlau-
Ponty writes that:

*Each time I experience a sensation, I feel that it concerns not my
own being, the one for which I am responsible and for which I make
decisions, but another self which has already sided with the world,
which is already open to certain of its aspects and synchronised
with them....I experience the sensation as a modality of a general
existence, one already destined for a physical world and which runs
through me without my being the cause of it.*[3]

Sensation - when we are open to it - challenges the self out of solipsism, into inhabiting that 'self which has already sided with the world'. The window - when we can manipulate and change its setting - echoes and amplifies this sense of ourselves. It affirms our individuality - because we can exert control over it - but at the same time reinforces our connection to everything outside ourselves - to the world of human society. We come to the limit of our private realm and are reminded that it is part of a much larger social organism. At the same time, we are reconnected to the natural world - primarily because the evidence of our reinvigorated senses reminds us that we too are a natural organism.

The architects of the Arts and Crafts movement of the late nineteenth century employed a diverse range of window types and sizes in the houses they designed, in what can be seen as a reaction against the increasing uniformity of the industrialised environment. In his book *Individuality*, C.A. Voysey laments that 'Democracy, as it becomes more articulate and better organised, becomes more mechanical and less able or willing to recognise individuality'[4] Voysey opposes the autonomy of the individual to the forces of mass-production which encourage only a dull conformity. It is the role of domestic architecture, in Voysey's view, to frame and reinforce individuality. In the typical Arts and Crafts house, the window does this by gathering some space to itself, so that it sits slightly apart from the room while remaining a part of it, echoing the desired relationship of the individual to society.

It is possible to find similar celebrations of the window in twentieth-century architecture. In Louis Kahn's Fischer House, the windows' multiple functions are made manifest to the point almost of exaggeration. As in Friedrich's painting, light enters from high up, while lower down, it is possible, by opening shutters and panes to vary the amount and quality of light and air. The window becomes a kind of index of inhabitation. The reciprocal relationship between inside and outside is strengthened by the presence of the window, with its heavy timber sections, its window-seat, its shutters. It is accorded the same symbolic and functional importance as the fireplace which it surrounds. They both serve equally as reminders of human society's essential needs (light, air, warmth, shelter) and our relationship to nature (gathering round the fire, looking out the window). The window becomes a space in its own right, a space where, using the evidence of the senses, we measure ourselves against our surroundings.

But more generally in twentieth-century architecture, there has been a tendency for this at-the-window moment to lose its particularity. For figures like Le Corbusier, Walter Gropius and Mies van der Rohe, architecture had to embrace the possibilities offered by mass-production, had to move towards universal solutions, in which the relationship of the individual to the world became more idealised and abstract. As a consequence, the function and nature of the window was largely rethought. An understanding of opening as meaning 'presence of window', is replaced by an understanding of opening meaning 'absence of wall'. In addressing the introduction of light and view into buildings, architects tend to think in terms of a general condition, rather than particular moments.

MIES VAN DER ROHE: LESS WINDOW IS MORE

In his skyscraper projects of 1922, Mies had famously reduced architecture to 'skin and bones'. Structure and skin were separated completely, the skin was freed from all load-bearing duties and could thus become a completely glass membrane. In one sense, then - the visual sense - the skin disappears. But of course it is still present - it is no less of a physical barrier than the load-bearing walls it replaces. And Mies was acutely aware of this. In his dramatic renderings of the *Friedrichstrasse* project, he exploits the reflective qualities of the glass, faceting the form to maximise its expressive possibilities. As Kenneth Frampton notes, he uses glass like 'transparent stone' [5] (which, of course, is not that far from what it actually is.)

In later projects however, and particularly in his domestic work, the glass facade figures more as absence than presence. In the famous collage drawings of the house Mies designed in Wyoming for Stanley Resor in 1938, we get no sense of the presence of the extensive glass wall. We are aware of interior space and an immense landscape beyond, but not of what lies between. The window disappears. Mies' intention is to have as little 'interference' as possible between his 'pure' slice of living space and what lies beyond. In order to achieve this, paradoxically, he must introduce continuous sheets of glazing, which in sensory terms cut off the interior completely. Nature is visible, but not palpable. Furthermore, its presence is inescapable - it is impossible to escape a continuous visual connection to the exterior.

In the Farnsworth House, Mies developed and extended the language of the Resor House. Now the house has been reduced to a suspended volume described by the planes of floor and ceiling and two lines of white-painted steel columns. Again, the glass skin is conceived as an absence, its frames reduced to a minimum and concealed behind the structural columns. The only openings are the front door and two small low-level vents in the least visible facade. Mies wanted to reduce architecture to 'beinahe nichts' - almost nothing - in order to accentuate the presence of nature:

> Nature, too, shall live its own life. We must beware not to disrupt it with the colour of our houses and interior fittings. Yet we should attempt to bring nature, houses and human beings together into a higher unity. If you view nature through the glass walls of the Farnsworth House, it gains a more profound significance than if viewed from the outside. This way more is said about nature - it becomes a part of the larger whole.[6]

This is a highly idealised reading of the relationship of person and nature. Visually, the connection to the surroundings is uninterrupted. Haptically, however, there is a complete disconnection. The external skin is impermeable; its very purity discourages any interaction - one is almost afraid to touch it. The relationship to the outside cannot be modulated in any significant way, so that the internal climate of the house often becomes almost unbearable: too hot in the summer, too cold in the winter. For the client, Edith Farnsworth, the house became a kind of 'glass cage', not only because she felt permanently on show, but also because she felt trapped, frustratingly sealed off from the ever-visible surroundings. Rather than complete transparency, she yearned for a more controlled aperture through which to connect to the world:

*'I would prefer to move as the women do in the Old Quarter of Tripoli, muffled in unbleached homespun so that only a hole is left for them to look out of'. Best of all she said, the world outside would 'not even know where the hole was.'*⁷

Following his celebrated dictum that less is more, we might say that Mies strove to make more transparency from less window - but that, paradoxically, more transparency resulted in a less complete connection between inside and outside.

LE CORBUSIER: THE UNIVERSAL WINDOW

Le Corbusier also experimented with the seamless glass skin. In his *Cité de Refuge* project of 1933 in Paris, he employed a glass curtain wall covering the entire southern facade of the main accommodation block. The interior was to become a completely sealed, controlled environment - Corb used the faintly chilling phrase 'respiration exacte', or 'exact breathing', in his descriptions of the project. Conditions in the building soon proved unbearable and Corb had to kit it out with opening sections and a fairly primitive *brise-soleil*, but the project exemplifies his vision of the relationship between inside and outside. His was an architecture which sought to distance its users from the immediate experience of the world. Buildings are raised up off the ground, the site reconstituted as a roof garden. The relationship of the building and its occupants to the surroundings is - as for Mies - an idealised, controlled one. In his sketches, the apartment is reduced to a giant eye in the sky, fed by essential services from below, overlooking, but not engaging with its surroundings. Le Corbusier was obsessed too with issues of standardisation and repetition:

Appeal to industry: It is possible to manufacture a new and indefinitely modular window on a new scale, based on the use of thin and thick glass and the mechanical application of slides and cam fasteners.... To give ourselves the mechanical window! We architects would be quite content with a fixed module. We would compose with this module. Attention please! Windows must not open with leaves inward because they get in the way, or outwards either. They must slide sideways..(All our bourgeois houses, all our workers houses and all our apartment houses are conceived with

276

the same window, the same unit..) but what we have had up till now is the work of the blacksmith and not of the mechanic.[8]

Corb wanted a window which was precision-made and endlessly reproducible. At the same time, it could not be allowed to interfere with the purity of his spaces, or his facades, by opening inwards or outwards. With the sliding opening, the zone of the window becomes slimmer, reduced essentially to a single plane. There is no longer a distinct place at-the-window. Corb replaces the traditional vertical French window with the continuous horizontal strip-window, which becomes a constant presence in his work of the twenties and thirties. He likes, among other things, the consistency of this type of opening: it lets in the same quality and amount of light along the whole length of the space; it permits more or less the same view at any point along its length. Beatriz Colomina has described how Corb designed a house for his mother on Lake Geneva with no particular site, but a general view of lake, mountains and sky, in mind. The strip window became, in his words, 'the chief protagonist of the house.... the unique protagonist of the facade.'[9] The house is completely identified with window. The same is doubly true of the Villa Savoye, where the strip window becomes an ever-present datum, so that the interface between the house and the world is always the same. There is no distinction between wall and window across the plan, only across the section.

Bruno Reichlin recounts the negative reaction of Corb's one-time employer, Auguste Perret, to this development of the window:

> *Whereas the horizontal window, as Perret declares, 'condemns us to the view of an unending panorama', the vertical window stimulates us by letting us see a complete space (un espace complète): street, garden, sky. But above all, these openings may be closed.*[10]

Le Corbusier had always contended that the horizontal opening provided a much more complete and immediate connection with the exterior, but Perret also identified its limitations in this regard: it could not reveal depth by exposing foreground, middle ground and background to view. Thus what was outside would always remain at a distance - in an idealised, slightly abstract relation to the person at the window. Also the horizontal window seems to preclude the possibility of surprise - which the insertion of a window in an otherwise blank wall might provide - or of individual autonomy - which a window that the occupant can freely alter might provide. The continuous horizontal slot lends itself less well to human engagement. With the obvious rhyme between its form and that of the upright person, and the sense that in opening it, one could connect bodily - from head to toe - with the outside world, the vertical window seemed to offer a richer sensory experience to the occupant. It is precisely this richness of experience which we find vividly expressed in the contemporary work of the painter Pierre Bonnard.

PIERRE BONNARD: THE WINDOW, THE SENSES AND THE SELF

In Bonnard's painting of 1925 *La Fenêtre* (1925), the canvas is filled by the frame of a French window. Its jambs form borders to the edges of the composition; its central mullion anchors the middle. From behind this mullion emerges the head and arm of Bonnard's wife Marthe, standing on the adjoining balcony, looking at the view. She is a vestigial presence, her skin tones blending with the timber of the mullion, her hair merging with the distant mountains. The right hand of the composition becomes a series of vertical bands, delineating the complex layers of the window space - curtain, blind, jamb, frame, glazing, shutter. The passage from interior to exterior is revealed deliberately through this banding. The window's sectional depth, its grading of light and air is emphasised. On the left hand side, the relationship between inside and outside is far more direct. There is an equivalence in tonal weight between the two. If anything, the darker colours of the landscape seem to fill the window frame and press into the room. Although the window is closed, the figure of Marthe outside allows the domestic space extend into the landscape. Meanwhile, we also feel Bonnard's presence on the inside of the window, looking out and glimpsing his wife. She becomes an element in his reverie as he looks up from writing and reading at his desk.

When Bonnard moved to Le Cannet with Marthe after their eventual marriage in 1925, his subject matter narrowed in its scope almost exclusively to the domestic realm of their villa and the landscape surrounding it. As Marthe became increasingly debilitated by illness, she rarely ventured from the house, and spent hours in the bath. In Bonnard's paintings, she seems to have become absorbed into the spaces of domesticity. He spoke of trying to capture *un arret du temps* - a stilling of time. And indeed, the paintings evoke those small everyday epiphanies when one is struck afresh by everyday settings and rituals.

In *La Fenêtre-ouverte* (1921), Marthe is again a wraith-like presence, her sleeping head sliding into the lower right- hand corner of the painting. And again, almost the whole picture is occupied by the window, this time thrown open to the outside. The controlling layers of curtain, window leaf, reveal and the silhouetted blind are all revealed to us, and behind them the rich blue and green landscape looms. The moment has a sensory richness, with the vibrant, richly layered colour invoking not only what is seen, but also the smell of flowers and foliage, the touch of a warm breeze and the sound of the cicadas. And it is the window which frames and facilitates the moment.

During this phase of his work, Bonnard painted not from life, but from memory, and memory is activated especially by smells and sounds (far more so than by sights) His paintings always have this quality of a remembered moment, where equally important to gesture and position is the precise atmosphere, or one might say, the climate, of that instant in time. Thus sensory information becomes of paramount importance. Bonnard's diary was filled with quick sketches of glimpsed moments to be worked up into paintings, but these were always accompanied by a note of the weather. In the paintings we sense the weather in the space.

Again and again the window asserts its presence in Bonnard's work. Beginning with *La Salle à Manger Sur Le Jardin* (1931), there is a whole series of works which show a laid table in front of a central window. The horizontal plane of the table rears up to meet the vertical plane of the window. Each contains a floating field of objects, which rhyme with and complement each other. Although the view and the room are clearly differentiated - there is no uncertainty as to where one begins and the other ends (as one might find, for instance, in many of Mies' drawings) - somehow this allows an even greater proximity between the two.

The whole visual field is imbued with a sense of weightlessness, of airy suspension. When facing one of Bonnard's works, we seem to be invited to inhabit it, to swim in a thick soup of painted space. In fact we cannot do otherwise. Our relation to the painting is the same as his relationship to what is portrayed - an extremely intimate one. Distance or objectivity are impossible. (This is perhaps what most clearly differentiated him from the mainstream of modernist aesthetics which even in the hands of a pleasure-lover like Matisse tended - much like the architecture of the period - towards more universal, abstract, objective methods.) We identify completely with this very particular moment of entering a room full of light and air and the invitation of food. The paintings speak directly to the senses. Timothy Hyman describes them as evoking 'a rediscovery of the fullness of being' [11]. They seem to capture those moments when, spurred by the sensation of light and air, of sound and taste, we pause at the window and become freshly aware of our own being.

Footnotes

1 - Bronte, C. (1985, first publ.1847) *Jane Eyre*. London: Penguin. pp. 39-40

2 - Schmoll, J.A. *'Window Pictures'* quoted in Stromberg, K. *'The Window in the Picture, the Picture in the Window'* *Daidolas*, No. 13, p. 58

3 - Merlau-Ponty, M. (1962) *Phenomenology of Perception* (trans. Smith, C.). London: Routledge. p. 216

4 - Voysey, C.A. (1915) *Individuality*. London

5 - Frampton, K. (1995) *Studies in Tectonic Culture. The Poetics of Construction in Nineteenth and Twentieth Century Architecture*. Cambridge: MIT Press

6 - Norburg-Schulz, C. *'A talk with Mies Van Der Rohe'* reprinted in Neumayer, F. (1991) *The Artless World; Mies van der Rohe on the Building Art*. Cambridge: MIT Press

7 - Friedman, A. (1998) *Women and the Making of the Modern Home*. New York: Harry N. Abrams

8 - quoted in *Domus*.....

9 - Le Corbusier (1954) *Une Petite Maison*. Artemis- Verlags. p.31-4

10 - quoted in Reichlin, B. *'The Pros and Cons of the Horizontal Window: the Perret-Le Corbusier Controversy'* in *Daidalos* No.13, p.72

11 - Hyman, T. (1998) *Bonnard*. London: Thames and Hudson

Twenty One.
Dermot Boyd

Interview with Pat Scott, 2002

Unpublished, originally commissioned for *Architecture Ireland*, Royal Institute of Architects of Ireland magazine

To mark the occasion of his retrospective at the Hugh Lane Gallery in Spring 2002, I was asked to interview Patrick Scott for Irish Architect (now Architecture Ireland). Unfortunately, the interview was recorded on a primitive tape machine and proved almost impossible to transcribe. Time passed; the article was not published.

I really enjoyed talking to Pat on that cold damp afternoon in his house. He was charming, generous with his memory but humorously evasive when talking about the meaning behind his work.

This was further illustrated when, weeks later, I asked him to review our students' work at DIT (Dublin Institute of Technology). I introduced Pat to the class, mentioning his involvement with the SIGNA agency and his design work for CIE amongst his oeuvre. Explaining that the orange, black and white livery travelling at speed through the green Irish landscape was both an ingenious and patriotic choice, I was quietly corrected. 'No' Pat explained, it was because he had an orange, black and white cat at the time.

Maybe it is this theoretical silence that Patrick Scott enjoys conveying through his work. He is a remarkable artist and for that reason, this conversation, lost in transcription, should not be 'totally forgotten'.

DB - Pat, what do you wish to convey in your work?

PS - That was the kind of question that I was hoping that you would not ask! That's why I gave up interviews about 40 years ago when people asked me that. That is an impossible question. I am usually thinking about sex or something when I am painting. I cannot answer that.

DB - Michael Kane once told me that all artists think about sex and all that architects think about is space. Is that why you became an artist?

PS - I cannot talk about why I do things I just do them because I want to do it, to give satisfaction, to re-charge my batteries.

DB - If you are not putting a message across, where do you think 'it' comes from?

PS - Sitting down and starting something.

DB - Is that an easy process?

PS - No, it is not easy. It is very difficult...very difficult. It is a bit scary. It is no good sitting around thinking about it, you just have to get down to it.

DB - Why did you study architecture?

PS - Simply because I left school in 1939, my father at the time was totally bankrupt. It was the war. The only option was to get a job in the bank. My father had been a bank manager and it was the last thing I wanted to do. One of my aunts was a well-to-do lady; she organised for an architect she knew in London to take me on to do my articles and take the RIBA (Royal Institute of British Architects) examination. However, it was 4th September 1939 so that was out. In time, she did however kindly pay for my education. She said to me 'What are you going to do now?' and I said I would go to study architecture in University College Dublin (UCD). She gave me one thousand pounds. I went to Dublin and lived on one thousand pounds for five years.

DB - Why particularly architecture?

PS - I didn't particularly want to be an architect. It was the nearest thing to being a painter. That's what I wanted to be, but there was no painter in Ireland making a living from his or her painting. I had no ambition to do portraits or commissions.

DB - How did your architectural training inform your work?

PS - I don't know... I do not know what it was like to be trained in architecture. It was self-teaching. There was the professor, Rudolf Maxmillian Butler - it took him four years to die. I saw him once in second year. I was doing a small country house in a Georgian manner. He suggested that I place a couple of urns on the parapet. There were no books in the library in UCD except Bannister Fletcher of course; we taught ourselves. As the teaching came straight out of Bannister Fletcher, we were always one step ahead.

DB - What interested you about studying architecture?

PS - We did not get very inspired projects to do. For our final thesis we were given the subject, it was to design a new Railway Station at Kingsbridge (now Heuston Station). We all did the same project. We were not given a choice. In our last year we had James Downes as professor; again, I saw him only once. The UCD library however also did have four books by Le Corbusier and these volumes were our bible.

DB - At Michael Scott's offices, can we talk about the influence of Le Corbusier?

PS - The reason the Busaras looks the way it does is because of this. It was pure Corb. I went to Paris immediately after war. I went to the Pavilion Suisse. When I came to Scott's office, the bus station was a little two-storey circular building on the same site

It was like the London Underground Stations of the 1930s. Michael persuaded the government of the time to add more programme and that is how it grew. Wilfred Cantwell and I did the first sketches.

DB - Was it your favourite project in the office?

> PS - I worked on it the whole time; towards the end I was in a supervising role, keeping an eye out.

DB - You worked closely on the application of mosaic to the building?

> PS - Yes, but I was involved in the building from the first sketch plans. Everything we did was anonymous: there was no credit. It was simply 'Michael Scott's Office'. I did not even see Michael Scott at a drawing board in my life. It was a great experience. Busáras is an incredibly inventive building. The side facing the Custom House followed the Abercrombie Plan, completing a crescent on Beresford Place.

DB - How long did the project take?

> PS - The first sketch plan was in 1945 and the building was completed in 1956. There was two years in this period when the government changed and the whole thing was dropped. Luckily, the concrete skeleton had been erected at that stage.

DB - And the mosaic?

> PS - I was sent by Michael to the Building Centre in London to look at what materials were coming on to the market after the war. I found this Italian glass mosaic tile and I brought samples back to the office but it was Michael who went to Venice.

DB - The curved roof over the parking bays?

> PS - Ove Arup designed that. It is structure, a thin shell of concrete. He drew it. He was full of ideas, all of the time. Varming (the mechanical engineer) was also full of ideas.

DB - When it comes to your artwork, I am puzzled that there is little exploration of three-dimensional space except maybe in your very early work. How would you define space?

> PS - I don't think about things like that. I do not analyse what I

do at all!

DB - But in the arrangement of space, you have a gift.

PS - I do not think about the theory behind what I do.

DB - Okay, what do you prefer: the horizontal or vertical?

PS - It is no good asking that question. It depends on what you are doing.

DB - (Firmly) Horizontal or vertical, Pat?

PS - I don't know. I like both. I paint the square so that gets over that question very smartly. My favourite is the square!

DB - How do you size your work? Define the plane of engagement. Is it those proportions that define the finished work?

PS - I stretch the canvases to the size I want and I paint on them.

DB - But I am very interested in the parameters that you set as an artist in making your work and the reaction you have to other spatial influences that surround you, especially as you did train as an architect.

PS - Yes, when I do a tapestry I go and look at the site and I decide how it should be filled. I do not make tapestries that look like pictures on the wall. I try to fill the space. Each tapestry in the exhibition (Patrick Scott Retrospective – Hugh Lane Gallery, 2002) is specially commissioned and each fills the space that they occupy. That is why I painted the background wall in the gallery so dark. The gold paintings also look well on a dark background; you can paint the wall behind them any colour, as there is no colour in the pictures.

DB - You are a gifted colourist. Is there a difference in its use between your work through canvas and tapestry?

PS - There is a different technique at work. Seventeenth-century tapestries for instance were woven to look like paintings.

DB - Your graphic approach does seem freer and more expressive in tapestry work.

> PS - When I started working with raw canvas I was strict with it. I believe that gold should not be used with colour so the canvas is un-primed. Gold eliminated the colour.

DB - And why use gold in your work?

> PS - I used gold leaf as an architect and I liked it.

DB - Your use of the gold circle (with a square hole), is this symbolic?

> PS - No, it is the shape of a Chinese coin, a reproduction.

DB - The use of the gold 'sun' is symbolic surely.

> PS - Yes.

DB - In the exhibition in 1959-60, you moved towards abstraction. Did this reflect your participation in the Guggenheim Prize in New York in the previous year?

> PS - 'Birds in a Field', this was probably my first move towards abstraction. 'The Bog' paintings, the first work using un-primed canvases.

DB - Was the New York art scene important to you?

> PS - I was exposed to new techniques that I started handling myself. I was always experimenting with new techniques. When I was working as an architect I only produced four or five paintings. A year after, 1960, I worked hard, was experimenting and making art all the time.

DB - In your work, you have kept a particular direction.

> PS - It was not an intellectual decision. It is something that came about through the work.

DB - What do you think your position is as an artist?

PS - There is more to explore if I had the strength. The work was the best I could manage in the time at my disposal.

DB - Transcendental or meditative are terms that are often applied to your work. How do you make the metaphysical?

PS - God only knows! How would I know?

DB - Tables?

PS - The design of tables...I am not a great meditator myself. The table does help: people get on the floor to meditate; it forms a place to enter meditation. Sometimes, I would go into a room and just draw a circle in chalk and that creates a little bit of peace.

DB - How important is it to be an Irishman?

PS - Very important. I have never lived outside Ireland. I have only been away for a couple months at a time.

DB - Is belief important to you?

PS - Belief in what? I don't believe in the afterlife if that is the question...I do believe in a lot of things I suppose.

DB - How would you like to be remembered?

PS - God knows, I don't know, I would just like to be remembered, not totally forgotten.

Twenty Two.
Ellen Rowley

Crisis Culture & Memory Making across Two Generations of Dublin Architecture, 2007 - 2008

Two unpublished presentations, *Bodytalkcity*, Dublin Docklands event, 2007 and *Afterthoughts*, Green on Red gallery, 2008

The following paper comprises a stitching together of two oral presentations: 'Crisis, what crisis?' (November 2007) for the *Bodytalkcity* forum and public art reaction (*Body City*) to the Dublin Docklands development; and 'King Kong comes to town' (March 2008) for *Afterthoughts*, an artist's response to the Central Bank building (Dublin, Sam Stephenson, c.1978) and to the issue of post-occupancy of buildings.

Body City www.bodycity.org was curated by Cliodhna Shaffrey, Nigel Rolfe and Sheila Morris and raised crucial questions to do with capitalist development (private business space) generating and determining the globalised contemporary city. Amidst the curators' questions, one struck me as most provocative and was explicitly linked to my research into Ireland's architectural history from 1940 to 1980: 'Why is history erased so readily for a bold new cityscape?'

The second forum, *Afterthoughts* http://dennismcnulty.com/afterthoughts.html was organised by artist Dennis McNulty as a non-prescriptive gathering which would confront the huge issue of the 'life' of a building after construction. In line with McNulty's engagement with the Central Bank for his own work (*Framework/ Rupture*), my paper sought to position such an architectural happening in its historical context but also - taking the Central Bank as an emblem - to consider our ever-shifting reception to and perception of our city.

Both events were initiated by Dublin's art community as open platforms for unpicking the processes of urban development (and architectural praxis). By questioning how the city is formed and how we the citizens react to the city and behave in its spaces, both were ultimately driven, in different ways, by the need to understand the mechanisms of developer-led architectural and planning practices.

Certainly *Bodytalkcity* was underpinned by a reactionary stance, thereby positing the controversial 'crisis' question; its manifesto demanded a revaluation of Dublin's new urban villages and their colonisation of former fringe communities. By pitching itself into the safer distance of 1970s Dublin, *Afterthoughts* was rooted in a less explicit and perhaps more measured and abstracted line of enquiry. But in both instances I interpreted my role and contribution to be a reflection on the nature of the built environment generally, through the case of Dublin's recent architecture particularly.

This essay constitutes my sentimental interpretation of the thinking and teachings of Dalibor Vesely (Architecture in the Age of Divided Representation (MIT, 2004)), applied to contemporary Irish history and architectural production therein.

Crisis and situatedness

The ubiquitous 'crisis' underlying Dublin's architecture during the past fifty years is as I perceive it, founded upon the universal crisis of the 'self-referential' nature of architecture.

Dalibor Vesely explains the meaning of self-referential architecture whereby a building or complex of structures 'may appear complete, even well-integrated and unified, while in reality they are only large fragments which are un-situated and without particular meaning'.[1] As such they present themselves as finished objects when in fact, objects are irrelevant in the experience of architecture: as Vesely explains, 'architectural experience is not generated in the context of buildings as objects, but it is always situational'.[2] Architecture is central to any person's life-world and as situations 'represent the most complete way of understanding the condition of our experience of the surrounding world' then architecture is situational.[3]

Crisis - if we are to call it that - pervades the city because the architectural and spatial constituents of the city, the buildings-streets-public spaces are conceived of in terms of appearance and the modes of design understand architecture as form. So while architecture is presented and experienced as just another type of production, that is aestheticised technological production, the reality of the built environment as fundamental to our orientation in world is lost.

Like language, architecture is essential to our possibility for communication and participation. And here the analogy with language is further enforced by a mutual so-called crisis: language, having denied the richness of the non-verbal gesture, its essential corporeality, has become a science of linguistics.[4] The call for a 'corporeal turn' in the realm of language is provocative and relevant to the more physically expressive nature of architecture because building, from its conception, must be directed by the body.

While a building is a concrete construct, founded and apparently unmoveable - though this is ironic considering the miserly forty-year lifespan of much recent architecture in Dublin - our experience of it is shaped by our bodily involvement with it. Truly our built environment does not simply appear to our sight in an organised definitive full-stop, but it arises and emerges in a shifting way according to a synthesis of inherent perceptual skills.[5]

The self-referential nature of the immediately legible spaces, in visual terms, of Dublin's new urban villages finds its roots in the science of perspective and perspective's genealogy of technological design tools such as the grid system and Computer Aided Drafting (CAD). Such that, in moving through Grand Canal Square – the apotheosis of the regenerated Dublin Docklands, landscaped by Martha Schwartz and framed by Daniel Libeskind's theatre (2010) and Aires Mateus' hotel (2008) - we are at once seduced and oppressed by the invasion of the virtual into the actual. Our real experience of the place is simultaneous with the CAD representation of the place. The process of designing the space is one and the same thing as, and is interchangeable with, the end-product.

Because architecture has for a long time been 'technologised' and as a result is governed by *zeitgeist* principles (the spirit of

the age), emphasis is always placed on an imagined future. History is understood as a tyranny of progress, forever driving Time forward; and the city as a product of this process becomes, to paraphrase Colin Rowe, a 'theatre of prophecy'.[6] Even the acknowledgement of existing buildings as documents to be respected and manipulated from the past ('theatre of memory') translates as a negation of the city as a continuum. Here, we inadvertently address the *Body City* curators' question, 'Why is history erased so readily for a bold new cityscape?' Development is driven by the Cartesian dictum: 'distance yourself from the world and you can restructure it anew'. Le Corbusier enforced this rationalist idea in relation to the city as a tabula rasa when he stated that, *'tout doit commencer a zero'.*[7]

The spaces of the city become non-situational through their overt openness and present-time zoning or mixed-use needs. Preferably our city will be visually-literate. It will not accommodate or enable defensive space such as that shaping the medinas of the Islamic world which are alienating, even hostile to the visitor; they cannot be navigated by means of a map but instead the spaces unfold through the experience of living there and participating in the community.[8]

Crisis-culture and the case of Ballymun

An activist and academic industry of crisis has run through Irish architecture during the latter half of the twentieth century - most especially in relation to the progression of our urban environments, thereby positioning Dublin at the helm of any crisis-culture. This industry has produced reports, studies, exhibitions and actions: *The Inner City of Dublin* (mental health crisis document, 1974), *Hands Off Dublin* (Deirdre Kelly, 1976), Dublin, *A City in Crisis* (Royal Institute of Architects of Ireland, 1975), *Manifesto for the City*, (Dublin City Crisis Conference, 1986/87); *Dublin City Quays* (School of Architecture, UCD, 1986), *Saving the City* (Frank McDonald, 1989), *Dublin in Crisis* (Dept of Geography, TCD, 1991) and *SubUrban to SuperRural* (Irish Pavilion, Venice Biennale, 2006).

All of these manifestoes were generated by non development/ thoughtless development/over development. Mostly those from the not-so-immediate past have been forgotten by our generation, intent as we are that it is only our millennial sprawling city that has been ravaged by economic exigency and heedless development. In reality, the crisis is ever present, evolving with each generation and made manifest most explicitly in the realm of housing. Just as today's problems stem from house-as-property rather than house-as-dwelling, housing has been at the centre of crisis culture across recent history. We are reminded of the slum-clearance inquiries of the 1930s and 1940s, and the consequent reconditioning of city-centre Georgian buildings and the erection of low-rise estates of terraced homes all over the green fields at Dublin's fringe.

In light of the mostly dire housing situation, the incitation of the term 'crisis' has been a useful means of engendering debate or better still of initiating change or renewal. However, in the situation of the housing crisis of 1963, the discourse and subsequent action was hysterical. In this instance, crisis gave rise to the lab-rat of Irish architecture and urbanism, Ballymun Estate.[9] I say 'lab-rat' because Ballymun is Ireland's legendary site of utopian and dystopian interchange. It is the formerly green-field stage turned edge-city where urban theories have been played out to the rhythms of the State's social and economic aspirations. And as such, Ballymun is a highly susceptible site; its susceptibility being something of an intangible reality which one local resident wryly summarises as, 'Dublin sneezes, Ballymun catches cold.'[10]

While this comment pertains to the place's negative fragility in social and physical terms, it also highlights its status as Ireland's singular reactive sub/urban phenomenon; a reality which we may forget due to the more visible and commercially biased presence of the Docklands development. It continues to be the place where crisis and subsequent experiment collide; where rationalist urbanist ideology created its spatial frame in the late 1960s, the communitarian Third Way principles of new urbanism are driving its current regeneration process.

Originally conceived of as the heal-all solution to an extreme housing crisis (the collapse of houses on Fenian and Bolton streets in June 1963 leading to four deaths) the scheme of 3,021

dwellings, represented a sub/urban grand projet which embraced
the contemporary ethos of modernisation. In such a climate
of crisis and forceful modernisation, it is not surprising that
the adopted architecture for the estate's housing championed
technological experimentation which unsurprisingly, did not
consider the situational nature of building as a vehicle for
memory making.

*I stake my reputation, for what it is worth, on the outcome of a new
system, an industrialised system, never before tried in this country
and on a scale not exceeded in money or volume in any country in
Europe, on a single contract for housing, and it is going well...*

- Neil Blaney, Minister for Local Government,
Committee on Finance, Dail Eireann, October 1966

By Dublin's contemporary architecture's standards, the seven
15-storey towers, the nineteen 8-storey deck access blocks and
the ten 4-storey walk-up blocks have lived a typically short life
of forty years. Their current demolition as part of the Ballymun
Regeneration Ltd (BRL) plan makes a drastic statement and
illustrates the place's tendency towards self-reinvention. This
is not to undermine either the careful negotiation specifically
since 1997 between community, local authority and planners/
architects which has arrived at the present regeneration plans,
or to negate the origins of the current project which lie in the
neglect during a twenty-five-year period by the State of a massive
community, pitched to the north periphery of Dublin. But rather
to draw on the poignant reality that through the demolition of
the 1960s buildings, the place is again rising like a phoenix from
the so-called ashes; where those ashes were green fields in 1965,
today they are the baseline of incredible community activism in
pursuit of physical rehabilitation.

The community's response here to the negligence by Dublin
Corporation of their most basic needs during the 1970s and
1980s led to the establishment of more than ninety local groups,
and their subsequent mobilisation had motivated the wholesale
refurbishment of their physical environment.[11] Interestingly,
the centrality of community participation in the reshaping of
Ballymun since 1997 is in line with both Blairite so-called 'Third

Way' politics and the philosophy of 'New Urbanism'. These corresponding principles use urban design and community empowerment to rehabilitate marginalized and disenfranchised communities; as in the example of Ballymun, whereby a sustainable community is sought through a combination of self-regulation and (regeneration) professional consultation, there emerges a 'new moral politics of community' which has not been challenged or really questioned so far.

> ...a thinly veiled moral crusade targeted towards vulnerable residents in disadvantaged neighbourhoods.[12]

It is timely now to remind ourselves of the fact that Ballymun, like the city where it belongs, is a multilayered cultural and social 'situated-artefact' with, as John Montague points out, its own fast-disappearing archaeology.[13]

Memory making and the case of Central Bank

The act of razing the tall towers of Ballymun to the ground (only three remain at time of writing, 2008) provokes our conundrum once again - 'Why is history erased so readily for a bold new cityscape?' The fact that we are even reflecting on the archaeology of this much-maligned complex of structures shows how, with the layering of time, our experience of our built environment shifts. Two contentiously bombastic structures in Dublin's centre are encountering a similar shift in public reception/perception, Liberty Hall (Desmond Rae O'Kelly, c.1965) and the Central Bank. Somehow, both of these buildings have become 'authenticated' over time.

Drawing on the latter as our example, it is interesting to situate the Central Bank in terms of its contemporary reception (that is, the reactions to it in the 1970s and early 80s) and then its subsequent legacy, so as to pose the problematic as to why it is, by now (in the early twenty first century), a welcome architectural event in one's experience of this place, Dublin. While the example represents a very particular set of conditions relating specifically to the local (in respect of Central Bank's history in the context of Dublin), it also raises a universal issue to do with our relationship with the city as a locus of collective memory: how in the past four decades we have moved from living unselfconsciously with the city, thereby destroying much of its fabric; to then celebrating it as a precious tapestry-like construct made up of architecture as layers of memory; to today, whereby we seem to feel our city as a collage with buildings becoming its fragments.

> *If the ESB's victory fires the starting gun for a wholesale onslaught on the remaining splendours of the eighteenth century, then it will be a victory most Pyrrhic indeed for the city of Dublin*

- Editorial, *Build Magazine*, September 1964

Born out of a climate of newfound concern for the built inheritance, the plans for the Central Bank were met from the offset with suspicion and scepticism. The controversy over the destruction of seventeen Georgian houses on Fitzwilliam Street in the summer of 1965, so as to house the offices of a large semi-government body (the Electricity Supply Board, ESB) in a four-storey warren of brick, glass and pre-cast concrete panels, which is then set back slightly from the street and articulated by serialised five-bay elements, resulted in public outcry and raised awareness of the validity of architectural conservation.

In many respects, the contextual design for the ESB - contextual in terms of respecting the neighbouring parapet height and using a repetitive fenestration pattern, echoing its Georgian forefathers – meant that the ESB building itself was well received in architectural circles; it was charged with an element of renewal in terms of the city's existing architectural order (to paraphrase Louis Kahn).

But the reality of the former Georgian terrace's wholesale demolition went hand-in-hand with the general crumbling of much of Dublin's Georgian infrastructure, thereby signalling an extensive reevaluation of the city centre and supposed heart and soul of Dublin. Housing was shifted outside the city's bounds while roads in the city-centre were widened and traditional institutions knocked down, to make room for cars and more and more office buildings.

As I passed the new Central Bank building with Jim Fitzpatrick, the

theatre producer, he remarked, 'It's two lift shafts going nowhere'.
Is that what the city itself is to become...The banks and insurance
companies want Dame Street for themselves, they are determined
to get it.

- Ulick O'Connor, cited in *Plan Magazine*, October 1973

Suspicion and scepticism began to make way for outright hatred.

While the Central Bank building was being constructed - a
structural system which attracted much attention due to the
novelty of it being hung from the top down as such - it became
apparent that the approved plans had evolved into quite a
different architectural creature. In fact, as it was going up, the
building was exceeding its approved height by 29 ft; a massive
controversy ensued and the building's construction was halted
at the end of 1973, while a hearing began in February 1974. [14] It
was a case of an extreme breach of planning laws - laws that were
only a decade old – and unforeseen energy went into making
sure that the Central Bank did not set a precedent! Already it had
become as much a symbol as a reality.

Here a narrow street...has been made literally claustrophobic by
the overwhelming presence of the Central Bank, which not only
closes the view and blots out part of the sky, but, which when
seen from part of the street, actually rides over the roofline of the
Trinity Bank...If the present height is seen to be tolerated, against
the decision of the Planning Authority, not only will the Planning
legislation and Authority lose all credence, but Dublin, I believe,
will be saddled with yet another cause for constant visual dismay.

– Edward McParland, Dublin Civic Group,
Central Bank Hearing, February 1974

The polemic against the unfinished structure raged from all
quarters: the preservationists, obviously enough, such as the
Dublin Civic Group, architectural students at Bolton Street and
even warnings and comments about scale came from such sworn
architectural modernists as Robin Walker:

Dame Street which, without changing its essential use, has changed the style and scale of its fabric and most certainly has changed its character. For the worse? Perhaps the historical lesson to be learned is that change must be gradual to be unnoticeable…To be unnoticeable, change must take place over as long a period as possible…

- Robin Walker, *City in Crisis*. RIAI, 1975

The Central Bank was built however; albeit with modifications to Stephenson's roofline. But inevitably the contempt railed against it lived on in public consciousness. Yes, it was unique to Dublin and yes, it signalled an alternative mid-twentieth-century technological corporate aesthetic in Dublin but, by the early 1980s, a few short years after its completion and occupation by the state institution of Central Bank in 1978, the country went into a rapid spiral of indebtedness and recession. [15]

With the reality of it costing £10 million by the end of its construction debacle, the Central Bank might be read as an emblem (in birth, subsequent form and ongoing function) for a collective sense of loss and lack of direction (in societal terms). As an excessively bombastic and unapologetic cog in the government machine, the structure embodied all that was hateful and not to be trusted at this confused time.

It is not an exaggeration to propose that Stephenson's civic building on Dame Street had become Kafkaesque and mythic in the first decade of its life in the city, and this symbolisation was not simply as a result of its defiant scale. As contemporary socio-economic studies reveal, the post-Central Bank mood was one of dejection and despondency. [16]

The architectural translation of this despondency was, unsurprisingly, reactionary, but reactionary in unbuilt blueprint form only. A climate of economic recession will push architecture more in the direction of architectural culture than architectural production; whereby building research develops in the realm of theory rather than practice, not as a dichotomy but as two sides of same coin. So, this reaction then to the systems which yielded the Central Bank was played out through an emerging generation, in an arena of exhibitions and visionary projects, one such being *Traditions and Directions. The Evolution of Irish Architecture* at the Royal College of Art, London in 1980. Old and new buildings were displayed, chosen for their integrity and essential Irishness. One of the generation's spokespeople explained the newer projects on exhibit:

> *These projects display a concern for the continuity and definition of urban space, the relationship of the individual building to the city and the relative importance of monument and fabric...particularly in projects at an urban scale, they are informed by the particular tradition of street, square and the ability of a repetitive unit to form space.*

303

- Derek Tynan, Traditions and Directions. RCA, 1980

Interestingly, this particular exhibition in London represents the only occasion (according to my research) whereby the Central Bank is illustrated or listed alongside other noteworthy buildings from Ireland's architectural history. One posits, rhetorically, whether the Central Bank has been excluded from significant histories of twentieth-century Irish architecture - that is, beyond a chastising mention - because it is simply and complexly too emblematic?

Dubbed the 'Irish Renaissance' (to quote Gerry Cahill, The *Architects' Journal*, October 1984), this 'school' developed in part into Group 91 and Temple Bar's renegotiation (c.1991). As an architectural disposition simmering during the 1980s, its key words were continuity, context, evolution, typology. And as a disposition rather than a definitive school, we might term it Irish Critical Regionalism or Contextualism. It was best recognisable by its reaction to, but not rejection of, modern architecture's penchant for object-buildings.

Ironically, in recognising the city as a palimpsest and all architectural-events as the city's constituent parts, the Contextualists of the 1980s into the 1990s made it okay (at last) to accept the Central Bank: nothing from the past should be rejected, but rather, re-shelved.

The dogma of memory &
the crisis of communitarianism

> *...that the city remembers its past and uses that memory through monuments; that is, monuments give structure to the city.*

> – Aldo Rossi, *Architecture of the City*, 1966

The influence of Aldo Rossi and his colleagues at Casabella, Greggotti et al., was profoundly felt on the endeavours of the emerging generation. Rossi's writing was pretty much contemporaneous with Colin Rowe's Collage City and was being absorbed by these younger Irish architects just as Sam Stephenson's infant monster was emerging on Dame Street in the early 1970s.

And it was through this newfound emphasis on memory as associational-with-architecture that we are left adrift today, feeling for memory's substance in the city and its spaces and places. We have inherited something of a dogma that memory is spatial and localised but this so-called dogma keeps evading us. [17] By its nature, memory is slippery and not fixed, while the architectural development of this dogma now sees us surrounded by glazed and mirrored skins and atria: these being our newfound architectural-events.

The proliferation on our cityscape of mid- and low-rise complexes, which maximise rentable space while minimising service space, [18] and are bounded by glazing systems which allow windows to act as walls, brings us beyond this urban appetite for openness to an almost-aggressive hunger for transparency. As Irenee Scalbert asserted, the city today is all about the interior, with the lobby becoming the markedly significant space.[19] In Dublin in 2008, the ubiquitous triple-height atrium-style lobby is always evident, yet never welcoming, behind its glass wall.

In contrast to the emphatic concrete and horizontal striped massing of Central Bank, the reflective skins of much current architecture deny the materiality of a building as artefact. Diane Agrest's analysis from 'Architecture of Mirror/Mirror of Architecture' brings us from the Central Bank-as-object to the

Dublin Docklands-as-transparent complex:

> *The architecture of object by the use of mirrors paradoxically negates its own objecthood. This is clear particularly if one considers this architecture in context. The presence of the object is subdued by the fact that it attempts to absorb its context; it is object and context at the same time.*

> – Diane Agrest, *'Architecture of Mirror/Mirror of Architecture'* 1984

The Central Bank, in all its solidity and exteriority, becomes a temporary and most welcome release from the incessant 'visual social penetration' of the new buildings around town. King Kong keeps us not just outside its slabs, but beneath its precarious overhang. Do we feel protected by its (by-now) reassuring as much as menacing omnipresence? In this way, we move from glibly accepting it to actually appreciating it. In short, it offers us a reprieve from the non-private.

The Central Bank's 'objecthood', like that of Liberty Hall and the Ballymun towers, has attained a situational character over time which embeds it into the experience of Dublin city. As Vesely might explain, the situational nature of any architecture 'endows experience with durability in relation to which other experiences can acquire meaning and inform memory'.[20] Beyond becoming a marker on the skyline or a place on and away from the street, the shift in character from the self-referential to the situational is illusive. Like the experience with which it is intimately bound, i.e., the experience of memory - this process is slippery. It must be about more than the patina of Time? Or perhaps not...

Unlike Liberty Hall and the architecture of 'old' (1960s) Ballymun, the Central Bank structure is not in danger of immediate obliteration. Having treated its vernacular neighbours as parasites in the 1970s, it was the implied perpetrator underlying this essay's rhetorical question, 'Why is history erased so readily for a bold new cityscape?'

Today we witness the disappearance of the Ballymun towers and are confronted with the imminent destruction of Liberty

Hall; in their place (actual: Ballymun, Dublin Docklands and projected: Liberty Hall) come the architectural products of New Urbanism. And so the issue of erasing collective memory from city is as pertinent as it was during the rapid modernisation project of 1960s Lemass's Ireland. Memory is replaced by the new heal-all solution: community. Now the business or culture community get shiny glazed structures for public buildings while the residential community get quirky mid-rise or engrained and colourful (twenty-first century vernacular) architecture for domestic buildings. The tendency towards reinvention, whether emerging as a Capitalist imperative or out of community activism, continues to inform our cityscape.

What is interesting to point out in terms of the community-based ideals driving New Urbanism in pockets of our city is the proposition that once again the shaping of spatial order is or can be the foundation for a new moral order. David Harvey suspects that the adoption of a new architecture, albeit generated by community decision, is guilty of similar prescriptive tendencies of Modernist utopian strategies; that underlying this is the persistent habit of privileging spatial forms over social processes.[21] He goes further in his criticism by highlighting the fundamentalism of community (as championed by New Urbanism):

> The New Urbanism assembles much of its rhetorical and political power through a nostalgic appeal to 'community!' as a panacea for our social and economic as well as our urban ills...[22]

So far, only Ballymun bears the fruits of this penchant for 'communitarism' but other neighbourhoods in Dublin (St. Michael's Estate, Inchicore) and in Limerick (Moyross and Southill) are undergoing similar processes (2008). Harvey's criticism of community-based regeneration is, in my mind, exaggerated, but there is wisdom in challenging the blind reverence paid to New Urbanism 'from the ground up' structures of change. At the most basic level, this process champions an all-new physical frame which will be inevitably made up of non-situational object buildings.

All we knew now disappeared, the promised landscapes and town centre eventually arrive, thirty years late but at last it has arrived. 'That place is getting regenerated, isn't it?' Changed beyond recognition, it no longer clings to your trousers like muck from the muck hills, it now sits in your pocket, like your ticket to the local disco, you take it out every so often and say, 'look where we're going'.

– Daniel Seery, *'A Short Story of my Town'* from
Ballymun writers group, *Tall Stories*

Reinvention, reinvention, reinvention...

Dublin must be lived-in, designed-as and experienced as a place where situations are in a dialectical relation to the architecture, streets and public spaces 'to which they give rise and which in turn contain them' [23] So that we can dwell in the streets, not as we do in the intimacy of the corridors in the house, but that the dualism of public/private is reconciled through a celebration of the city as a continuum rather than fought against through transparent walls of object-buildings set on a grid of directional-streets.

In the words of Colin Rowe: that the city should enable 'the joint existence of permanent reference and random happening, of the private and the public, of innovation and tradition, of both the retrospective and prophetic gesture.'[24]

Footnotes

1 - Dalibor Vesely, 'Architecture and the Ambiguity of Fragment' in Robin Middleton (ed.), *The Idea of the City* (London: Architectural Association, 1996), p. 111

2 - Dalibor Vesely, 'Architecture and the Poetics of Representation' in *Daidalos* (No.25, September 1987), p. 26

3 - Ibid., p. 32

4 - See Horst Ruthrof's discussion of this in *The Body in Language* (London: Cassell, 2000)

5 - For discussion of this perceptual process, see Maurice Merleau-Ponty's essay 'Cezanne's Doubt' in *Sense and Non-Sense* (Evanston: Northwestern University Press, 1964), pp 12-19

6 - Colin Rowe (with Fred Koetter), *Collage City* (Cambridge: MIT, 1978), p. 49; see Frances Yates, *The Art of Memory* (London: Routledge, 1999)

7 - This brief discussion is taken from Dalibor Vesely: In an overview of historicism, Vesely discusses the historicist understanding of time as 'a tyranny of progress'. He also refers to the historicist nature of Le Corbusier's ethos (M.Phil seminar, History and Philosophy of Architecture, School of Architecture, Cambridge University, 2000-2001)

8 - I am grateful to Emma David for this explanation of defensive space within the traditional Islamic city. Emma David (ongoing PhD Cantab.), 'The Islamic City', unpublished lecture, January 2002, Visual Arts Society, Trinity College Dublin

9 - The following analysis of Ballymun is extracted from my review of Seamus Nolan's Hotel Ballymun (March 2007) which was originally commissioned by Sandra O'Connell, *Architecture Ireland*. See Ellen Rowley, 'Hotel Ballymun: Site for Reflection in the Heady Days of Regeneration' in Aisling Prior (ed.), *Hotel Ballymun. Seamus Nolan* (Dublin: Breaking Ground, Ballymun Regeneration Ltd., 2008)

10 - From Ballymun Oral History Project, cited in Dr Robert Somerville-Woodward, *Ballymun, A History. Volumes 1 + 2 c. 1600 – 1997* (Dublin: BRL, 2002), p. 51

11 - Somerville-Woodward summarises the evolution of Ballymun's community groups, *Ballymun, A History. Volumes 1 + 2 c. 1600 – 1997*, p. 47 - 60

12 - These words are used by Mark Boyle and Robert Rogerson, 'Third Way' Urban Policy and the New Moral Politics of Community: a Comparative Analysis of Ballymun in Dublin and the Gorbals in Glasgow' in *Urban Geography* (Vol. 27, No. 3, April – May 2006), p. 6

13 - John Montague, 'Ballymun: an architectural history', unpublished lecture, Hotel Ballymun art action/event, April 2007

14 - For a lively and informative outline of the events surrounding the Central Bank's construction, see Frank McDonald, *The Destruction of Dublin* (Dublin: Gill & Macmillan, 1985), pp. 165 - 210

15 - 1977 net foreign debt = £78 million

    1978 net foreign debt = £297 million

    1979 net foreign debt = exceeded £1,000 million

    1983 net foreign debt = £6,703 million

16 - In 1982, the Institute of Public Administration (IPA) published a series of reports on the situation of government since the late 50s, in which the preface emphatically states: 'Unemployment is rising and the social problems which follow from economic stagnation are growing. Despondency seems to be on the increase, as though the intractability of our problems had at last sapped our will to solve them.' Frank Litton's Preface, *Unequal Achievement: The Irish Experience, 1957 – 82* (Dublin: IPA, 1982), cited by Terence Brown, *Ireland. A Social and Cultural History 1922 – 2000* (London: Harper Perennial, 2004), p. 319

17 - For a useful overview of the concept and workings of memory in architecture, see Adrian Forty, *Words and Buildings* (London: Thames + Hudson, 2004) p. 215

18 - Mitchell Schwarzer, 'The Spectacle of Ordinary Building' in William Saunders (ed.) *Sprawl and Suburbia. A Harvard Design Magazine Reader* (London: UMP, 2005), p.84

19 - Irenee Scalbert, 'Lobbying for Space' unpublished conference paper, *Defining Space Conference*, October 2007, University College Dublin

20 - Dalibor Vesely, 'Architecture and the Poetics of Representation' in *Daidalos* (No.25, September 1987), p.32

21 - David Harvey, 'The New Urbanism and the Communitarian Trap: On Social Problems and the False Hope of Design' in William Saunders (ed.) *Sprawl and Suburbia. A Harvard Design Magazine Reader* (London: UMP, 2005), p.23

22 - Ibid.

23 - Ibid.

24 - See the conclusion of Colin Rowe (with Fred Koetter), *Collage City* (Cambridge: MIT, 1978)

Twenty Three.
Dominic Stevens

Natural Artificial

From *Rural* (Leitrim: Mermaid Turbulence,
The Arts Council, 2007)

The society that we live in has very clear ideas about what is natural and what is artificial. The word artificial is from the Latin *ars* 'art' and *facere* 'make'; implicit in this is that it is man that does the making. Natural, as defined in Oxford English Dictionary, is something *'not made, caused by, or processed by humans'*. We were all educated with this understanding of a division, whether science, architectural theory or environmentalism, the world was always divided into two, the natural and the artificial.

One of the bases of our society is religion, and certainly Christianity is firm in the notion that God gave man dominion over the animals and over nature, that the universe centered on man. Environmentalism, for many a science, for others a new religion, similarly places man in the centre as custodians of nature, the ones responsible, the ones in charge. It seems that the rich and powerful have centered their science, culture and art on this sense of self-importance for as long as modern civilisation has existed.

Architecture exists in this cultural construct as well; we always view the building as being something that sits on the landscape, separate to it both in definition and visually. When we look at a farmed hillside with a new house built in the middle of it we ask does it fit in? Does it not spoil the view? There is the view, which is understood as nature, and the house, that is understood as an artificial addition.

Animals

Keeping animals was an eye-opener for me. I had never given much thought to how animals interact with their environment before, and it surprised me how much animals form where they live to suit their needs and feeding habits. Our ducks roam free range; however, they chose the dampest place around our house and set to work on their mud-flat, wet-land landscaping project. What used to be grass is now muddy, puddly and wet, the ducks wander around rooting in the soft ground, drinking and generally doing all the things that ducks like to do while not swimming. So I learnt that animals through their activities alter landscape just as we do, do they feel in control? Do our goats as they are chewing the cud see themselves also at the centre of the universe? Did the 'goat god' give them dominion over us?

Sciences have always supplied us with the proof that we are different, and over the years many different theories have existed to keep us neatly separated from nature. The most important was that man uses tools and animals do not.

It was in Africa in the 1960s that Jane Goodall, a research scientist working with Louis Leakey the anthropologist, first observed a chimpanzee using a stem of grass to extract termites from a nest. It caused scientific uproar - Louis Leakey responded to the news with the famous remark, "Ah! Now we must redefine man, redefine tool, or accept chimpanzees as human."

Termites, Tool Makers

Some animals are extremely effective at making their environment comfortable using limited means; this allows them to thrive.

There are a huge amount of termites in the world; it is estimated that there is five hundred kilograms of termites for every human alive, on a much tinier land area. They accomplish this primarily because of the skillful architecture and engineering of the termite mounds. The termites of sub-Saharan Africa build mounds in mud which stand on average three metres high and contain a complex system of channels and ducts of different sizes. The termites do not live in these mounds, rather, their nest lies in the ground underneath it, the mound serves to regulate the temperature and humidity of the nest while ventilating it. Its exact size and design is continually modified to deal with changing populations and seasonal climatic differences.

Within the nest, temperatures fluctuate no more than one degree Celsius while outside, daytime temperatures exceed forty degrees and night time plummets to below freezing. The million or so inhabitants produce collectively the same respiratory gas exchange as a cow, and this is also dealt with in the mound. They farm a fungus just above the nest, which is allowed to rot prior to eating to aid digestion. This is carried out with a minimum of energy, the construction and upkeep of a typical mound involves no more than 10% of the colony's annual expenditures of energy.

In making such a perfectly-tuned tool, the termites have been able to externalise many bodily functions, particularly temperature control, digestion and respiration. This is done with no input of external energy apart from what is passively available on site. Thus their race is able to thrive with little environmental damage.

It seems that there is a lot that we can learn about the construction of environmentally stable structures from these mounds, and a multi-disciplinary team from Loughborough University in England is carrying out an amazing research project that is studying the mounds and trying to apply what they are discovering to the task of proposing more intelligent structures for human habitation.

This termite mound, in its extreme complexity of form, simplicity of material and functional effectiveness, is a compelling object. It stands however as something ambiguous; for me it is an example of an artifact that does not rest happily in a natural classification, nor in an artificial one. It starts to question this classification system entirely.

Structures in the Landscape

If we look at it coldly, rationally, leaving religion and philosophy to the side, the building work done by animals is no different to that carried out by man; perhaps it is less concerned in general with aesthetics (though the bauer bird constructs functionless monuments to attract a mate). The thing that often makes it stand out is its effectiveness with regard to survival within a

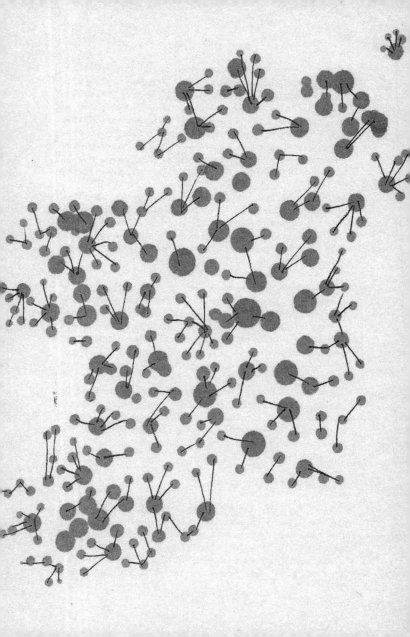

given landscape, using limited means.

If we accept man as a part of the natural world, it leaves us in a very different position when examining our houses and settlements, they become simply natural phenomena that are either effective for their use or not. We are just one of countless millions of interdependent living and inanimate systems that have a complex web of relationships with each other, and our survival as one of these systems depends on our ability to co-exist in a sensitive balance with the others.

All we really ask of our houses is that they keep us warm and dry, and protect us from intruders. At the moment we achieve this with huge wastages of energy and material. These simple demands should be obtainable through passive means utilising only local materials in all but the least hospitable landscapes. Over the last century, using fossil fuel reserves has made us lazy in this regard, because in fact, like the houses of animals, our vernacular buildings (architectural heritage) were simple, smart and easy to construct. If we learn from our past and from species around us and add to this our contemporary technical know-how and our intellectual cleverness as a species, we can once more make houses that are a balanced part of the landscape in which they are sited as opposed to being hosted by that landscape.

If we examine our houses and settlements unfettered by our inherited feelings of superiority, they appear to be inefficient in their use of resources, and to be too reliant on energy inputs from afar, from out of our direct control.

Twenty Four.
Grafton Architects,
Shelly McNamara & Yvonne Farrell
Bocconi University Extension,
Milan, 2008

Oral presentation from World Architecture
Festival, 2008 (with preface by Shane O'Toole,
Architecture Ireland, Issue 242, November 2008)

World Architecture Festival Diary
Friday, 23 October, 2008, Barcelona

722 entries from 63 countries have been whittled down over the past two days from a shortlist of 224 to 17 category winners and finalists. News of Grafton's (Grafton Architects, Shelley McNamara and Yvonne Farrell) learning category win on Wednesday has broken at home. *The Sunday Times* wants an article for next weekend. Lord Foster resigns from the Super Jury, as his Smithsonian Institution won the New & Old category yesterday. Bob Stern takes over as chair and Süha Özkan joins the jury alongside Cecil Balmond, Ricky Burdett and Charles Jencks.

Foster sits in the front row for most of the 17 presentations, while Stern keeps things rattling along at a good pace. Wolf Prix antagonises the jury as much as Sou Fujimoto charms them with his Final Wooden House. Shelley (McNamara) and Yvonne (Farrell) give the performance of their lives. They spent all day yesterday refining their ten-minute pitch. Balmond is their champion, although he criticizes Bocconi's 'anemic' glazing. Jencks thinks Milan needs less stone. Özkan supports the urban concept. Burdett keeps his powder dry. Is that good or bad? It's clear that the Graftons will be in the final shake-up. Yvonne reckons Fujimoto is the biggest threat and I agree.

While the Super Jury deliberates, we listen to critic William Curtis describe how Le Corbusier is an architect for all seasons. Two hours later, in the Fòrum's cavernous Grand Auditorium, Paul Finch announces the winner of the largest-ever architectural awards programme – the first World Building of Year. Irish architecture will never be the same.

– Extracted from Shane O'Toole's '*World Architecture Festival Diary*', published in *Architecture Ireland* 242, November 2008.

The following is a two-person oral presentation by Grafton Architects, Dublin, at the first World Architecture Festival, 2008. The architects are presenting their building (an extension to the Bocconi University, Milan) to the judges and they have 10 minutes to do so. This discourse is an exemplar in how to reduce the making and experience of architecture to words and by the ticking of the clock. This is the art of the architectural presentation. Students, learn!

Shelley McNamara:

This is an extension to Bocconi University which is embedded into the urban grain of central Milan.
The idea was to make two worlds, one hovering over the other, with the space of the city flowing between.
We wanted to the make the university as a 'place of exchange' and Il Broletto, the medieval market building in the centre of Milan, was a reference point.
We were affected and influenced by the solidity and robust monumental quality of the walls of the city.
In the scheme, 1,000 professors occupy an inhabited roofscape. The carved ground forms the public spaces below.
A large scale structure allows us to hang the offices from the roof, liberating the public spaces below.
We took the public space of the city through the building bringing with it the stone floor of Milan. This opens the university to the life of the city. In fact the building feels like a city in miniature.
Conference and professors foyers co-exist on this stone plate. The entrance courtyard placed centrally in the plan is the point at which the organization and spatial complexity reveals itself.
There is a shift in scale to the repetitive grain of the offices above which form a labyrinth of courts, voids and routes making a perforate canopy to the public spaces.
Offices form beams of space which span 25m. Public spaces cascade to 9m below ground.
This is a non-compositional approach to making space. The strategy of holding two worlds apart forms a third more open-ended world which allows the life of the city to enter in.
We came to Milan with a strategy but the struggle was to find a language appropriate to that city.
Close by on Corso Italia is the heroic Moretti building but we

also looked to the character of the ordinary city for direction.

Viale Bligny with its stone floor; Milan, a city of hard exteriors and light interiors.

The big move was to place the Aula Magna on the most public corner. As Hugh Campbell states, 'It rises out of the underworld as a kind of invitation to the city.'

We gave the university a 'window to Milan'. A type of Chinese lantern which engages with the citizens of Milan.

The solid elements are the carved ground, the auditorium and the library wall or shield.

These form a hard exterior within which the lighter more aerated world of the offices and courts exist.

It was the programme that required that the conference facilities be placed below ground.

Courts and voids provide light and ventilation to both the offices as well as to the spaces below.

The outer urban crust rises out of or hovers over the ground.

Yvonne Farrell:

The cantilivered Aula Magna draws the space of the city into the lower foyer at 5 metres below street level.

The Aula holds 1,000 people.

Three light-scoops (periscope roof-lights) interlock with the office courtyards above.

Interlocking volumes of the Departmental Libraries encourage social overlap.

These interlocking volumes are represented on the facade.

This forms a vertical urban 'crust'.

The horizontal urban 'crust' of the city floor is also worked and carved.

The primary structure is placed at 25-metre intervals. We thought about the building as a piece of infrastructure at the scale of the city.

Inhabited diaphragm walls form the main circulation at office levels.

Roof beams span the 25 metres onto these diaphragm walls.

Steel rods hang from these roof beams to support the floors of the offices below.

This section describes 'lightness', where elements are hung from above, forming undulating soffits.

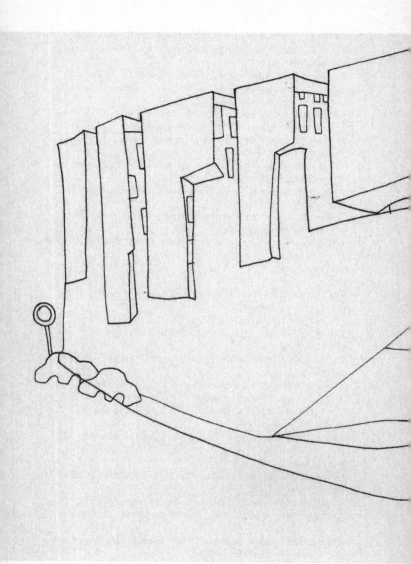

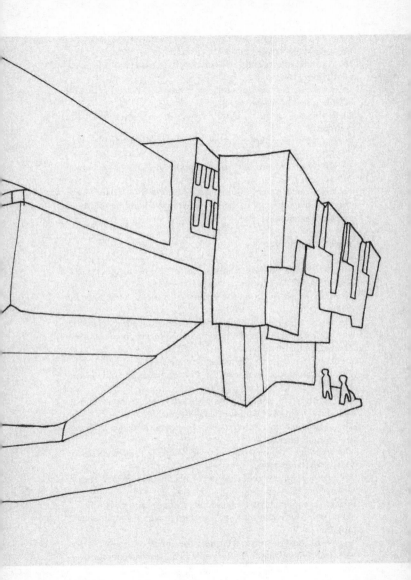

Whereas, this section describes 'weight', where the element of the Aula Magna erupts out of the ground.

In previous projects and in this one, we have made multi-layered, ventilating glass skins.

Here we see the pivotal entrance courtyard, placed centrally, both in plan and in section.

Glass shingles form the light – reflective, airy interiors of the courtyards,

in contrast to the hard external 'crust', which presents itself to the city.

We have used a local stone called 'ceppo', which is like geological concrete.

We have used a fixing system used traditionally in Milan, where 'ceppo' is fixed directly to the walls, giving the buildings of Milan a monolithic quality.

Shelley McNamara:

The entry sequence penetrates the solid form of the building
A new public space forms an urban threshold.
The delayed entry allows the visitor, en-route, to view into the sunken foyer.
The cantilevered Aula Magna almost touches the library element.
The library hovers over the street to make an entrance canopy.
The façade folds and laps.
Light and views are through cracks in the surface.
The interlocking volumes of the library are expressed on the street.
The south edge has a loose informal relationship with the boundary in contrast with the Viale Bligny edge.
The offices, bridges, courts and connections make a three-dimensional weave.
The building takes its place in the Milan skyline with Torre Valaska in the distance.
The elements come together to form a distinct corner and to make a public space.
Space is compressed and released horizontally and vertically.
Skewered connections to the city are made throughout the building.
A sense of compression is felt under the entrance canopy.
Offices bridging 25m form the entry to the central courtyard.

The level of the city runs through. Outdoor courts light the conference halls below.

A stepped courtyard functions as a public space.

The private independent world of the professors have their own grand staircase slung in the navelike space behind the library shield.

Other stairs in the building are carved but this one feels as if it is suspended in the space.

The balustrade forms a beam to support this staircase and the landings and galleries form the social space for the professors.

Yvonne Farrell:

A stepped external ramp forms an independent connection for students...to the conference facilities 9 metres below ground.

Here, we are standing 9 metres below ground, looking up at the entrance courtyard.

The entrance courtyard is held like a bridge, over the public spaces below.

From the entrance courtyard, you can see cascading public spaces.

By night, the atmosphere of the Foyer is waiting for life to enter in.

By day, the lower foyer is full of light, reflected by the Bianca Lasa marble floor.

As the light fades, the glass screen seems to disappear....and the city comes more into play.

Here, we see the diagonal spatial connections, the undulating soffits and...clerestory light coming from suspended gardens.

The finer stone is like the interior of an oyster shell...which continues into the Aula Magna.

While the rest of the building is about making spatial connections beyond the individual space.

The Aula Magna is a 'cocooned' space, animated by natural light.

Conclusion:

An inspiration for us was the theatricality of the Duomo roof where one moves through and within the structure and one is visually connected with the multiple layers and ledges of this construct.

We are inspired by the labyrinthine multi-layered quality of the space which has been described as 'a kind of light Piranesi'. Our client says:

> *I believe that one can feel the soul of the people who designed this building and who built it. For everybody day by day it has been the discovery of a new volume, of a new surface, and this has been for me a very beautiful experience.*

We wanted to make this building feel like a 'piece of Milan'. We feel that this building has come out of Milan. We have anchored the building into this city culturally and physically. We have made a building with mass and weight, like the buildings of Milan. But we have opened it up to the life of the city, connecting the life of the university with the life of the city.

<u>Twenty Five.</u>
<u>Catherine Marshall</u>
Re-location/Dis-location, 2008

New Piece of writing

We tend to think of architecture as 'civilized' as opposed to 'natural' and therefore as an urban rather than a rural art-form, notwithstanding the many great buildings in rural settings. A number of Irish architects have broken surface in the last few years with projects that embrace their rural heritage. It is important to pay attention when someone like Tom De Paor calls on both the rural and his Irish heritage at one and the same moment with a house made of turf briquettes for that most cosmopolitan and sophisticated of contexts, to represent his country at the Venice Biennale.[1]

Another Irish architect, Dominic Stevens, has gone even further, moving to live and work in rural County Leitrim, where he has designed a number of very contemporary houses that are specifically planned to embrace the age-old traditions of country life and the needs of both the communities who live there and of the local ecology. Stevens is taking a long view of the needs of his chosen environment and the socio-ecological systems that currently sustain it and, hopefully, will continue to do so. In a thoughtful rationale, *Rural*, Stevens defends his move from Dun Laoghaire - a highly developed and long-established metropolitan heartland on the outskirts of Dublin - to County Leitrim, traditionally one of the most under-populated areas of the country.[2] Perhaps the most profound of the many of powerful discoveries he has made as a result of this move is the depth of knowledge he is acquiring from engaging with his new surroundings physically, by working his five acres of land, rather than merely observing them. As he writes in *Rural*, *'I had entered a world where it seemed more creative to dig the ground than to think about digging it.'*[3]

It is here that his work most closely approaches the work of another expatriate from Dublin South County – the artist Juliana Walters. After years in London and Paris where she earned a glamorous living accessorising for the stars of the international music world, Walters came home to Ireland to settle with her husband and young family, not in suburbia but in the middle of farming land in north Co. Wexford.

Interesting questions of identity arise for both Stevens and Walters. How do they fit into their new environments? In accommodating themselves to their respective new homes and habitats, do they abandon their former identities as they develop new ones? Can their urban selves co-exist alongside the rural ones?

Juliana Walters is a conceptual artist. That inevitably means that her community of peers is relatively small and fairly widely scattered throughout Ireland, with an equally inevitable concentration on larger urban centres. Unlike Stevens, the work that she does is not easily seen as fulfilling a community service and meeting a visible need. Whether we like it or not, architecture is perceived to have more relevance for most people than contemporary art. While Stevens can go back to the essential elements of domestic architecture and happily divide humankind into 'tenters' and 'burrowers', as they alternatively settle and farm or pursue a more mobile, nomadic existence, Walters is less sustained by community perceptions.[4] For her, the experience of dis-location has to be analysed and explored primarily in a very personal way.

The isolation of rural life has led her to question her very visibility. Since her former life locked her to the world of fashion, where appearance is everything, Walters began by investigating the very things that had fed that life. In place of the make-up that she might have used to present herself as a city dweller, she now used mascara and false eyelashes to create images of natural creatures such as butterflies and insects and measured the passage of time by cleaning the filter of her washing machine at calibrated intervals and creating sculpted objects from the fluff she gathered as a result.

Potato Picking in Ballyfad was one of the most powerful artworks she made after her return to Ireland. As Walters points out, 'It formed part of a series of small events linked to some investigations/research I was carrying out titled 'Rethinking the Rural.' [5] The work involved digging potatoes on the land of a neighbouring farmer. She could hardly have picked a more archetypal image of agricultural labour in Ireland, celebrated in literature by Brian Friel, Seamus Mac Grianna, and Patrick Kavanagh, and in painting by Paul Henry and Gerard Dillon, to name but a few. Walters eschewed the bare feet and red flannel skirts of Paul Henry's potato pickers in favour of a designer coat in bright yellow, while her high-heeled shoes sink into the wet Wexford clay, dragging her down like the leg irons of a chain gang.

Perhaps the most significant thing about this performance was that she did not film the process or invite an audience. The question for her was does the artwork happen if it does not have an audience? Must visual art be visible and if it must be, how visible can it be in a rural setting without altering the rural? If Dominic Stevens feels that it is better to dig than to think about digging, Juliana Walters suggests that it is better to make art than to think about audiences and visibility.

The labour of digging in her urban outfit is the metaphor for the two polarities she seeks to reconcile:

> At the time I made a decision not to record the potato picking event by way of images - it was more an intimate project based around dialogue, exchange - the bartering of time between the local farming family and myself, where potato picking was one of a few tasks I undertook.[6]

Walters chose to make ephemeral work that left no trace on the landscape, to make the act of digging in her city clothes a performance, the reward for which was the exchange that took place between her as an artist and the community of which she is now a part.

In 2006 Walters made the short film *Spaltung* in which she is seen, dressed in another urban outfit - a bright, red coat - running into a forest along a grassy path with an elastic rope in her hand. The elastic is tied to a tree and Walters runs into the forest clutching it until it can stretch no further. It snaps backward, forcing her to repeat the process again, and again, in a vain attempt to measure her place:

> I feel the recorded performance Spaltung, the sculpture Between a Beach Stone and a Metal Ball, the mascara compositions and a site-specific work I made in the local forest, all form part of a body of work which is based on the shift from urban to rural - my attempt to find balance, mark of space, test limits and 'fit in' etc.[7]

Stevens has referred to the Irish countryside now as a 'serviced landscape' rather than a place in which the craft of farming is still current.[8] Walters' attempt to measure space in *Spaltung* might be possible in the geometry of the city but is harder to pin down when the co-ordinates are organic and therefore constantly changing, expanding, even dying. Her personal dilemma is emphasized in this work through the use of digitally generated mirror imagery of the measuring process. The effect of this is to create a number of digital clones of herself, of the wooded laneway and the surrounding trees, questioning further our hold on our sense of individuality and our knowledge of our surroundings.

Far from Stevens' 'spread-out-city' that is most people's experience of the countryside now, Walters re-asserts the power and the otherness of nature.[9] The figure in red recalls archetypal folk images such as Rose Red, or Little Red Riding Hood, lost in a terrifying forest, with paths that inevitably confound and confuse. The term 'spaltung', meaning 'splitting' was used by Freud to refer to fracturing of the individual personality. Confronted with the wilderness in this instance the lone figure splits into an infinite number of selves while the forest similarly divides but also appears to re-group to form brooding, totem-like presences that could be either menacing or comforting. The craftsmanship of the countryside that Dominic Stevens yearns for may provide the ultimate solution, but within the terms of Walters' work that solution is a long way off, and the wilderness, far from being the serviced landscape that Stevens denounces, grows more mysterious and elusive as the figure in the city dress fragments.

Faced with the eternal dilemma of how to define themselves in different contexts, both architect and artist resort to their creativity. When challenged by their new environments, they look to their art forms to help them to make sense of them. While Stevens makes houses that acknowledge the primeval 'tenter' and 'burrower' needs of a particular community in a particular place, Walters' art balances the urban and rural in a personal way that is ultimately so in tune with archetypal anxieties it reaches out to the universal. The final positions of artist and architect may be different but for both of them, the important thing is to make work using the tools they have available to them.

Doubting his ability to emulate his father's craftsmanship in another potato field, the poet, Seamus Heaney said,

> Between my finger and my thumb
> The squat pen rests.
> I'll dig with it.[10]

Walters and Stevens are in good company.

Footnotes

1 - Tom De Paor, N3, Irish Pavilion, Venice Biennale, 2000

2 - Dominic Stevens, *Rural*, (Cloone: Mermaid Turbulence, Arts Council – Kevin Kieran Award, 2007)

3 - Ibid, p.13

4 - Stevens discusses tents and caves, using the terms 'tenters' and 'burrowers' in Ibid, pp. 73 - 74

5 - Juliana Walters, unpublished correspondence with the author, November 2007

6 - Ibid.

7 - *Spaltung* and the other works referred to here were shown in the exhibition *Surface Tension*, Wexford Arts Centre, and through the Arts Council's *Touring Experiment* in Raheen, Co. Clare, May 2007; The Source Art Centre, Thurles, July 2007; and Broadstone Studios, Dublin, December 2007-January 2008.

8 - Stevens, *Rural*, p.19

9 - The term 'spread-out city' is used by Stevens in Ibid, p.27

10 - The final 'verse' of Seamus Heaney's famous poem *'Digging'* (1966), in *Death of a Naturalist*. London: Faber & Faber

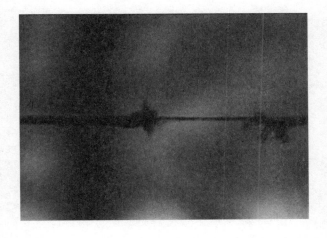

Practiced Distance, 2007, video still, © Juliana Walters

<u>**Twenty Six.**</u>
<u>**Anna Ryan**</u>
<u>*Writing Architecture, 2009*</u>

New piece of writing

A small boy holds his mother's hand. Together, they walk to
school, traversing a network of poor, wet fields.

> The fields between the lakes are small, separated by thick
> hedgerows of whitethorn, ash, blackthorn, alder, sally, rowan, wild
> cherry, green oak, sycamore....In their branches the wild woodbine
> and dog rose give off a deep fragrance in summer evenings, and on
> their banks grow the foxglove, the wild strawberry, primrose and
> fern and vetch among the crawling briars....A maze of lanes link the
> houses that are scattered sparsely about these fields, and the lanes
> wander into one another like streams until they reach some main
> road. These narrow lanes are still in use. In places, the hedges that
> grow on the high banks along the lanes are so wild that the trees
> join and tangle above them to form a roof, and in the full leaf of
> summer it is like walking through a green tunnel pierced by vivid
> pinpoints of light.[1]

An elderly woman holds a carpet bag. Alone, she walks through
the city, away from her room in an austere boarding house.

> Ice on the pavement, on the gratings and architraves, the street like
> a wedding cake in a dream. In one of the houses a pipe must have
> burst, for water is trickling down the steps and into the servants'
> area at the front and three hapless men with mops are looking at it.
> But touches of weak sun redeem the council-grown shrubberies and
> the trees in the tiny triangle of park. [2]

I choose to open this essay on Writing Architecture with these
two written moments, moments that offer the settings for
particular lives at particular times. Precisely constructed, these
short passages immediately present the reader with fully formed
worlds; yet there is room in those worlds of words for the reader
to imagine, to inhabit, to experience. The reader walks with the
young boy, walks with the old woman, is physically present in

their tangibly described worlds. Taken from Irish writers of the twentieth- and twenty-first centuries – John McGahern and Joseph O'Connor – these texts are different in time, location and intent. From a memoir beginning in Leitrim in the 1930s and a novel opening in London in the 1950s, the craft of these writers relies on them constructing believable worlds of words. There is a close intensity to their observations and projections, at the same time as a complete ordinariness. There is consideration given to the subtle details of light, to variations of texture and materiality, to the sense-able presences of temperature, touch and smell, along with a definite awareness of scale. In attending to these aspects of the experiential world, their writing is powerfully spatial, deeply architectural.

Within the discipline and practice of architecture, however, writing is rarely architectural in and of itself. In the professional world of architecture, writing generally tends to operate in two main ways. Firstly, writing is used to prosaically describe an architectural project – its brief and its construction. Secondly, writing is used to critique an architectural project – its concept, its built form, its relationships within history and society. In both approaches, the writing is separate to the architecture. An opportunity is being lost. It is this lost opportunity that I wish to here address.

Having stepped to one side of the discipline of architecture for a number of years, and having engaged myself fully in the discipline of geography, I returned to architecture with a much more perceptive understanding of its operation. I now help to immerse first-year students into the world and culture of architecture – a very significant challenge as it is all wholly new to them – and through this teaching I have come to recognize very apparent similarities between the processes of designing and those of writing. Through introducing and reinforcing the conceptual and practical activities of architectural design, I have realized that I am teaching them how to manipulate space in order to express an (architectural/spatial) idea. My writing practice follows the very same motivations. I manipulate words to express an idea. Selecting brick as the sole material with which to define the thresholds, direct the light, texture the ground, sculpt the courtyards, and vault the ceilings of, for example, a domestic house – pushing the use of brick to its very limits – operates in an analogous way to shifting word order, varying sentence length, developing fluid yet coherent movement between paragraphs, and intensifying vocabulary. One practice constructs and manipulates three-dimensional space. One practice constructs and manipulates one-dimensional words. But both volumetric enclosure and written text can work through and define spatial ideas. What links both processes of spatial understanding is the person (author-architect) and their negotiation of their surroundings. I turn to Wittgenstein to articulate this. As philosopher, teacher and self-taught architect he wrote, 'Working in philosophy – like working in architecture in many respects – is really more a working on oneself. On one's own interpretation. On one's way of seeing things. (And what one expects of them).' [3] In other words, the production of (spatial) knowledge, in whatever form it emerges, is grounded in personal situation. [4]

This understanding of architecture as a working on one's way of seeing things is well understood. Amongst practitioners of the discipline, architecture is recognized as far more than building; architecture is a way of thinking about the world; architecture is a way of approaching and engaging (with) the world. At its most interesting and influential, this architectural thinking, these architectural engagements, embrace the political and social, the visceral and emotional, the logistical and environmental, the historical and strategic. It can be argued that the ultimate most important aspect of architecture is when such thinking, such approaches, result in a physical building – a set of spaces in which one can talk, eat, laugh, sleep, work. Architecture becomes functional space...?

When architecture emerges as built form, however, it is always striving for something more than pure function. This searching is at the core of the ideal practice of constructing architecture. In its ambition for itself, built architecture searches for a technological exploration, or a visual beauty, or a quality of material texture, or a sequential clarity of spaces, or a spatial intensity that moves the emotion, that strikes the body – a wholeness of experience that effects the person whilst in the space and when no longer there. Thus architecture, at its most powerful, changes the individual, even temporarily; changes their sense of themselves and their relations with others and with their surroundings. If and when it doesn't, architecture collapses into building. Architecture becomes a search for moments of experience, and the after-life of those experiences...?

In recognizing architecture thus, as both tangible presence and aspiration towards presence, architecture has the potential to be practised in many ways. Making physical buildings – building architecture – is the most obvious and most accepted mode of practising architecture. But writing architecture, writing as architecture, needs to be considered just as central to the motivations and interests of the discipline – as a way of thinking and operating spatially, as a way of inspiring particular ways of being and acting in the world. One can question why the role of writing within the discipline of architecture generally tends to separate the creative activity of the discipline from the critical. One can question why the role of writing within architecture is generally not regarded as an integral part of the discipline's creativity. Practices of architecture generally rely on representations to put forward and explore ideas in and for the world. Drawing and model-making – both real and virtual – are currently the central means of representing these architectural ideas. However, as a starting point for considering writing architecture – writing as architecture – it is important to first consider the (potential) role of writing as mode of representation within the process of constructing architecture. To consider this relationship between representation and reality, I look to the work of James Corner and Dalibor Vesely.

In his investigation of the once purposeful and future-oriented sense central to the concept of landscape, Corner observes how, 'Changes in cultural practices and modes of understanding may precede or follow from innovations in representation.' [5] He notes that 'The pictorial impulse denies deeper modes of existence, interrelationship, and creativity,' [6] and continues to observe that landscape architects prioritize visual and formal imaging over other forms of imaging such as acoustic, tactile, cognitive or intuitive imaging. [7] Corner proposes the development of new idea-imaging techniques – he calls them eidetic operations – that embrace the full dimensions of being, beyond only vision and the picture-able, maintaining that,

> *how one 'images' the world literally conditions how reality is both conceptualized and shaped. That representation exercises such agency and effect is precisely why images in design cannot properly be considered as mute or neutral depictions of existing and projected conditions of secondary significance to their object; on the contrary, eidetic images are much more active than this, engendering, unfolding, and participating in emergent realities.*[8]

Thus Corner is challenging the discipline to develop new representational approaches and methods in order to imagine, participate and project in ways relevant to contemporary conditions. He is endeavouring to open up practice beyond the limitations inherent in the mechanisms of the discipline's existing representational modes. His interest is not so much in the images themselves but in the activities and experience of imaging – and what can emerge from them.

Corner's emphasis on the activity of imaging, his sense of representation as participation with the world, and his call for an exploration of representations – or idea-images – relevant to the fullness of our human embeddedness in the world all resonate with the work of architectural theorist Dalibor Vesely. Vesely's writing challenges contemporary and future architectural practice to recognise the potential embedded within a situated or contextual approach to spatial creativity. By placing importance on that which comes before the act of thinking, Vesely foregrounds prereflective experience. He presents how, because of the challenges of communication, the significance of this deep aspect of the world often goes overlooked; however, he calls for a new poetics of architecture that places importance on the emergence of architecture from this close acknowledgement of situation, context and natural world. This attitude to architecture is concentrated on the everyday-ness of life, what Vesely terms as 'typical situations'. Addressing representation is central to this call for a new poetics of architecture. Vesely presents the purpose of representation as having a mediating, communicative and participatory role 'because it enhances our ability to participate in phenomenal reality.'[9] However, he examines how modern science's search for order and certainty brought about a significant change in the representation of reality. This transformation led to the belief 'that our life can be entirely represented in terms of scientific, technical rationality, leaving behind all that cannot be subordinated to this vision – mainly the domain of personal experience, praxis, and the natural world.' [10] Vesely's difficulty is with representation that claims to be independent, with what he terms emancipatory representation: representation that separates the results from the original communicative context.[11]

Both Corner and Vesely are motivated by the potential of opening up ways of exploring and communicating (spatial) ideas. For both, this openness to the myriad possibilities of process-led and participatory representation is key to the development of relevant and grounded architectural projections. How could writing, as creative practice, fit with their visions for a new poetics of architecture, for a recovery of the agency of landscape? As with any representational technique, writing has its own limitations as a mode of communication, different, but no less important, than the limitations of drawing as representational tool, or model-making as representation tool. Writing is bound up with the complexities of language, and language is embedded within established structures of meaning. However, in embracing the potential within any set of limits, new possibilities can emerge. So, what vision can be had for architectural writing within the discipline? How can architecture as enveloping spatial sequence, be explored through the medium of words? Can a proposition at the scale of the body be presented, and thus visualised and viscerally (if virtually) experienced through an arrangement of words? To respond to this, it is important to draw attention to the capabilities critical within literary fiction. This pushes the discussion to consider writing, not as mode of representation for architecture, but as architecture.

This sense of the power of projection and agency within literary writing was very well expressed by Colm Tóibín in his opening address to the 2009 Listowel Writers' Week in Co. Kerry. He spoke of how 'writing...is, at its simplest, a way of changing the world.' Like Corner emphasising the activity of imaging over the image itself, or Vesely emphasising the potential of representations to participate with the world, Tóibín discussed the importance for writers not to focus on the product – the book – but rather on the process of writing. Constructing a piece of writing offers a particular outlook on the world, an outlook that is shared through a communication of words with the reader. Tóibín articulated such a relationship.

> *Instead of changing how we live [the reading experience], can intensify it, offer it shape and meaning... Writing is not a way to offer the reader a window on the world, but a way of closing the curtains, darkening the room, so that something previously invisible, something that before now feared the light, can now become privately present.*[12]

There is a great intensity of focus in making visible and tangible an aspect of the world; this making involves a great precision on the part of the writer. Raymond Carver describes the work of a writer as trying to find 'a unique and exact way of looking at things, and finding the right context for expressing that way of looking.'[13] The architect, intent on constructing the world in a physical sense through the assemblage of three-dimensional matter, could perhaps open interesting opportunities for his or her work in embracing the fiction writer's approach to the observation, projection and construction of the world through the assemblage of language. Indeed, perhaps the descriptions of the fiction writing process as touched on by Tóibín and Carver offer a lead to contemporary architectural practice; the ways in which they articulate the agency of the writing process could perhaps give a direction towards an architecture encouraged by Vesely that emerges from a creative engagement with context and with the deeper levels of everyday life.

Thinking about writing as intensifying and (re)shaping the world prompts a consideration of the role of writing within the architectural design process. In architecture, the relationship between the design process and writing predominantly remains one of reportage, documentation, detached pragmatic description, or intellectual discussion that clearly supports, but is not central to the proposal in its concrete-ness. Though there are a few minor exceptions, in general writing is not explored as a design tool. Within my current role guiding the learning experiences of undergraduate architectural students, I have made various forays into exploring with students the potential of writing within the design process. These explorations offer moments for them to develop and deepen aspects of their growing design abilities, as well as revealing ways of beginning to address, in a more widespread manner, the lost opportunity of writing practices within the discipline: explorations of writing that presents the spatial character of the project in a compelling manner; writing that explores the boundaries or limitations of the architectural drawing or model in communicating the experiential qualities of the spaces being proposed; writing that intensely suggests the materiality of the project, its relationship with its inhabitants. In many ways, this writing could be described as phenomenological – concerned with communicating as direct an experience as possible of the proposal. In a school of architecture, if a student does not have drawings and models on the wall, there is deemed to be no architectural project; however, establishing writing as a central design tool can only lead to a more fruitful situation for architectural representation. Experiential and exploratory writing has something significant to offer the architectural design process.

We must wonder why writing – as an activity central to the formation of imagined and projected literary worlds – is generally sidelined within architectural design processes in favour of drawing and making. We must test how writing can develop alongside drawing and making as a representational activity essential to the development of architectural propositions for the world. We must explore how writing practices within the discipline can become – in and of themselves – valid as architecture. Writing architecture; architectural writing; within these lie the starting threads of a narrative, potent and perhaps provocative, worth being woven towards a pattern of thought and practice.

Footnotes

1 - John McGahern, *Memoir* (London: Faber and Faber, 2005), pp. 1-2.

2 - Joseph O'Connor, *Ghost Light* (London: Harvill Secker, 2010) p. 27.

3 - Ludwig Wittgenstein, 1931, quoted in Robert Mugerauer, *Interpreting Environments: Tradition, Deconstruction, Hermeneutics* (Austin: University of Texas Press, 1995), p. 13.

4 - This personal situation is, of course, contingent on many factors including societal, educational, geographical and embodied contexts.5 James Corner in James Corner and Alex S. MacLean, *Taking Measures Across the American Landscape* (New Haven and London: Yale University Press, 1996), p. 18.

6 - James Corner, 'Eidetic Operations and New Landscapes,' in *Recovering Landscape: Essays in Contemporary Landscape Architecture*, ed. James Corner (New York: Princeton Architectural Press, 1999), p. 158. 7 - Corner, 'Eidetic Operations,' p. 153.

8 - Corner, 'Eidetic Operations,' p. 153.

9 - Dalibor Vesely, *Architecture in the Age of Divided Representation: The Question of Creativity in the Shadow of Production* (Cambridge, Massachusetts: The MIT Press, 2004), p. 19.

10 - Vesely, *Divided Representation*, p. 29.

11 - Vesely, *Divided Representation*, p. 19.

12 - Colm Tóibín, opening address to Listowel Writers' Week, June 2009

13 - Raymond Carver, 'On Writing,' in *Fires: Essays, Poems, Stories*, Raymond Carver (London: The Harvill Press, 1985), p. 22.

Twenty Seven.
Paul Kearns/Motti Ruimy

Can't See The Scale Of It, 2010

From Kearns & Ruimy, *Redrawing Dublin*
(Kinsale: Gandon Editions, 2010)

Architects, urban designers and planners increasingly talk about 'scale' or more importantly 'appropriate scale' in city making. Understanding what is an 'appropriate scale' for a development on your street, your block or your city is apparently a magical formula for unearthing a critical component of successful city making. Get the scale right and you're more than half way there in the best practice of designing and managing successful and attractive urban spaces.

Scale is important in city making. It is the building blocks of form, determining positive and negative space, the places we inhabit and the places we walk through. Pinning down what constitutes appropriate scale is altogether more difficult. Definitions are somewhat elusive. 'Appropriate scale' seems, well, just that, obviously appropriate. Can imaginative, transformative, altered, or daring scales ever be 'appropriate'? Delightful, inspiring even? Who decides?

The experts or arbiters of 'appropriate scale' seem to find this pretty instinctive. Whilst each city obviously differs from the next, the 'appropriate scale' for each city, and each district in that city seems somehow intuitive or unconsciously understood for the arbiters of 'appropriate scale'. Whilst the rest of us struggle to decipher the laws of the science or rules governing 'appropriate scale', for others it feels, well, just right, it's a spontaneous and almost involuntary innate design reflex.

'Appropriate scale' in the context discussed above is instinctively understood to mean the height or massing of a single building or group of buildings relative to another building or group of buildings in a city block and its relationship to the width and length of the adjoining patterns of streets and public spaces.

We suspect however that the insightful invocation of 'appropriate scale' is fed less by either an astute understanding of mathematical volumetric relations, or an innate aesthetic sense or insight into universal laws of geometrical beauty, but by the rather simple but acute awareness of what we call the 'reality of the now', in other words a knowledge of what currently exists on or near the site in question.

Is it possible that the staunch advocates of 'appropriate scale' tend to confuse bad architecture with radical change of scale? For many they are simply one and the same thing. Perhaps that is understandable. There is a lot of average architecture around and increased scale only magnifies its mediocrity.

There is however nothing more disturbing or dislocating to the mind of those who fastidiously adhere to the received wisdom of 'appropriate scale' that there may in fact be a multiplicity of answers to what is 'appropriate scale'. That an infinite spectrum of possibilities exists, a kind of 'relativism of scale', informed by and dependent upon excellence in design and execution, each with a terrifyingly different but equally aesthetically and functionally satisfying answer to the question of 'what is the appropriate scale?'.

If the 'appropriate scale' is to be reduced to a kind of architectural moral relativism, then all sorts of urban delightful architectural designs are in theory at least imaginable. For the adherents or proponents of 'appropriate scale' however this is nothing short of a vision of urban dystopia, in effect a potential uncontrollable 'Pandora's box' of built possibilities, a form of perverse abnormal urban expression that is uncensorable or uncontrollable.

It is somewhat intriguing that many of those who most eloquently dissect the language and extol the virtues of the importance of 'appropriate scale' in city making - in Dublin at least - rarely extend their use of the word beyond a narrow range of, well, certain urban scales. It is interesting that the passionate interest and defence of the 'appropriate scale' of individual buildings rarely extends to a discussion of either the macro urban city scale (how big our city should be) or the micro liveable urban scale (how big our apartment home should be).

Somehow the importance of the appropriate scale of a building is instinctively understood in designing attractive sustainable urbanism whilst the scale of the city itself or the scale of the homes within it are either of marginal interest or somebody else's responsibility. We suspect the reason for this is rather simple. Just as the wisdom of appropriate scale is dependent on, the pedestrian observation of the now, the size of somebody else's apartment (it is invariably somebody else's), the size of the city is not as easily imagined or visually consumed and thus of little interest.

Yet effective designers of real urbanism require an understanding or at least an informed opinion of the very large and very small scales at which effective city making takes place.

City makers need to ask the intriguingly and increasingly more important question, how big should our city be? Should we plan to double the population or keep it stable? Reduce it or half it? Would doubling the population of Dublin City over the next twenty years significantly reduce Ireland's CO_2 output if over that same period the overall population of the State only marginally increased?

Similarly there is an urgent need for a robust debate on the role that the provision of spacious apartment design plays in consolidating urban living and a compact city. Would providing high density apartment family friendly homes, akin to suburban houses in Meath or Kildare affect consumer housing choice and thus potentially CO_2 output? What are the real, perhaps unspoken barriers to the desire to live in urban Dublin?

If Dublin is to understand the importance of scale in designing for its future - if scale is not to be interpreted as narrowly as how many floors is acceptable on a particular building - the city needs to broaden its understanding the importance of scale; a scale that is both really experienced and economically and environmentally understood and not just one that is simply casually observed or seen.

Twenty Eight.
Sandra O'Connell
Poetic Memory & Urban Imprint, 2010

Unpublished paper for Irish Studies conference,
Tromso, Norway, 2010

'When I think about architecture, images come into my mind', writes the Swiss architect Peter Zumthor.[1] While some images contain Zumthor's 'professional knowledge', the more marking appear to flow from deep within his childhood memory, as he illustrates:

> There was a time when I experienced architecture without thinking about it. Sometimes I can almost feel a particular door handle in my hand, a piece of metal shaped like the back of a spoon. I used to take hold of it when I went into my aunt's garden. That door handle still seems to me like a special sign of entry into a world of different moods and smells. I remember the sound of the gravel under my feet, the soft gleam of the waxed oak staircase, I can hear the heavy front door closing behind me as I walk along the dark corridor and enter the kitchen, the only really brightly lit room in the house.[2]

Poet Thomas Kinsella relates a similar sensory experience of domestic architecture and space in the poems collected in *A Dublin Documentary* (2006) – a dense volume that weaves together selected poems with childhood memoir, family chronology and black-and-white photography. Like Zumthor's re-imagined door handle, which offers 'a special sign of entry into a world of different moods and smells',[3] Kinsella refers in the poems repeatedly to the door itself as a threshold or gateway into an inner world, where the architecture is defined by sharp black and white contrasts of darkness and light – the 'black hole' set against the brightness of the 'whitewashed wall'.[4] The domestic interiors of Kinsella's childhood are womblike, dark passageways that lead into a rich sensory experience of sounds, textures and smells. In the poem 'Hen Woman':

> [....]
> The cottage door opened,
> A black hole

In a whitewashed wall so bright
The eyes narrowed.
Inside, a clock murmured 'Gong...'

The French philosopher Gaston Bachelard discusses in his seminal work *The Poetics of Space*, the importance of the house on our consciousness, from which we continuously draw: 'For our home is our corner of the world...it is our first universe, a real cosmos in every sense of the word'.[5] According to Bachelard's phenomenological study, the house *'furnishes us dispersed images and a body of images at the same time'* – while it is up to the 'imagination' to augment reality.[6] Bachelard refers to poetry as way of completing these images of the house, which have a 'psychological elasticity', as past and present merge: *'Through poems, perhaps more than through recollections, we touch the ultimate poetic depth of the space of the house'.[7]*

Kinsella's *A Dublin Documentary* delves deep into this childhood imagery of the home to portray both domestic space as well as a growing consciousness of the wider urban territory, as the protagonist's world expands from the enclosed courtyards and familiar back lanes into long journeys through the South Inner City streets. Kinsella's complex relationship with his birth city is formed, as we will see, by the tension between the perceived *'rural'* idyll of the *'white-washed cottage'*, lodged in the back lanes and low-rise working class neighbourhood of Inchicore and Kilmainham, above which towers the vast industrial complex of the Guinness Brewery, closely connected with Kinsella family history.

Imaginative Beginnings

The poems collected in *A Dublin Documentary* span several decades from Kinsella's literary beginnings in the 1950s with *Another September* (1958) to the 1999 collection, *The Familiar*. However, Kinsella devises his own chronology, as the poems are reprinted not in their order of original publication but in the poet's personal timeline of encounters with central characters and with his urban environment. *A Dublin Documentary* is organised in two parts. Part I – entitled *'...imaginative beginnings...'* – traces the poet's childhood and family background in the south inner city area of the Liberties, Inchicore and Kilmainham. Painted in black and white (as in the case of the accompanying photographs), the childhood world is one of marked contrast between the *'black hole'* domestic interior ['Hen Woman'] [8] and that of *'silent square courtyard[s]'* and *'white-washed cottages'.*[9] Set several years later, Part II discusses the poet's *'...second roots...'* as he returns to Dublin as a family man from lecturing in universities in the United States and settles in an altogether different middle-class environment:

> *...a pleasant house in the city centre, on Percy Place beside Husband Bridge, across the Canal from the Peppercanister Church, within sound of the church bell on Haddington Road, and with a coalman and his horse in our mews on Percy Lane.*[10]

'The History of the Kinsella or Kinchella Family' concludes the book as an epilogue. Based on a *'handwritten history of the family, by Jack Brophy, an uncle of Thomas Kinsella'*, it discusses the rural origins of the family in Wicklow, Wexford and Carlow, which are of central importance to the poet.

Kinsella's poems are densely populated with characters from his childhood and youth but the central protagonist is the city itself – from the industrial Liberties, Kilmainham and Inchicore to the Georgian City of Percy Place and the Peppercanister Church on Upper Mount Street. Yet the book's very title, *A Dublin Documentary*, is ambiguous, suggesting an objective, fact-based account, whereas the city is explored from the highly personal and subjective viewpoint of the poet. This ambivalence is hinted at in the selection and reproduction of the urban photographs, contributed mostly by Seamus Fitzpatrick. Kinsella's selected scenes range from urban details – a street sign, a cobble stone, a fountain, a monument – to the larger streetscapes of Ely Place, Baggot Street and Haddington Road. The hard urban infrastructure is softened by images of the leafy Grand Canal. Printed in black and white, darker than normal and somewhat blurred, the photographs are evocative rather than specific. Their gritty and grainy nature evokes the dark atmosphere that is central to many of the poems as well as the very process of remembering.

A *Dublin Documentary* traces through these streetscapes and urban objects the intrinsic relationship of maturing self and expanding city, documenting the impact of place and locality on individual experience. For the reader, Kinsella's urban environment is specific and identifiable, recounted and retraced with almost forensic detail. His mental map of Dublin is imprinted with full-life characters and vivid memory: 'Basin Lane, off James's Street, near the Canal, not far from the Brewery' is the home of his maternal grandparents – the Casserlys; whereas the Kinsella grandparents live in 'Bow Lane, on the other side of James's Street, close to the end wall of Swift's hospital, and at the start of the road leading towards Kilmainham out of Dublin'. [11] Kinsella writes: 'It was in a world dominated by these people that I remember many things of importance happening to me for the first time'. [12]

In Kinsella's poetry, urban locations are closely linked, and made identifiable, through people. Streets, back lanes, houses and courtyards are only made meaningful by the presence of their occupiers. This awareness of place and its relationship with people, begins for Kinsella in the domesticity of the family home, where the dark interior of the Casserly home – a 'dark passageway' leads to two equally 'very dark' rooms, 'where the grandparents spent a lot of their time'[13] – becomes associated in the poem 'A Hand of Solo' with the 'black taffeta'[14] of the grandmother's dress and with the 'indigo darkness'[15] of the exotic pomegranate fruit he buys in her shop – a subtle hint at the expanding world outside.

The experience of interior space – the proportions, furnishings, smells and sounds – becomes also closely linked to the experience of losing a beloved family member or friend: The poetic self is 'swallowed' by the 'chambery dusk' and by the 'smell of disused / organs and sour kidney' emerging from the darkened bedroom where Grandmother Kinsella passes away in 'Tear'; [16] St James's bell is the only sound that penetrates the solitary silence of the 'Union ward', where a treasured elderly neighbour dies ['Dick King']; [17] while the 'grandparents' bed' in the poem 'Bow Lane' evokes the suffering of Uncle Tom Kinsella:

He died in here in 1916
of cancer of the colon/My father heard him
whispering to himself: 'Jesus
Jesus, let me off.' But nothing worked.

- 'Bow Lane' [18]

The urban environment of both grandparents' homes – Bow
Lane and Basin Lane – is decidedly working class, characterised
by single-storey cottages and two-storey terraced houses, owing
to the presence of two large employers, the Guinness Brewery
at St. James' Gate and the Great Southern Railway in Inchicore.
According to architectural historian, Christine Casey, *'Guinness
is the largest industrial complex in the city centre, covering a site of
almost 60 acres... from Marrowbone Lane and the former Grand Canal
Basin to the s(south) bank of the Liffey'.*[19] The Kinsella family is
closely associated with the Guinness brewery, where both the
poet's father and grandfather worked. Their memory is evoked in
the long poem *'The Messenger'*, when a Guinness representative
attends the funeral of Kinsella's father John Paul, who died May
1976:

> *Somebody well dressed*
> *Pressed my hand in the graveyard.*
> *A thoughtful delegated word or two:*
>
> *'His father before him...Ah, the barge captain...*
> *A valued connection. He will be well remembered...*
> *He lived in his two sons.'*

Thus, for Kinsella the area and activities of the historic Guinness
brewery in Dublin's inner city Liberties area are intrinsically
linked to the father and grandfather. The Guinness barge, sailing
the Rivery Liffey, evokes for Kinsella a dynamic and industrious
image of the grandfather – *'the barge captain'.*[20] Kinsella's Dublin
is an active city of industry, built in and around the marginal
areas of the city – the back lanes and back yards. The elderly
family friend, remembered in the poem *'Dick King'*, who worked
for the Inchicore Railworks – a vast 75-acre complex enclosed
by a high limestone wall, which provided employment to some
2,000 workers – moves through this complex urban maze and

enters the poet's world via a small gate across the backyards:

> *The Railway works were [...] reached by a walled-in passageway,*
> *through a turnstile directly facing St Mary's Terrace. This*
> *passageway led nowhere but into the works, and was called the*
> *Khyber Pass. And here is where Dick King emerged when he came*
> *to visit us in our house on Phoenix Street.*[21]

Alongside these vast industrial complexes of Guinness and the Inchicore Railworks, Kinsella also remembers the 'cottage industry' of the makeshift shop that supplemented the family income. Grandmothers Kinsella and Casserly are described as industrious *'formidable women' who 'both managed small shops in their houses'*.[22]

While for Kinsella, people give meaning to a place, places in turn evoke the memory of people. From the fountain on St. James's Street, for example, spring memories of the treasured family friend Dick King:

> *Clearly now I remember rain on the cobbles,*
> *Ripples in the iron trough, and the horses' dipped*
> *Faces under the Fountain in James's Street,*
> *When I sheltered my nine years against your buttons*
> *And your own dread years were to come:*
>
> *-'Dick King'* [23]

In the poem *'Irwin Street'*, it is the experience of 'morning sunlight' on the familiar well-trodden path that triggers memory for the school child:

> *Morning sunlight – a path of clear memory –*
> *warmed the path and the crumbling brick wall*
> *and stirred the weeds sprouting in the mortar.*

Exile & Second Roots

Kinsella's urban environment is gradually expanding, as he attends the Model School in Inchicore, although, as he recalls, 'a great deal of Dublin outside of these two small districts

[Inchicore and Kilmainham] would have seemed threatening and strange'.[24] After a brief spell in Manchester during the Second World War, Kinsella returns with his family to the inner city and recalls their re-settlement to the place of his early childhood years: 'our finding a tiny house in Basin Lane – a few doors from the Casserly shop'.[25] From there, Kinsella cycles across town to 'the North side', where he attends O'Connell's School on North Richmond Street. Although Kinsella's journeys are largely confined to Dublin's inner city, they can be read in the literary tradition of the Bildungsroman, where the protagonist embarks on his educational journey, as he uproots from the domestic environment and begins to mature and gain essential life experience in an ever-expanding world.

While the urban fabric is central to the development of Kinsella's voice, there is also a growing sense of distance and alienation from the familiar territory, as the poet questions his very belonging to the city. In the opening comments of *A Dublin Documentary*, Kinsella writes:

> *I am not, technically a Dubliner; despite being born and reared in Inchicore. I am told that for the full qualification three generations born in the city are needed. My children would qualify, if they wished; my parents were born in Dublin. Their own parents were all born in the country. My mother's parents, the Casserlys came from Ballinafid in County Westmeath; the Kinsellas from Tinahealy in County Wicklow.*

This poetic distance to the city permeates much of the poems collected in *A Dublin Documentary*. Although the poems are set in the city, the voice seeks belonging to another generation, celebrated by Kinsella for its connection with the country. In an interview with John Haffenden, Kinsella admits: 'I have a fairly complicated sense of Irish origins mixed up with my own first memories of life on a fringe of Dublin, an almost rural village'. The 'whitewashed wall' of the urban backyards, at the heart Dublin's industrial activity – a recurring architectural feature – evokes in Kinsella therefore ultimately a sense of belonging to the country.

Written some 70 years earlier than *A Dublin Documentary*, Samuel

Beckett's first collection of poems – *Echoe's Bones and Other Precipitates* – which was published in Paris in 1935 by the avant-garde Europa Press, might serve as a precursor to Kinsella's self-exile from the very city he celebrates. Beckett's urban territory is less confined than Kinsella's, as his Dublin map stretches from the very centre of O'Connell Street to Portobello harbour, where he follows along the Grand Canal a *'dying barge / carrying a cargo of nails and timber'*. Turning his back on the city, Beckett's poetic voice travels south where the world is 'opening up':

> *Then for miles only wind*
> *and the weals creeping alongside on the water*
> *and the world opening up to the south*
> *across a travesty of champaign to the mountains*
> *and the stillborn evening turning a filthy green*
> *manuring the night fungus*
> *and mind annulled*
> *wrecked in the wind.*
>
> - 'Enueg I' [26]

Beckett's haunting imagery of the 'still born' evening and 'night fungus' clearly enter the surrealist realm of the subconscious. Written in Paris and Dublin during the 1930s, the *Echoe's Bones* poems are equally influenced by James Joyce's experimentation with language and location, and by the stark, placeless interior landscapes of the French surrealists. Although Beckett's and Kinsella's urban wanderings rarely cross path in their respective collections, they share common ground in their growing estrangement from their environment. Kinsella's poetic voice is torn between belonging and a Beckett-like sense of self-exile and isolation.

In the poem *'The High Road'* Kinsella depicts in minute detail urban objects that populate his immediate environment and have become imprinted on his poetic memory – *'the shop door'*, *'the parapet of the bridge'*, the *'barred window'*, *'the brick pillars'*, *'the feathery grass'*. Yet the poem radiates, above all, a profound sense of loss. On his journey along *'The High Road'*, driven by impulse, he drops the grandmother's farewell gift of *'A silvery / little mandoline, out of the sweet-box'* from high ground, *watching*

*it fall into empty air/ and watched it turning over with little flahes /
silveryshivering with loss'.*[27] This ambiguity between belonging and
alienation is further developed in the poem *'Baggot Street Deserta'*.
Looking out from the Baggot Street attic window, the poet seems
closer to the *'arch of stars, and the night'* than the city, although he
is conscious that *'A mile away the river toils'.* [28] Contemplating a
'call of exile', the poet watches: *'My quarter-inch of cigarette / Goes
flaring down to Baggot Street'.*[29]

The poet and critic Gerald Dawe considers exile in a wider sense
as *'a useful metaphor of artistic space'.*[30] Although Kinsella remains
rooted in his explorations of the city – such as in his acclaimed
poem *'Nightwalker'* (1968) – it is an experience marked by inner
exile and isolation from poetic tradition. For Dawe, this sense
of isolation becomes, however, a positive act of *'reworking...the
tradition'*, leading ultimately to *'the creation of an imaginative space
beyond it'.*[31]

Kinsella's poetic search is a highly personal one and his central
motif is distilling individual experience – in particular the
experience of loss – into a precise poetic response. *'I see poetry as
a form of responsible reaction to the predicament one finds oneself in'*,
writes Kinsella and adds:

> The experience of an individual can be significant and, if the
> impulse is there, it is a responsible thing to record the particularities
> of that experience...accompanying the record of the experience with
> a record of the response.

When Kinsella records therefore his own urban experience and that
of his family in A Dublin Documentary, it is not to make a document
of the city; rather it is a creative re-working of Dublin so as to make
a territory beyond it. Through the poems and accompanying prose,
Kinsella re-imagines his city - he searches for a balance between his
need to belong in the back lanes and 'silent square courtyards', and
the poet's sense of necessary distance and self-exile. Delving deep
into his 'first universe' of domestic space – according to Bachelard,
'a real cosmos in every sense of the word' – Kinsella offers a richly
layered narrative that points, above all, to the poet's essential role
within society to re-imagine experience. Kinsella's very detachment
from his city allows him to make a true documentary of Dublin.

Footnotes

1 - Zumthor, Peter. *Thinking Architecture*. (Basel: Birkhäuser, 2010), p.7

2 - Ibid.

3 - Ibid.

4 - Kinsella, Thomas. *A Dublin Documentary*. (Dublin: O'Brien Press, 2006), p.14

5 - Bachelard, Gaston. *The Poetics of Space*. First published 1958. (Boston: Beacon Press, 1994), p.4

6 - Ibid., p.3

7 - Ibid., p.6

8 - Kinsella, Thomas. *A Dublin Documentary*. (Dublin: O'Brien Press, 2006),p.14

9 - Ibid., p.13

10 - Ibid., p.78

11 - Ibid., p.8

12 - Ibid.

13 - Ibid., p.13

14 - Ibid., p.12

15 - Ibid.

16 - Ibid., p.24

17 - Ibid., p.19

18 - Ibid., p.21

19 - Casey, Christine. *Dublin. The Buildings of Ireland*. (New Haven and London: Yale University Press, 2005), p.646

20 - Kinsella, Thomas. *A Dublin Documentary*. (Dublin: O'Brien Press, 2006), p.36

21 - Ibid., p.63

22 - Ibid., p.8

23 - Ibid., p.18

24 - Ibid., p.68

25 - Ibid., p.69

26 - Ibid., p.15

27 - Ibid., p.56

28 - Ibid., p.71

29 - Ibid., p.70

30 - Dawe, Gerald. *'Absence of Influence: Three Modernist Poets'*. In: *The Proper Word. Collected Criticism*. Edited by Nicholas Allen. (Omaha, Nebraska: Creighton University Press, 2007), p.142

31 - Ibid., p.14332 Kinsella, Thomas. *A Dublin Documentary*. (Dublin: O'Brien Press, 2006), p.1333 Ibid., p.4

Notes

Harmon, Maurice. Thomas Kinsella, Designing for the Exact Needs. (Dublin & Portland (US): Irish Academic Press, 2008)

Jackson, Thomas H. The Whole Matter. The Poetic Evolution of Thomas Kinsella. (Dublin: The Lilliput Press, 1995)

O'Brien, Eoin. The Beckett Country. Samuel Beckett's Ireland. (Dublin: The Black Cat Press in association with Faber & Faber, 1986)

Harmon quotes from John Haffenden's interview with Thomas Kinsella published in Viewpoints: Poets in Conversation with John Haffenden. London: Faber and Faber, 1981.

The Europa Press was set up in Paris in 1935 by the enterprising Irish-Russian publisher, literary agent and poet George Reavey (1907-1976). Alongside Beckett's Echo's Bones, the Press published poems by Brian Coffey, Denis Devlin and Reavey himself as well by the French Surrealist Paul Eluard and the American expatriate Charles Henri Ford. The Europa Press formed collaborations with artists from the legendary Atelier 17 in Paris, including S.W. Hayter, Pablo Picasso and Max Ernst.

Kinsella quoted in Harmon. Harmon quotes from Badin, Donatella Abbate. Thomas Kinsella. 1996. (New York: Twayne Publishers) pp. 199-200

Authors' details

Compiled by Neil Ardiff and Ellen Rowley

Sources for authors' biographies include the Dictionary of Irish Biography (Royal Irish Academy and Cambridge University Press, www.dib.cambridge.org), the Dictionary of Irish Architects (Irish Architectural Archive/Ann Martha Rowan, www.dia.ie), John Olley et al, <u>Ireland. Twentieth-Century Architecture</u> (Prestel, 1997), individuals' obituaries (such as that by Shane O'Toole for Noel Moffett), family notes (such as those by Simon Walker for Robin and Dorothy Walker) and practices' websites.

Frank Gibney was born in 1905 and is considered one of the most significant contributors to town planning in Ireland after independence. He worked in collaboration with Patrick Abercrombie, Ernest Aston and Manning Robertson in the preparation of various town plans including Waterford and Tralee, Drogheda and Tullamore. During the 1950s he worked for 16 Local Authorities. He is probably best known as the architect of the Bord na Mona housing schemes which are an early example of contextual housing and as such, have influenced subsequent generations of Irish architects. Frank Gibney died in 1978.

Noel Moffett was born in Cork in 1912. He was educated at Trinity College Dublin and Liverpool University, from where he gained an honours degree in architecture. He went on to study town planning, and worked in the offices of Serge Chermayeff, Burnett, Tait and Lorne, and Joseph Emberton. He practised in Dublin during the 1940s and was associated with the White Stag group through his wife Margot. During this time he designed major public exhibitions in Dublin (for the Mansion House) on tuberculosis and post-war planning. He also designed and built an outdoor amphitheatre on Achill Island in 1941. He returned to London at the end of the 1940s whence he ran a successful architectural practice, was the head of town planning at the Kingston College of Art, was active in RIBA and was President of the Architectural Association in 1974-5. Noel Moffett died in 1994 in a traffic accident.

Dorothy Cole moved to Paris in 1946 at the age of 17, having graduated from the Dominican Convent in Wicklow. She worked for the New York Times bureau in Paris, spending some seven years in the city. On her return to Dublin she worked as personal secretary to Michael Scott, in addition to managing the SIGNA design agency, which she co-founded with Scott and Louis Le Brocquy. Having married the architect Robin Walker in 1961, she became Dorothy Walker and is well known by that name as an internationally respected writer, critic and curator; she worked tirelessly in promoting Irish art at home and abroad and notably, was instrumental in setting up ROSC from the mid-1960s. She successfully campaigned for the establishment of an Irish museum of modern art (later IMMA), serving on the Board of Directors of IMMA until her retirement in 2002. Dorothy Walker died in the same year.

Arthur Gibney was one of the foremost architects of the second half of the twentieth century. He was born in 1932 and educated at the Dublin Institute of Technology and the National College of Art. After working as an assistant to Michael Scott, he established - with Sam Stephenson - the partnership Stephenson Gibney Associates in 1960. Fifteen years later, he established Arthur Gibney and Partners, winning the RIAI Gold Medal a year later for the Irish Management Institute Building in Sandyford. He was Professor of Architecture and President of the Royal Hibernian Academy, as well as President of the Society of Designers of Ireland and of the RIAI. He completed a PhD at Trinity College on the building materials of 18th-century Irish architecture. Arthur Gibney was a renowned architectural draftsman and watercolourist who became increasingly interested in architectural conservation during his career. He died in 2006.

Sean Ó Faoláin was an acclaimed short story writer whose work reflected the changing landscape of modern Ireland over a period of 60 years. He was born in Cork in 1900 and was educated at the Presentation Brothers, Cork. He fought in the War of Independence and earned MA degrees from the National University of Ireland and Harvard University. He lectured briefly at St. Mary's College, Strawberry Hill, and served as Director of the Arts Council of Ireland. He was a founder member and editor of the hugely influential literary periodical <u>The Bell</u>. He was elected Saoi of Aosdana in 1986. Among his many works are <u>The Man Who Invented Sin</u> (1948) and <u>The Talking Trees</u> (1971). Sean O Faolain died in 1991.

Maurice Craig was one of Ireland's most distinguished architectural historians and campaigners. He was born in Belfast in 1919 and was educated at Magdalene College, Cambridge, before completing a doctorate at Trinity College Dublin. He was a member of the Inspectorate of Ancient Monuments in England for 17 years before working as Executive Secretary of An Taisce. He wrote extensively on Irish architecture to wide critical acclaim and was a tireless campaigner for the preservation of Dublin's Georgian architecture; Dublin 1660-1860: The Shaping of a City (1952) is widely considered to be his masterwork. Maurice Craig died in 2011.

Robin Walker was a seminal figure in Irish modern architecture. He graduated from UCD in 1946 and spent the next ten years working in Michael Scott's office as well as periods abroad, including a year in Le Corbusier's Paris atelier and later, at the Illinois Institute of Technology, Chicago where he studied under Ludwig Hilberseimer and worked for stints in Skidmore Owings Merrill. In 1961, Robin Walker and Ronald Tallon were made partners of Scott's firm which would become Scott Tallon Walker. Alongside each other, Tallon and Walker designed a huge body of important modernist buildings including the RTE campus, UCD restaurant building, Bank of Ireland Baggot Street and Bord Failte HQ. Walker taught at both UCD and Bolton Street (now DIT, Dublin School of Architecture), and made invaluable contributions to architecture through his writing and his lectures over three decades. He was passionately interested in Georgian architecture and its relationship to modern architecture and continued to draw, exhibit and write about architecture until his death in 1991.

Gerry Cahill, born in 1951, has been Principal in GCA Gerry Cahill Architects since the early 1980s. He is also director of Urban Projects, a group set up in 1997 to explore and pursue urban design studies and major city regeneration proposals. The group won the RIAI Silver Medal for Housing in 2007 for the large mixed-use development at Clarion Quay as part of the regeneration of Dublin's Docklands area. Gerry is passionate about energy conservation and has been involved in the design of energy conscious buildings since the 1990s. He served as Director of SEI – the Sustainable Energy Authority of Ireland -

from 2000 to 2006 and in 2001 received the Lord Mayor's Award for his contribution to Dublin. He continues to teach studio in UCD and is a leading figure in Irish architectural culture through his lectures, writing and walking tours.

John Tuomey was born in Tralee in 1954. In 1976, he graduated in architecture from UCD, before taking up a position in the office of Stirling Wilford Associates in London. Upon returning to Dublin, he worked as an architect at the Office of Public Works for six years, while also lecturing at UCD. In 1988 he established O'Donnell + Tuomey Architects with Sheila O'Donnell – this practice has won many accolades, including the RIAI Gold Medal for the Ranelagh multi-denominational school (Dublin) in 2005 and a Stirling Prize nomination for An Gaelaras Cultural Centre, Derry in 2011; and has represented Ireland in Venice Architectural Biennale three times. John Tuomey was elected a Fellow of the Royal Institute of Architects of Ireland in 1994 and an Honorary Fellow of the American Institute of Architects in 2010. In 2011 he was elected to Aosdana. He has served as President of the Architectural Association of Ireland and is currently Professor of Architectural Design at UCD. Exciting recent buildings include the Sean O' Casey community centre in East Wall, Dublin, and the ongoing student centre for the London School of Economics.

Frank McDonald is the Environmental Editor of the Irish Times. He graduated in History and Politics from UCD in 1971, after which he worked with the now defunct Irish Press, serving as its New York Correspondent from 1972 to 1973. He joined the Irish Times in 1979, and was appointed its Environment Correspondent in 1986, before being appointed Environment Editor in 2000. A native of Glasnevin in north Dublin, he is passionate about the conservation of Dublin's architecture, winning a Lord Mayor's Millennium Medal in 1988 for his work in highlighting the destruction of the traditional fabric of Dublin during the 1960s and 70s. His publications include The Destruction of Dublin (1985) and The Construction of Dublin (2000). He lives in Temple Bar, Dublin.

Seamus Heaney is a poet, writer and lecturer. He was born in 1939 into a farming family in County Derry, Northern Ireland and studied English Language and Literature at Queens University Belfast. He worked initially as a teacher and began to publish poetry in 1962. His first major volume, <u>Death of a Naturalist</u> (1967) was published to much critical acclaim. He has lectured at the University of California, Berkeley, Queens University Belfast and Harvard University, among others. He has been awarded several honorary doctorates worldwide and his work has won many international awards, including the Geoffrey Faber Memorial Prize and the EM Forster Award. In 1995, he won the Nobel Prize for Literature. He lives in Sandymount, Dublin.

(Dr) John Olley is a lecturer in the School of Architecture, UCD where he has been teaching courses in history and theory of architecture and landscape, among others as well as supervising postgraduate research into architecture and music, and architecture and sustainability. He co-edited the significant publication <u>Ireland. Twentieth-Century Architecture</u> (Prestel, 1997) and has published on a wide range of architecture subjects, from history to building reviews in Architecture Research Quarterly and elsewhere.

Raymund Ryan is Curator of the Heinz Architectural Center at the Carnegie Museum of Art in Pittsburgh, USA. An architectural graduate of UCD, and Yale, he worked for architect Arthur Erickson in Los Angeles until 1990, returning to Ireland as Co-Director of the Urban Design Group of Ireland's National Building Agency before moving to the School of Architecture at UCD in 1993. He has written extensively on architecture for numerous publications and has collaborated on architecture proposals in Brussels. He was Irish Commissioner for the Venice Architecture Biennale in 2000 and 2002.

(Dr) Eddie McParland is a retired lecturer of history of architecture at Trinity College Dublin. He was educated at UCD and Cambridge University, having a background in mathematics and art history. He is the co-founder of the Irish Architectural Archive and founder of Irish Landmark Trust. Since the 1970s, Eddie has been studying Irish eighteenth-century architecture, publishing widely on the subject in local and international journals. His contribution to Irish architectural history, through his campaigning, researching, teaching and supervising postgraduate research, is huge. His acclaimed books are <u>James Gandon: Vitruvius Hibernicus</u> (Zwemmer, 1985) and <u>Public Architecture in Ireland</u> (Yale, 2001). He is currently widening his investigations beyond Ireland, to explore aspects of classicism in architecture.

Shane O'Toole is an architect, international critic, historian, campaigner and broadcaster. He has been a director of Group 91 consortium of architects during the 1990s (Temple Bar), Tegral company architect and Irish architecture critic for <u>The Sunday Times</u>. He was the Irish Architecture Foundation's Commissioner for the Venice Biennale's 10th International Architecture Exhibition. He is an award-winning architect, and, as a member of the International Committee of Architecture Critics (CICA), was named International Building Press Architectural Critic and Writer of the Year in 2008, 2009 and 2010. He is founding member of DoCoMoMo International and a leading force in DoCoMoMo Ireland. He has contributed to, co-edited and co-written several books including <u>Liam McCormick: North by Northwest</u> (Gandon, 2008) and continues as a freelance critic writing reviews in BD online and elsewhere.

Tim Robinson was born in Yorkshire in 1935. He graduated in mathematics from Cambridge University before going on to work as a visual artist in Istanbul, London and Vienna. In 1972, he moved to the Aran Islands, County Galway, from where he worked as a cartographer, mapping the islands themselves, the Burren and Connemara. He is now based in Roundstone, Connemara (Galway). <u>Stones of Aran</u>, his two-volume study of the islands, was published to much praise. He is currently preparing the third volume of <u>Connemara</u> and recently exhibited his artworks and some maps in the Hugh Lane Gallery in Dublin (2011-2012) while a visiting fellow to Magdalene College, Cambridge. He is a member of Aosdana.

Fintan O'Toole is a journalist, author and broadcaster and is one of Ireland's leading political and cultural commentators. He has been drama critic of <u>In Dublin</u>, the <u>Sunday Tribune</u>, the <u>New York Daily News</u>, and the <u>Irish Times</u>, and literary adviser to the Abbey Theatre. He edited <u>Magill</u> magazine and, since 1988, has been a columnist with the <u>Irish Times</u>, of which he is currently assistant editor. His award-winning work has appeared in many international publications. His more recent books include <u>Enough is Enough: How to Build a New Republic</u> (2010) and <u>Ship of Fools: How Stupidity and Corruption Sank the Celtic Tiger</u> (2009).

(Professor) Roger Stalley is the retired Professor of History of Art at Trinity College Dublin. Educated at Worcester College Oxford and the Courtauld Institute of Art, he has taught and written extensively on both Irish and European medieval architecture. His books include <u>The Cistercian Monasteries of Ireland</u> (Yale, 1987) and <u>Early Medieval Architecture</u> (Oxford, 1999). He is an elected member of the Royal Irish Academy and the Academia Europaea. As principal investigator, Roger recently oversaw the development of the significant IRCHSS research project, "Reconstructions of the Gothic Past" (2008-12) www.gothicpast.com

Tom de Paor was born in London in 1967 and grew up in County Clare. He studied architecture in DIT and UCD, graduating in 1991. In the same year, he won the competition (with Emma O'Neill) to build the Visitor Centre at Ballincollig, Cork. He was awarded the contract for the strategic master-plan of the A13 motorway by the Council of Dagenham in 1996. His work has won many awards and he has exhibited widely. In 2000 he represented Ireland in the first Irish pavilion (N3, published here) for the Venice Biennale. Then in 2010, De Paor presented <u>4am</u>, a piece that formed part of the main show at the 2010 Venice Biennale. He also co-curated the 2010 Irish national pavilion exhibition <u>Of deBlacam and Meagher</u> along with Peter Maybury, Cian Deegan and Alice Casey. He has taught at UCD since 1992 and his practice has designed such public projects as the Picture Palace in Galway and the pump house in Clontarf, Dublin, as well as many notable private buildings including the Stoney Road Press in East Wall, Dublin.

(Professor) Hugh Campbell is an architect and architectural historian. He graduated from UCD with first class honours in 1988, after which he worked with de Blacam and Meagher on a number of noteworthy Irish projects. In 1998, he completed a PhD on the politics of urban development in nineteenth-century Dublin. During this period, he taught in UCD and in the Architectural Association in London, becoming Senior Lecturer at UCD in 2005. He has been Professor of Architecture in UCD since 2008, always enabling new scholarship in Irish architecture by promoting young researchers and the culture of Irish architecture internationally. Hugh's ongoing research interests include photography, space and the self and he is currently joint editor of Volume IV (Irish Architecture) of <u>Art and Architecture of Ireland</u> (Royal Irish Academy, Yale University Press, 2014).

Dermot Boyd is an architect and lecturer. He was born in Belfast and is a graduate of the Dublin Institute of Technology (DIT) and Trinity College Dublin. Following graduation in 1990, he worked with Alberto Campo Baeza in Madrid and for John Pawson in London. He returned to Dublin in 1992, working for many years with McCullough Mulvin Architects before establishing Boyd Cody Architects with Peter Cody in 1997. In the same year, he served as President of the Architectural Association of Ireland. His work has won many awards, including first prize in the AAI/FIS Collaboration in 1996 and the RIAI award in 1998. Currently he is the head of 5th year studio at DIT (Dublin School of Architecture) and in his teaching role he has overseen the publication of exciting studio projects such as <u>Wasteland</u> (2009) and <u>NamaLab</u> (2011).

Dominic Stevens was born in London in 1965. He graduated in architecture from UCD in 1989, after which he worked for Christoph Langhof and Leipe Stegelmann in Berlin. He established his practice in 1995 and relocated to Cloone, County Leitrim, in 1999. He was architect-in-residence with Roscommon County Council in 2005 and exhibited at the Venice Biennale 10th International Architecture Exhibition in 2006. He won his first AAI Award in 1999, receiving many accolades and mentions through these awards since. In 2005 Dominic won the Arts Council / Office of Public Works research bursary, the Kevin Kieran Award. A former editor of <u>Building Material</u>, the journal of the AAI, he has written extensively on architecture and society, including <u>Rural</u> (2009) and <u>Domestic</u> (1999), both of which were published by Mermaid Turbulence. Currently, Dominic is assistant head of 5th year, DIT (Dublin School of Architecture).

Grafton Architects was founded in 1978 by **Shelley McNamara** (b.1952) and **Yvonne Farrell** (b.1951). The work of the practice has received many awards and has been published widely. Recently, in 2008, Grafton Architects won world building of the year for the Luigi Bocconi university extension in Milan. Both Yvonne and Shelley were members of the Group 91 consortium (Temple Bar, Dublin), are members of Aosdana and have designed significant buildings in Ireland - such as the Department of Finance (Dublin), the President's House (University of Limerick) and Parson's Building for mechanical engineering (Trinity College Dublin) - and abroad, such as the Bocconi extension and ongoing educational buildings at Toulouse (France) and Prato, Rome (Italy). They are keen educators, teaching studio at UCD, as well as taking visiting positions in architecture schools at Menrisio and Lausannne (Switzerland, 2008-11), holding the Harvard Kenzo Tange Chair in 2010 and the Yale Louis Kahn Chair in 2011.

Catherine Marshall was the first head of collections at the Irish Museum of Modern Art. Prior to taking up this position, she lectured in History of Art at Trinity College Dublin and at the National College of Art and Design, and she continues to guest lecture all over the country. She is former chairperson of the Irish Association of Art Historians, has served on the board of the Douglas Hyde Gallery and was a consultant to the Arts Council of Ireland. She is an accomplished writer; her writings include Irish Art Masterpieces (1995) and Making Visual Art Visible (2002), and she has edited numerous collections and catalogue essays on contemporary Irish artists. Catherine is currently joint editor of Volume V (C20th Art and Artists) of Art and Architecture of Ireland (Royal Irish Academy, Yale University Press, 2014), and she is writing a PhD on collections in Irish art.

(Dr) Anna Ryan has been lecturer in architecture at the University of Limerick since 2007. Among her areas of expertise are design studio and the history and theory of architecture. In 2000 she graduated with a B.Arch. from UCD, after which she worked with Grafton Architects for two years and was editor of Building Material, the journal of the AAI. In 2008, she graduated with a PhD from the Department of Geography, University College Cork. Her first book, Where Land Meets Sea:

Coastal Explorations of Landscape, Representation and Spatial Experience, (Ashgate, 2012) has received great critical acclaim.

Paul Kearns is a Senior Planner at Dublin City Council. In 2010, in collaboration with the architect Motti Ruimy, he published _Redrawing Dublin_, a book that challenges policy-makers and citizens to confront the contradictions of the city. One of the main themes of the work is the inherent tension between urban and suburban Dublin. The book brings together mapping, graphics, photography and statistics to examine issues of how Dublin functions as a city.

(Dr) Sandra O'Connell is a graduate of the School of English, Trinity College, where she completed an M.Phil and a PhD. She is passionately interested in Irish architecture and literature and has written extensively on these areas. She is editor of the RIAI's journal _Architecture Ireland_ and of the _RIAI Annual Review_. She is the founding curator of the popular OPEN HOUSE Dublin weekend. She is currently editing the _Selected Poems_ of the Irish-Russian poet and modernist, George Reavey (1907-1976), for the Lagan Press, Belfast, and a volume of essays on Reavey for the Lilliput Press, Dublin.

372

The makers of the book

The editor & compiler

Dr Ellen Rowley is currently a research associate and formerly award-winning lecturer on the subject of architectural history and theory with the School of Histories and Humanities, Trinity College Dublin (2003 – 2008). Ellen researches and writes about the history and culture of architecture in Ireland from 1940 -1970. Along with fellow DoCoMoMo Ireland cofounders, she is working to safeguard key buildings of this period from destruction and careless redevelopment. She is assistant editor of Irish Architecture 1600 – 2000, Volume IV of Art and Architecture of Ireland (Royal Irish Academy, Yale University Press, 2014), and enjoys collaborating with architects, artists and film-makers around the culture of building.

The publisher & compiler

Maxim Laroussi is an architect and principal of Dublin-based practice Architecture Republic which he established in 2005. The office has since garnered numerous awards, as well as a nomination for the Mies van der Rohe prize. Maxim was President of the Architectural Association of Ireland in 2005/2006 and currently teaches studio design at the School of Architecture, University of Limerick. He is interested in architecture as a critical practice, engaging with engineers, artists, scientists, policy-makers, and other professionals through research, analysis and cross disciplinary collaboration.

The designer

This book was designed by graphic designer David Duff. David is a graduate of Visual Communications at IADT, Dun Laoghaire (2009). He is an invited member of the International Society of Typographic Designers, and has been working (primarily in Dublin) individually and collaborativeley on a wide range of projects for the last 3 years.

- *www.ninepictures.com*

The illustrator

The line drawings in this book are by artist, researcher, illustrator and creative facilitator Fiona Hallinan. After her art history studies, she undertook a MSc in Interactive Digital Media Systems (2007) and since this she has been working in relational art, researching and creating digital audio walking tours, co-ordinating events, writing and drawing. She illustrates maps supplementing her own work, articles and artist's books and her work can be found online.

- *www.notalittlepony.com*

The copy-editor

Neil Ardiff is a writer, cartoonist, painter and freelance editor based in Dublin.

Twitter: @nardiff